BIOLOGY
Lives

KT-152-279

NORWICH CITY COLLEGE LIBRARY

Stock No.	208247		
Class	570 JEN		
Cat.	O/S	Proc.	3Mee

MORTON JENKINS

Hodder & Stoughton

A MEMBER OF THE HODDER HI

208 247

Acknowledgements

I have been very fortunate to have had the assistance of Roger Frost for the sections on use of information and communications technology. For this help, I express my sincere thanks. It is also a pleasure to thank the science team at Hodder & Stoughton Educational for generating the idea of the book and for their help and encouragement throughout its production. Last but not least, I would like to thank the many students who I have had the pleasure to teach over the last 36 years. They have made my teaching career both enjoyable and interesting. By their often perceptive questioning, I have been stimulated to try to organise the contents of this book into a form which is accessible to them and which I hope they will enjoy reading.

Morton Jenkins, 2001

The publishers would like to thank the following individuals, institutions and companies for permission to reproduce photographs in this book. Every effort has been made to trace ownership of copyright. The publishers would be happy to make arrangements with any copyright holder whom it has not been possible to contact:

Associated Press (114); Benetton (166 left); Biophoto Associates (42 both, 144, 240 both); Bruce Coleman Limited (41 all four photos, 72, 127 both, 177 top left, 190 bottom right, 207 top left, middle right and bottom (both), 208 top (both), 210 top (both) and bottom left, 211 top (both), 233 (both), Holt Studios/Inga Spence (253 left), /Nigel Cattlin (112 both, 155 right, 189 bottom left, 208 bottom left, 210 bottom right, 211 bottom), /Primrose Peacock (26); Life File (88 bottom right, 171 top left, 207 top right and middle left, 209, 226, 227 both), /Angela Maynard, (180 middle left), /Emma Lee, (37, 39, 258), /Lionel Moss, (155 left); Mark Wagner, (88 left); Mary Evans Picture Library, (61, 152 left, 164 both, 228, 264 top right); 'PA News' Photo Library, (179) Natural History Museum (172 both); Science Photo Library (81, 156, 239 both, 264 top middle, 269 left), /A. Barrington Brown, (149 left), /Alexander Tsiaras, (264 bottom), /Andrew Syred, (8 bottom right), /Andy Crump, (269 right), /Astrid & Hanns-Frieder Michler, (116), /Bill van Aken, (180 bottom right), /Biophoto Associates, (34 both, 95), /CC Studio, (230 left), /CNRI, (8 top right, 142 left, 143 all), /David Scharf, (253 right), /Dr Jeremy Burgess, (7, 8 bottom left, 152 right), /Dr Yorgos Nikas, (141), /Eye of Science, (40, 80, 195, 205), /Hank Morgan, (267), /Hattie Young, (170 top right, 190 top right), /James King-Holmes, (187), /JC Revy, (11 right, 73 right), /John Durham, (11 left, 180 bottom left), /Joseph Nettis, (190 top left), /Manfred Kage, (100), /Marcelo Brodsky, (230 right), /Martin Dohrn, (270)/National Cancer Institute, (57), /National Library of Medicine, (170 bottom, 264 top left), /Novosti, (177 right), /Peter Menzel, (177 bottom left, 189 top), /Prof K Seddon & Dr T Evans, (149 right), /Prof P Motta/Dept of Anatomy/University "La Sapienza", (142 right), /Quest, (124), /Science Pictures Ltd, (123), /Secchi-Lecaque/Roussel-UCLAF, (5, 8 top left), /Sheila Terry, (38), /Simon Fraser, Royal Victoria Infirmary, Newcastle upon Tyne, (94, 222), /Vanessa Vick, (224), /Will McIntyre, (87); Still Pictures, (234); Sue Cunningham, (254); Wellcome Library, London, (274).

Thanks go also to the following examining bodies for permission to reproduce examination questions: Assessment and Qualifications Alliance, Northern Ireland Council for the Curriculum Examinations and Assessment, Welsh Joint Education Committee and Edexcel.

Orders: please contact Bookpoint Ltd, 130 Milton Park, Abingdon, Oxon OX14 4SB. Telephone: (44) 01235 400414, Fax: (44) 01235 400454. Lines are open from 9.00–6.00, Monday to Saturday, with a 24 hour message answering service. You can also order through our website www.hodderheadline.co.uk

A catalogue record for this title is available from The British Library

ISBN 0 340 79051 2

First published 1999

This edition published 2001

Impression number   10 9 8 7 6 5 4 3 2
Year   2006 2005 2004 2003

Copyright © 1999, 2001 Morton Jenkins

All rights reserved. No part of this publication may be reproduced or transmitted in any form or by any means, electronic or mechanical, including photocopy, recording, or any information storage and retrieval system, without permission in writing from the publisher or under licence from the Copyright Licensing Agency Limited. Further details of such licences (for reprographic reproduction) may be obtained from the Copyright Licensing Agency Limited, of 90 Tottenham Court Road, London W1T 4LP

Cover photo from Bruce Coleman.

Typeset by Fakenham Photosetting Limited, Fakenham, Norfolk.

Printed in Italy for Hodder & Stoughton Educational, a division of Hodder Headline , 338 Euston Road, London NW1 3BH.

Contents

Preface

For the teacher

The author has always believed that the process of studying should involve a mastery of certain basic concepts, rather than the learning of 'laundry lists' of names and facts for the sake of expanding a memory. A knowledge of these essential names and facts should be seen as only a part of the studying process rather than an end in itself. Beginning with an understanding of first principles, a systematic approach to the study of biology is possible. The approach to learning by understanding and investigation has evolved successfully in thousands of schools and is preserved in *Biology Lives*.

The author has attempted to keep the readability at a level suited to the average year eleven student. All new words and terms stand out in bold type. These words are defined the first time they are used, and a Glossary is provided as a further reading aid for developing a 'working' vocabulary. The text is colour coded throughout to enable pupils to determine which sections are aimed at which level. Sections aimed at those taking Single and Double Award Biology are indicated by a pink line alongside the text, along with pink bullet points in the Learning Objectives boxes. Triple Award topics are shown by a blue line and blue bullet points.

The need to present concepts to students of varied abilities is recognised. In order to present the subject in a form that allows for comprehension at various levels, Learning Objectives for the student are indicated at the beginning of each chapter. These objectives serve to guide the student in studying the major concepts of the chapter. The questions for homework at the end of each chapter reinforce the student's understanding of the material. Each theme ends with sample questions of the standard to be expected at GCSE level which are there to help those preparing for this standard of examination. The value of these questions is based on the premise that, for revision, *failure to prepare is preparation for failure*.

Within the text are alternative approaches to experiments using sensors, as well as pointers to using software or the Internet. These are indicated by an IT logo in the margin of the text.

Morton Jenkins, 2001

Preface

For the student

Biology is a most fascinating and exciting subject. Its range is vast – from the study of something as wonderful as the human body, to the study of the simplest virus that may infect us. All plants and animals, and countless tiny micro-organisms of thousands of types and shapes, lie within its scope. Living things are the most important features of our colourful planet, and may be unique in our galaxy. They have many different structures, designs and patterns of behaviour, which astonish us even in our advanced computerised age.

The biologist's understanding of living things cannot be separated from other branches of science. The biologist must record experimental results in forms which can be readily interpreted. We find that living things can be compared with machines. In studying them we use terms like 'energy' and 'work'. Biologists also need to know something about physics and chemistry. Elements, compounds, ions and molecules are frequently in their minds, as are such concepts as solubility, diffusion, pH and the effects of temperature on rates of reaction. When it is realised that mathematics, physics and chemistry are all bound up with biology, it is easier to understand how the different branches of science are connected. Humans have made the sub-divisions of science for their own convenience. The divisions do not exist in the things they study. The biologist studies life, but a plant, for example, cannot properly be considered separate from the soil in which it grows, or from the air, the weather, sunlight or gravity. The tools of the biologist are observation and investigation.

Information and communications technology are essential to today's scientists. Computer sensors allow monitoring of changes of factors such as temperature, pH and oxygen over long periods of time. A word processor helps them to plan and write up their work, while a spreadsheet helps them to analyse data. Computer software and CD-ROMs help them to model their ideas, while the Internet helps them to find out what other scientists are doing elsewhere in the world. As a student scientist, you too may find these tools helpful, time saving and just as indispensable in your study of biology. Sections concerned with IT are marked throughout the book with these logos.

As you look through the book, you will notice that some sections are marked with a pink line and some with a blue line. If you are taking Single/Double Award Biology (ask your teacher if you are unsure) look out for all the sections coloured pink. If you are studying for Triple Award Biology you also need to look out for the blue sections.

Sections dealing with the nature of science are marked throughout the book with this logo.

Morton Jenkins, 2001

Introduction to Coursework

Scientific methods

A scientific method is a logical, orderly way of trying to solve a problem. It is this logic and order that makes scientific methods different from ordinary, hit-or-miss approaches. Remember, though, that scientific methods are not magic. Even the best planned investigations can fail to produce meaningful data. Yet failure itself may lead to eventual success. By careful study of each result, the scientist may find a new direction to take. Often this new direction leads to an even more important discovery than the one first expected.

Several methods are used in science, depending on the nature of the problem. Perhaps the most important is the investigative method.

Investigations

It is by investigating that new knowledge and new concepts are gained. There are many opportunities to investigate in your study of biology. The steps in this investigative method are logical and orderly. In fact, they are simply a system of common sense:

Decide what you want to investigate

You can't understand why something is happening unless you observe it in the first place. Science calls for the kind of mind that makes observations and asks questions about them. For example, why does your heart beat faster when you run? Why does the pupil of your eye change when light changes? Why do stems grow towards the light?

Well-planned investigations can answer each of these questions. However, in science, every answer raises new questions. Successful research leads to new research and new knowledge and sometimes solves problems.

Collect information

Scientists must build on the work of other scientists, otherwise science can not advance beyond what one person can learn in one lifetime. Before beginning an investigation, the scientist studies all the important information that relates to the observations. Often it turns out that someone has already answered many of the questions involved. For this reason, a library of scientific books and journals is an important part of investigating. As a special kind of library, the Internet will be of help too. In addition, there are biology CD-ROMs and general encyclopaedias on computer packages which may also assist. This textbook will serve as an aid to this background reading.

Make a prediction

The information available may not fully explain the observations. The researcher must then begin to investigate. At this point, an hypothesis is needed. The hypothesis is a sort of working explanation or prediction. For example, you might predict that the rate of action of an enzyme will increase as the temperature increases.

An hypothesis gives the researcher a point at which to aim. However, no matter how reasonable the hypothesis seems, it cannot be accepted until supported by a large number of tests. A research worker must be open minded enough to change or drop the original hypothesis if the evidence does not support it.

Test the hypothesis

The scientist must plan an investigation that will either support or disprove the hypothesis. This means that the investigation must test only the idea or condition involved in the hypothesis. All other factors must be removed or otherwise accounted for. The one factor to be tested is called the **single variable**.

Often, a second investigation, called a **control**, is carried out along with the first. In the control, all factors except the one being tested are the same as in the first investigation. In this way, the control shows the importance of the missing variable.

Observe and record data from the investigation

Everything should be recorded accurately. Correct, internationally standard units should be used. The record of the observations may include notes, drawings, graphs and tables. From time to time **sensors**, devices which plug into the computer, will be of help in making measurements in investigations. Observations and measurements are called **data** and in modern research, data are often processed using information technology. For example, computer spreadsheet packages can help draw graphs and analyse data, and a word processing package can help with the preparation of your experiment reports.

Draw conclusions and evaluate

Data have meaning only when valid conclusions are drawn from them, and validity can be assessed only when the investigation has been evaluated critically. Such conclusions and evaluations must be based entirely on observations made during the investigation. If other investigations continue to support the hypothesis, it may become a theory.

GCSE coursework

The coursework element of science in GCSE in the UK, whether it is biology or double award science, is worth 25% of the assessment. It therefore forms an important part of your course. The skill areas that are assessed in coursework correspond to:

- planning experimental procedures
- obtaining evidence
- analysing evidence and drawing conclusions
- evaluating evidence.

Throughout this book there will be indications of where activities may be designed to develop the experimental and investigative skills listed above.

ALL PRACTICAL WORK INVOLVING APPARATUS AND CHEMICALS MUST BE CARRIED OUT WITH DUE REGARD TO THE CONTROL OF SUBSTANCES HAZARDOUS TO HEALTH (COSHH) REGULATIONS AND THE MANAGEMENT OF HEALTH AND SAFETY AT WORK REGULATIONS WHICH ARE ESSENTIAL IN ALL SCHOOLS AND

COLLEGES. APPROPRIATE RISK ASSESSMENTS OF ALL PROCEDURES INVOLVING POTENTIAL HAZARDS MUST BE CARRIED OUT BY TEACHERS BEFORE ANY EXPERIMENTAL WORK.

Here is a check list showing how credit is given for the assessment of coursework in the GCSE examination for biology or science. When you decide on an investigation, use this to help you identify what an examiner is looking for in your written report.

Planning experimental procedures

Requirements for credit:

- Plan a safe procedure.
- Plan a fair test or a practical procedure.
- Make a prediction.
- Identify key factors to vary and control.
- Decide on a suitable number and range of observations.
- Select appropriate equipment.
- Use scientific knowledge to plan to obtain reliable evidence.

Obtaining evidence

Requirements for credit:

- Use equipment safely.
- Make precise observations.
- Make relevant and reliable observations.
- Recognise unpredictable observations.
- Repeat procedures as a check.
- Record observations clearly.

Analysing evidence and drawing conclusions

Requirements for credit:

- Present data clearly.
- Present data as graphs with lines of best fit.
- Identify trends or patterns.
- Use graphs to identify relationships between data.
- Present numerical results accurately.
- Show that results are consistent with evidence.
- Show that results support predictions.
- Explain conclusions using scientific knowledge and understanding.

Evaluating evidence

Requirements for credit:

- Show that evidence is enough for valid conclusions.
- Give reasons for unexpected observations.
- Show that evidence is reliable.
- Suggest improvements to procedure.
- Suggest further investigations to support the prediction.

Life processes

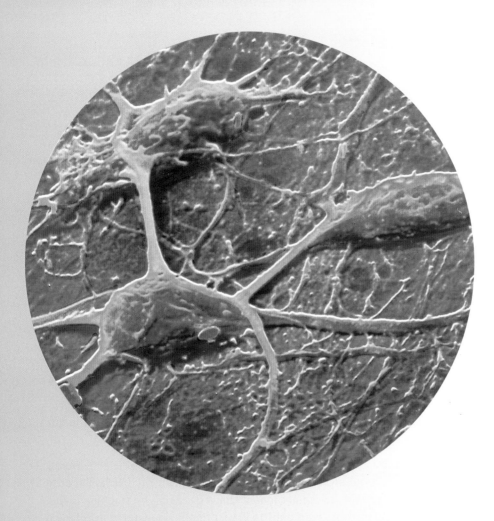

Nerve cells in the human brain. The nervous system allows animals to detect and respond to stimuli in their environment.

1 The basis of life

Learning objectives

By the end of this chapter you should be able to understand:

- that plant and animal cells have some similarities in structure;

- that respiration releases energy from glucose in all cells;

- how substances enter and leave cell membranes by diffusion, osmosis and active transport;

- that enzymes are important to cells.

The cell as the basic unit of life

Did you know?

There are about 50 million million cells in an average person and about 2000 times as many in a whale. The largest cell produced by any animal alive today is the egg of an ostrich which is up to 200 mm long, while red blood cells can be as small as 0.008 mm.

With the exception of bacteria and viruses, all organisms are made of one or more cells consisting of, at least, a **nucleus**, **cytoplasm** and a **cell membrane**. More complex organisms may have thousands, millions, or even billions of cells. An organism's size depends on the number, not the size, of its cells. In general, elephant cells are no bigger than the cells of an ant – the elephant simply has more cells.

A working knowledge of cells and their functions is fundamental to the study of biology. Almost every branch of biology deals, in some way, with cells.

The discovery of cells

More than three hundred years ago, in the 1660s, the British scientist Robert Hooke studied some thin slices of cork under one of the first microscopes. He noted that the cork was a mass of cavities. Since each cavity was surrounded by walls like the cells in a honeycomb, Hooke called the structures he saw 'cells'.

Robert Hooke did not realise that the most important parts of the cells were missing from the structures he had described. The empty cavities had once held living materials, yet Hooke did not follow up his discovery by studying living cells in detail. In fact, it was not until 1835 that the living material in cells was discovered. The French scientist, Dujardin, viewed living cells with a microscope and found what we now call cytoplasm. Three years later, the German plant scientist Matthias Schleiden claimed that all plants are made of cells. The following year, Theodor Schwann, a German zoologist, suggested that all animals are also made of cells. Such discoveries contributed to the cell theory which states:

- The cell is the unit of structure and function of all living things.
- Cells come from other cells by cell reproduction.

Since Dujardin's discovery, other biologists have added greatly to our knowledge of cells. However, in the early days they could not work beyond the limits of the light microscope which relies on light passing through lens systems.

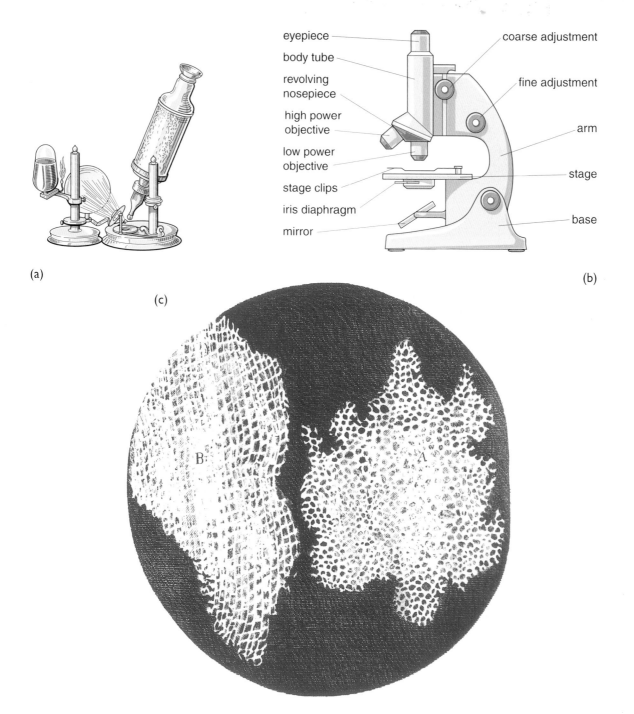

eyepiece

body tube

revolving
nosepiece

high power
objective

low power
objective

stage clips

iris diaphragm

mirror

coarse adjustment

fine adjustment

arm

stage

base

(a)

(b)

(c)

Figure 1.1 *(a) The microscope Hooke used when he first saw cork 'cells'. (b) A modern school microscope. (c) Hooke's drawing of the cells in cork*

In the mid-twentieth century, new tools and methods began to push back the limits of discovery. The most important of these was the **electron microscope**, which relies on a totally different system from the light microscope. It can produce magnifications significantly greater than that of a light microscope.

www

Cells alive
http://www.cellsalive.com/
The Biology Project: Cell Biology
http://www.biology.arizona.edu/cell_bio/cell_bio.html

The Cell
http://library.thinkquest.org/3564/
The Virtual Cell
http://personal.tmlp.com/jimr57/tour/cell/cell.htm

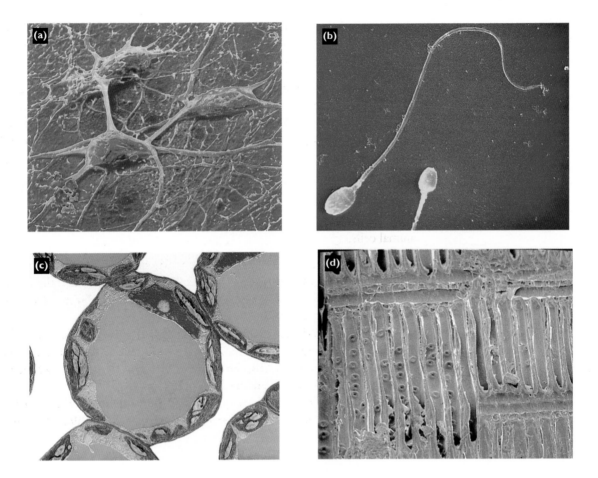

Figure 1.2 *There is enormous variety in plant and animal cells: (a) nerve cells, (b) sperm cells, (c) mesophyll cells, (d) xylem cells*

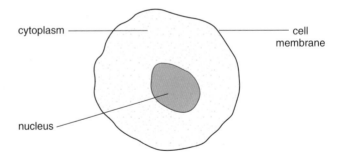

cytoplasm

cell membrane

nucleus

Figure 1.3 *A typical animal cell*

The essential components of cells

The nucleus is the control centre of all cell activity, without which it would die. It is usually spherical or oval in shape, often lying near the centre of the cell. It is surrounded by a thin, double-layered membrane which has pores to allow certain substances to pass between the nucleus and the rest of the cell. Spread through the nucleus are fine strands of chromatin that make up the chromosomes which are involved in cell division (see p. 144).

Cell chemicals outside the nucleus comprise the cytoplasm. Under the light microscope, cytoplasm appears as a clear semi-liquid filling most of the cell. It often streams within the cell, carrying with it the nucleus.

The cytoplasm is bounded by a cell or plasma membrane which separates the cell from other cells and from surrounding fluids. Like the nuclear membrane, it is not a solid barrier – molecules can pass through it in a controlled manner. It acts like a gate, allowing some molecules to pass and keeping others out (see p. 13).

Plant cells – specialists in food production

A typical plant cell has a number of specialised structures which are not found in animal cells.

- A **cell wall** made of a carbohydrate (see p. 38) called **cellulose**. This is a non-living, thick, rigid layer around the cell membrane which helps the plant to support itself. As a result of the cell wall, plant cells are distinct shapes – they may be angular, rectangular or rounded.
- A **vacuole**. This is a fluid-filled space enclosed by a membrane. The fluid contains dissolved food materials, minerals and waste products and is called **cell sap**. In older plant cells, the vacuoles are large and their main function is to support the cells by the pressure of the cell sap.
- **Chloroplasts**. These discs contain the green pigment called **chlorophyll** which is essential for the process of **photosynthesis** (see p. 24). Chloroplasts are only present in the parts of the plant that are exposed to light.

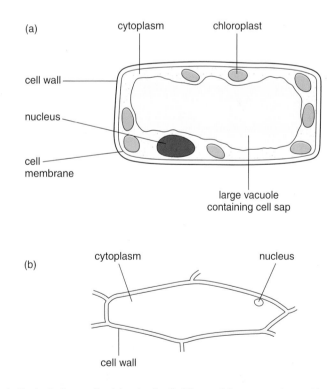

Figure 1.4 *Typical plant cells: (a) a leaf cell, (b) a cell from an onion epidermis*

Coursework Activity

Looking at cells

1 Take a clean microscope slide and, wearing eye protection, place a drop of iodine in potassium iodide in the centre of it.

2 Take a small piece of onion.

3 Using a pair of forceps, start at a corner and lift up the thin layer which covers the outside of the onion. Peel off as much of this layer as you can.

4 Place the layer onto the iodine on the slide so that it unrolls and lays flat. Carefully lower a cover slip over the onion with a mounted needle.

5 Remove eye protection only when all students have finished with the iodine. Now examine the layer under the microscope. Use low power magnification at first, focus, then examine it under high power.

You will not be able to see chloroplasts – explain why.

An easy way to see chloroplasts is to look at a whole leaf of the Canadian pond weed (*Elodea canadensis*), obtainable from most ponds or garden centres. Just place a leaf from the growing point of the pond weed in a drop of water on a microscope slide. Focus on low power, then on high power.

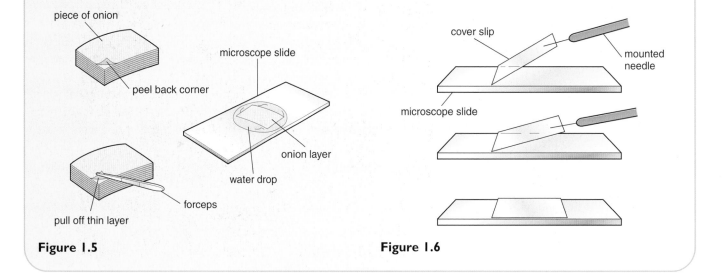

Figure 1.5

Figure 1.6

Cells acting together

A collection of similar cells with similar functions which grow in the same way is called a tissue. Tissues make up **organs**, which make up **organ systems**, which in turn make up **organisms**.

Cells within tissues are usually specialised to carry out their job. Muscle cells, whose function it is to shorten by contracting, are shaped like long cylinders. Nerve cells have long extensions with tree-like branches at either end. These are entangled with the branches of the next nerve cell to form a chain of interconnected cells functioning as a single unit. It is an ideal arrangement for getting messages from the brain to the rest of the body. Cells in the moist surfaces, such as the inside of the nose or throat, may have tiny **cilia**, or hair-like projections, sticking out of the surface to move particles or mucus along.

Other types of cells include:

● gland cells that make and release special fluids or secretions;

- connective tissue cells that fill spaces between tissues;
- epithelial cells that cover surfaces either inside or outside the body.

In plants, cells tend to be joined together more firmly than they are in most animal tissues. Some specialised plant cells are detailed below.

- **Parenchyma** are packing cells for support and storage.
- **Mesophyll cells** in the leaves have chloroplasts for photosynthesis.
- **Xylem** tissue contains cells with firm woody walls. They are often hollow like drain pipes and are used to carry water and minerals from the roots to the stems and leaves.
- **Phloem** tissue contains tube-like cells similar in structure to those in xylem, but which transport food from the leaves to the rest of the plant.

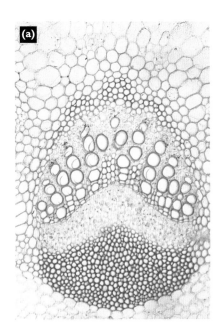 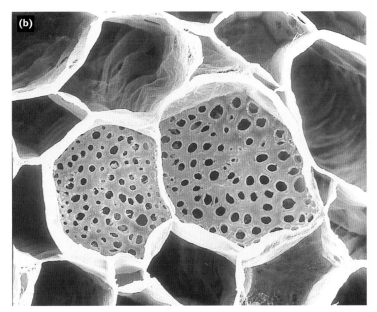

Figure 1.7 *(a) A vascular bundle in transverse section. (b) Phloem tissue under high power magnification showing the perforated sieve plates*

Cells at work

Life is dependent on the movement of certain materials into and out of the cell. Digested food and oxygen are among the essential materials to be taken into cells while waste products, such as carbon dioxide, are removed. To enter the cell, materials must be able to cross the cell membrane. Some molecules pass through freely, some less freely, and others not at all. The membrane is thus responsible for selecting materials for entry and exit. Several factors are important in determining this 'right of way'. Some of these are given below.

- The size of the particles. In general, small molecules pass through the cell membrane more readily than large molecules. Large charged molecules are, however, the exception to this rule and may pass through easily.
- The solubility of the particles in water. The liquids that bathe cells are usually solutions of molecules and ions in water. Substances which do not dissolve in water cannot pass through the cell membrane.

- The conditions inside or outside the cell. If the concentration of particles is greater on the inside of the cell compared with the outside, particles tend to leave the cell.
- The structure of the cell membrane. There are spaces between the molecules that make up the cell membrane which allow the passage of certain substances. These spaces may be too small for large molecules to pass through, but large enough for smaller molecules.

The rates and degrees at which certain substances penetrate the cell membrane varies. If a substance passes through a membrane, we say that the membrane is **permeable** to that substance. If a membrane lets some substances pass but not others, we say that it is **selectively permeable** or **differentially permeable**. The cell membrane is selectively permeable.

Diffusion

To understand better how substances pass through cell membranes, we need to understand more about molecules and their motion. In any substance, the molecules are constantly moving. This motion results in kinetic energy within the molecules themselves. Molecular motion is slight in solids, but much greater in liquids and gases. The movement of molecules is completely random, that is, the molecules move in straight lines until they collide with other molecules. After the collisions they bounce off and move in straight lines again until they collide with other molecules. It is easy to understand why this kind of movement results in a gradual spreading out of the molecules. Eventually the molecules will be spread evenly through any given space. This gradual, even spreading out of molecules is called **diffusion** or passive transport.

The principle of diffusion can be illustrated by opening a bottle of perfume. As soon as you open the bottle, the molecules start diffusing into the air. The people close to the perfume will smell it first and, as diffusion continues, the smell becomes stronger. More and more molecules spread out at random among the molecules of gases in the air. Finally, a state of equilibrium is reached. The molecules, though still in motion, are spread evenly among the gas molecules in the air.

In reality, as the perfume diffuses into the air, molecules of gases from the air also diffuse into the perfume bottle. This brings us to a basic law of diffusion. According to this law, substances diffuse from areas of greater concentration to areas of lesser concentration. In this case, diffusion will continue until the concentration of gas molecules from the air and the perfume is equal in all parts of the room.

Diffusion is affected by:

- *concentration* – the greater the difference in concentration between two substances, the more rapidly diffusion takes place.
- *temperature* – the higher the temperature, the greater the speed of molecular motion.
- *pressure* – the higher the pressure on particles, the greater the speed of diffusion from a region of high pressure to a region of low pressure.

Diffusion through membranes

How does a membrane affect the movement of molecules in diffusion? The answer depends on the nature of the membrane and the substance being diffused. You can demonstrate this with visking tubing and glucose solution. A sac is made out of the visking tubing and is filled with glucose solution.

The visking tubing sac containing the glucose solution is then placed in water. Since the visking tubing is permeable to both water and glucose molecules, two things will happen: water molecules will diffuse into the glucose solution and glucose molecules will diffuse into the water. Eventually, the concentration of glucose and water molecules will be the same on both sides of the visking tubing. This is a state of **dynamic equilibrium** because both types of molecule will be passing in both directions at equal rates. The visking tubing had little effect on diffusion in this case.

www

Transport in and out of cells
http://gened.emc.maricopa.edu/

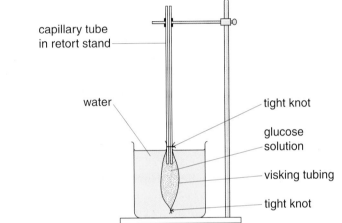

Figure 1.8 *Apparatus required to monitor the diffusion of glucose through a membrane*

What if the cell membrane were completely permeable? The answer is simple – the cell would die. Although molecules of water and other substances would be able to enter the cell more easily, the cell's own molecules would diffuse out into the surroundings at the same time. Clearly, the cell membrane must be only selectively permeable if the cell is to survive. You can demonstrate how a membrane can be selectively permeable by carrying out the above experiment using larger molecules. Water molecules can pass through visking tubing but sucrose molecules, for example, cannot as the sucrose molecule is almost twice as large as the glucose molecule. If the apparatus is set up as before but using sucrose solution rather than glucose inside the visking tubing sac, water will pass into the sucrose solution but sucrose cannot pass into the water.

After about half an hour, the level of the solution in the tube will have risen, while the level of water in the beaker will have dropped. This is an example of **osmosis** where there is diffusion of water through a selectively permeable membrane from an area of greater concentration of water molecules to an area of lesser concentration of water molecules.

So what does all this mean to our cells? If the solution surrounding our red blood cells had less water than the cytoplasm of the cells, water would pass out of the cells faster than it would enter. The cells would then shrink and die. If the opposite occurred and there was more water outside, there would be a net gain of

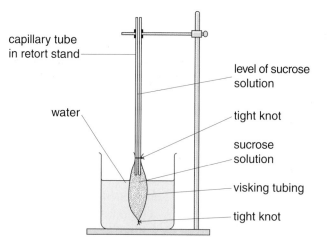

Figure 1.9 *The experiment can be repeated using sucrose solution*

Did you know?

It is possible to make ill-fitting leather shoes bigger by pushing potatoes to the ends of the toes. If they are left for a few days, the shoes will be a bigger size than before. Slugs will shrivel and die if you sprinkle salt on them. Try to explain these phenomena in terms of osmosis.

water and the cells would burst. Therefore, it is vital that the composition of our blood and other body fluids is regulated. This is an example of **homeostasis** or regulation of our internal environment (see p. 92).

Coursework Activity

To investigate osmosis in a potato

1 Label the lids of five Petri dishes as shown below.

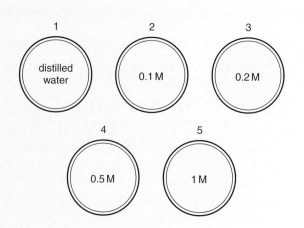

Figure 1.10 *Labelling the Petri dishes*

2 Put 30 cm³ of the solution marked on the lid into the Petri dishes.

3 Put the lids on the dishes.

4 With a cork borer, cut five cylinders from a potato making sure that they are each 50 mm long × 5 mm diameter.

Be careful that the borer cannot be pushed through into the hand.

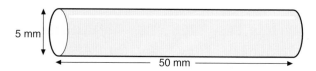

Figure 1.11 *A potato cylinder*

5 Weigh this batch of chips accurately on a top pan balance and record the mass in a table of results.

6 Place these chips in the Petri dish marked 'distilled water' and place the lid back on the dish.

7 Repeat stages 4 to 6 for each of the other dishes.

8 Leave the dishes for 20 minutes.

9 Remove the chips from the distilled water. Blot them gently with a paper towel. Weigh them accurately and record the mass in the table of results.

10 Repeat stage 9 for the chips in the other dishes.

Table of results

Solution in Petri dish	Mass at start/g	Mass after 20 min/g	Change in mass (±g)	% change (±)
Distilled water				
0.1 M sucrose				
0.2 M sucrose				
0.5 M sucrose				
1 M sucrose				

To calculate the % change:

$$\% \text{ change in mass} = \frac{\text{change in mass}}{\text{original mass}} \times 100$$

Draw a graph of the % change in mass against concentration of sucrose. Prepare the axes as follows:

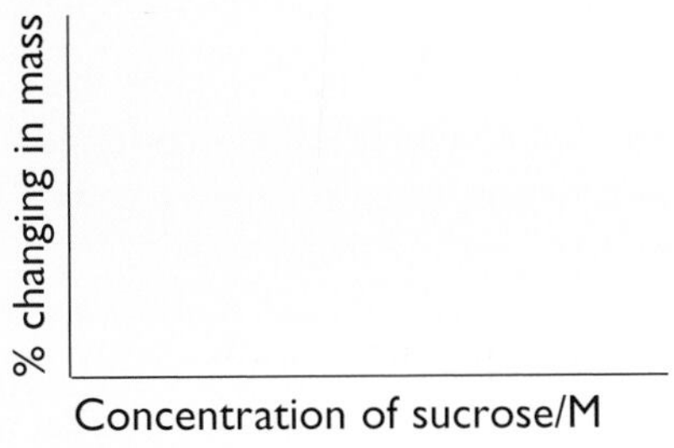

(graph axes: y-axis "% changing in mass", x-axis "Concentration of sucrose/M")

Questions

1 Why is it important to calculate the % change in mass?

2 In which solutions did water enter the cells of the potato?

3 In which solutions did water leave the cells of the potato?

To monitor osmosis – an alternative procedure using a computer

1 Fill a sac made of visking tubing with sucrose solution and place this in a beaker of distilled water.

2 Fit a pressure sensor to the sac with a tube and connect the sensor to a data logging system.

3 Start recording to test the system. You should have a graph trace on the screen that deflects when you squeeze the sac gently.

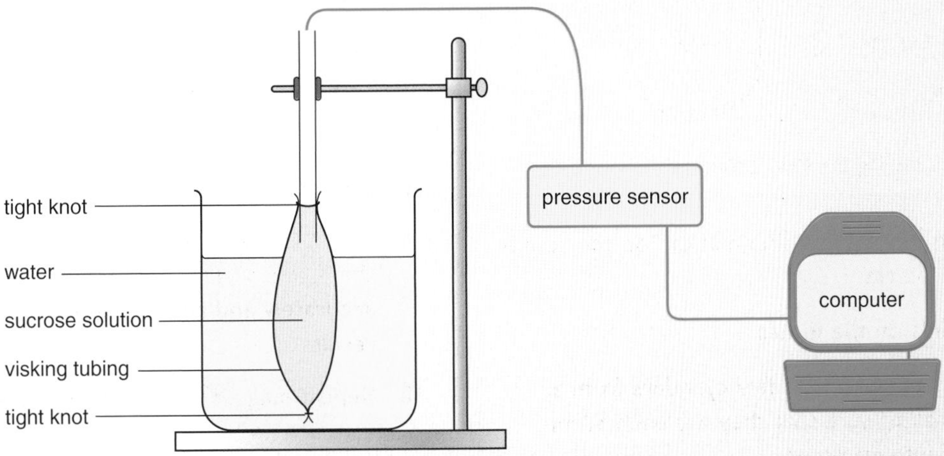

labels: tight knot, water, sucrose solution, visking tubing, tight knot, pressure sensor, computer

Figure 1.12 *Using a computer to monitor osmosis*

4 Continue recording for an hour or more. In the meantime, write up the experiment and answer the questions.

1 The graph trace should initially be a flat line, but it will change direction over time. What will cause the trace to change direction?

2 Draw a sketch to show how the graph will change during the experiment. As a clue, your sketch graph should have three sections you can label: (a) an initial flat line, (b) a section where the pressure rises and (c) a section where the pressure no longer changes.

3 Suggest how your graph explains what happens during osmosis.

4 You could use this method to investigate osmosis using a more concentrated solution of sucrose. Sketch the graph you would expect to obtain and explain why it may be different from the original one.

5 Look at the results of your experiment. Change the scale of the graph to see the results more closely. Find and label parts of the graph that represent equilibrium and the flow of water into the sac.

6 Repeat the experiment with a different concentration of sucrose solution.

Coursework Activity

1 Plan an investigation to find out the concentration of sugar which is equivalent to the concentration of cell sap.

2 Beetroot tastes sweeter than potato. Compare the sugar concentrations of the cell sap of beetroot and potato. Apply the procedure used on page 14 and refer to the Introduction to Coursework (p. 1).

Active transport

In many cases, particles pass into or out of cells against a diffusion gradient, i.e. against the direction of flow of particles. Sodium and potassium ions are examples of this – they are actively transported into or out of cells under certain circumstances. Whereas diffusion is a passive process, **active transport** requires energy released by the cell to be used to 'pump' ions in a particular direction.

Enzymes – tools of a cellular factory

Cells are living chemical systems in which substances are constantly changing: molecules react with other molecules; large molecules are built up and broken down. What starts these changes? What controls them? What keeps one change from interfering with another? The answer is **enzymes**. These are proteins made by living organisms which alter the rate of chemical reactions. They can be extracted from organisms and still retain their properties. We make use of this in biotechnology (see p. 246) when we use enzymes in washing powders and certain food manufacturing processes.

It is important not to think of all enzymes as chemicals which break large molecules into small ones like digestive enzymes. There are over one hundred thousand chemical reactions going on in your body at any given instant. Almost all of these are controlled by one or more enzymes, the vast majority of which have nothing whatsoever to do with digestion. Most are involved in the release of energy by the process of **respiration**.

All enzymes have certain properties in common:

● they are proteins.
● they are **denatured** when they are boiled. This means that their molecular structure is altered so that they can no longer work.
● they increase their rate of reaction with an increase in temperature up to a maximum. This suggests that the optimum temperature for our enzymes will be body temperature.
● their rate of reaction can be altered by changing the **pH** (degree of acidity or alkalinity). This means that each enzyme has an optimum pH at which it works fastest.
● they are **specific** in their action. This means that each one has a certain job. For example, enzymes used for energy release cannot be used for anything else, such as digestion or building up proteins.

Many possible models of enzyme action have been suggested. In one model, the enzyme is seen to act like a piece in a jigsaw puzzle. Another compares the action to a lock and key fitting together.

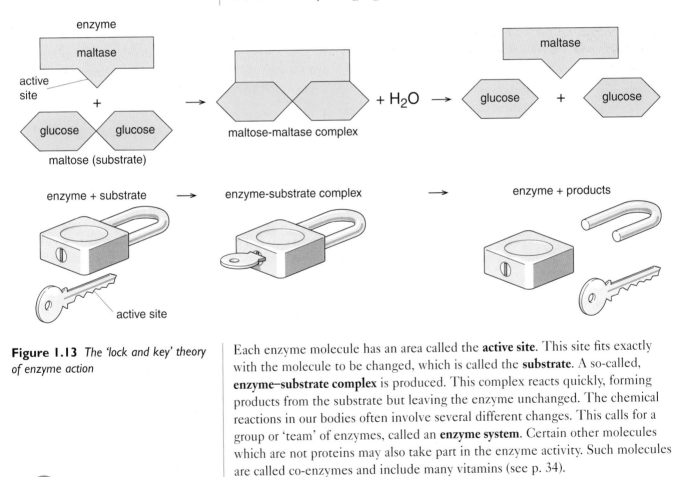

Figure 1.13 *The 'lock and key' theory of enzyme action*

Each enzyme molecule has an area called the **active site**. This site fits exactly with the molecule to be changed, which is called the **substrate**. A so-called, **enzyme–substrate complex** is produced. This complex reacts quickly, forming products from the substrate but leaving the enzyme unchanged. The chemical reactions in our bodies often involve several different changes. This calls for a group or 'team' of enzymes, called an **enzyme system**. Certain other molecules which are not proteins may also take part in the enzyme activity. Such molecules are called co-enzymes and include many vitamins (see p. 34).

www

The Online Biology Book – Enzymes
http://gened.emc.maricopa.edu/

The Biology Project – Biochemistry
http://www.biology.arizona.edu/

Enzyme activity

Catalase is an enzyme which is found in all organisms. It works by breaking down a group of poisonous substances called peroxides which are waste products made in cells. The peroxides are broken down to harmless substances, oxygen and water. Catalase has to work quickly to prevent the peroxides from killing the cells which produce them. It is, therefore, the fastest working enzyme.

Did you know?

Catalase is used in industry to make foam rubber and polystyrene products. The reaction between the enzyme and a peroxide will produce oxygen which is used to make the bubbles in the foam rubber or plastic. The same principle is used in the production of some first aid dressings for military use. The oxygen produced is used to kill certain bacteria which might otherwise cause gangrene.

Coursework Activity

To demonstrate enzyme activity

You will need to wear eye protection and a laboratory coat, if available, and must have access to a tap to wash any spillages away quickly with water.

The activity of catalase can be demonstrated using hydrogen peroxide and either plant tissue, such as potato, or animal tissue, such as liver.

You will need a piece of fresh liver from the butcher or a fresh potato, 3% hydrogen peroxide, three test tubes, a splint to test for oxygen, water, a Bunsen burner, tongs and labels.

1 Take two pieces of tissue (liver or potato), each about 1 cm³. Place one in a test tube half filled with water and boil it.

2 *Carefully* pour hydrogen peroxide into each of two test tubes until they are about half full. Label them A and B.

3 To A add a piece of unboiled tissue. Test any gas given off with a glowing splint.

4 Repeat stage 3 with test tube B and the boiled tissue. Wash your hands carefully once you have finished your investigation.

5 Describe your observations.

6 Explain your observations.

To demonstrate enzyme activity – an alternative procedure using a computer

1 Take two pieces of living tissue, each about 1cm³. Place one in a test tube, half filled with water, and boil it.

2 Carefully pour hydrogen peroxide into each of two test tubes until they are half full.

3 Connect two temperature sensors to a data logging system and place a sensor in each tube.

4 Start recording – you should have a graph trace on the screen. To one tube add a piece of unboiled tissue, to the other add the boiled tissue.

5 Explain your observation.

6 You can use a similar procedure to investigate the effect of changing the enzyme concentration. Sketch the graphs you would expect to obtain by adding more or less enzyme. Try the experiment.

Coursework Activity

Investigate the effects of one or both of the following on enzyme activity:

- temperature
- enzyme concentration.

Carry out the investigation using the apparatus shown in Figure 1.14 below and measure the volume of gas produced in the reaction.

Apply the procedure described above to the investigation and refer to the Introduction to Coursework (p. 1).

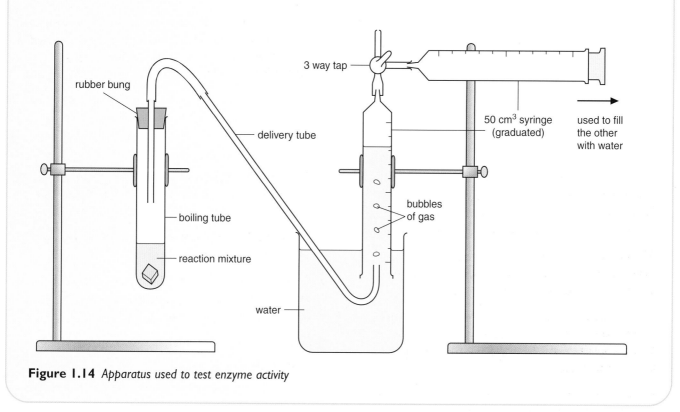

Figure 1.14 *Apparatus used to test enzyme activity*

Respiration – energy release in cells

Energy is the 'push' that makes things happen – it is the ability to do work. If you wind up the spring motor of a clock, the tightly wound spring will have stored or potential energy in it. As the spring begins to unwind and turn the mechanism of the clock, the stored energy is changed into movement or kinetic energy.

When carbon atoms are joined to make large carbohydrate molecules, the bonds which join the atoms are a form of potential energy. The bonds can be compared to wound-up springs.

A log burning in a fireplace is undergoing a chemical change in which the energy stored as chemical bonds is released. The carbohydrate in the log breaks down into carbon dioxide and water and the bond energy is rapidly converted into heat and light. In a similar way, our bodies give off carbon dioxide and water in a process which can be likened to burning. Although the end products of the two processes are the same, cells 'burn' their fuel, glucose, in a completely different way. Instead of releasing energy rapidly, cells must save it to be used for many functions in the body.

Chemical reactions in cells therefore take place in small steps that release energy slowly. The overall reaction can be represented by the following equation:

$$C_6H_{12}O_6 \;+\; 6O_2 \;\rightarrow\; 6CO_2 \;+\; 6H_2O \;+\; E$$

glucose · · · · · · · oxygen · · · · · · · · · carbon dioxide · · · · · water · · · · · energy

However, the equation does not tell you much about the energy. It does not tell you the form that the energy takes and it does not show you that the energy is released in stages. In fact, the energy is stored for a very short time before it is used, in the bonds of a chemical called **adenosine triphosphate (ATP)**. The ATP is a kind of chemical storage battery. In the ATP molecule, the three phosphate groups form a chain linked to the rest of the molecule.

$$A—P—P—P$$

The most important chemical fact about ATP is that the last phosphate group and bond can be separated relatively easily from the rest of the ATP molecule and can join to other compounds. The loss of the phosphate ion changes ATP into **adenosine diphosphate**, **ADP**, which can eventually be recycled to form ATP once more. Energy from the chemical bond in ATP becomes available for the use of the cell in building up molecules and to drive all living processes. The release of energy from glucose in every living cell is called **respiration** and is a characteristic of all living organisms. The energy released allows us to demonstrate the other six characteristics: movement, growth, reproduction, sensitivity, excretion and nutrition.

Coursework Activity

To demonstrate energy release by respiring seeds – an alternative procedure using a computer

Set up three thermos flasks as shown in the diagram, and record the temperature of each flask at the beginning and end of a week.

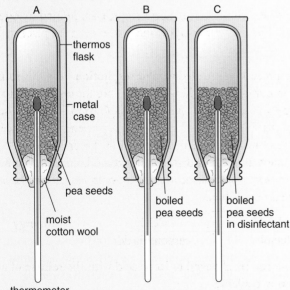

Figure 1.15 *Apparatus used to show that germinating peas respire and give off heat*

Questions

1 What is the purpose of the disinfectant?

2 What is the advantage of using thermos flasks rather than beakers?

3 Why are cotton wool plugs used rather than rubber bungs?

4 Which one of the flasks is the control?

5 Explain the results in each flask.

IT To demonstrate energy release by respiring seeds – an alternative procedure using a computer

1 Set up the thermos flasks as shown in Figure 1.16.

2 Connect three temperature sensors to a data logging system and place a sensor in each flask.

3 Start recording and continue to record for a day or more.

4 Sketch the graphs you would expect to obtain and compare these with your results. Add your comments to the graphs and print them.

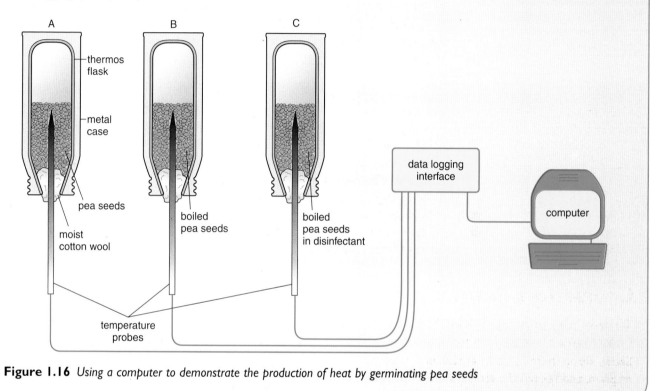

Figure 1.16 *Using a computer to demonstrate the production of heat by germinating pea seeds*

Respiration is a controlled process and occurs in small steps, each helped by one or more respiratory enzymes. These enzymes allow the process to take place at normal body temperature.

When oxygen is used in the process, it is called **aerobic respiration**. It is this form of respiration which occurs in our cells. It is, however, possible for respiration to take place without oxygen by a process called **anaerobic respiration**. This releases only a fraction of the energy that is released when oxygen is present. Glucose can be broken down with the use of respiratory enzymes without the presence of oxygen. In some organisms, such as yeasts, ethanol and carbon dioxide are formed by this process. This reaction is very important in industry because it is the basis of both baking and alcoholic fermentation.

$$C_6H_{12}O_6 \rightarrow 2C_2H_5OH + 2CO_2 + \text{Energy}$$
$$\text{glucose} \qquad \text{ethanol} \qquad \text{carbon dioxide}$$

In our muscle tissues, glucose can be changed to lactic acid with the release of a little energy when no oxygen is available.

$$C_6H_{12}O_6 \rightarrow 2C_3H_6O_3 + \text{Energy}$$
$$\text{glucose} \qquad \text{lactic acid}$$

This is useful during physical exercise when muscle cells are sometimes starved of oxygen because the energy demand exceeds the supply of oxygen by the blood. Under these circumstances, the body can still release energy for a short time, although there will be a build up of lactic acid causing muscle fatigue. After such exertion, when we rest, we breathe more deeply and more rapidly. This is essential because a greater intake of oxygen is needed to pay off the oxygen debt incurred by the extra demand. The fitter we are, the more efficient is our circulation, and the less lactic acid is produced.

Summary

1 The cell is the basic unit of structure and function in living things.

2 Living things are organised according to different levels of structure. Some are made of a single cell, others are made up of many cells organised into tissues, organs and organ systems.

3 The different kinds of cell in an organism support each other when they perform a particular function.

4 In order for the cell to remain in balance with its environment, the cell membrane controls the movement of molecules into and out of the cell.

5 The cell membrane is selectively permeable so different particles pass through at different rates. Useful materials can pass through the membrane, but cell structures remain within the cell.

6 Some particles may move through the membrane as a result of diffusion. When water passes through it is said to move by osmosis.

7 Movement of particles by diffusion is called passive transport.

8 When cells absorb ions against a diffusion gradient, energy is used by the cell and the process is known as active transport.

9 Enzymes are special proteins made by all living things. They are used to speed up chemical reactions taking place in the body.

10 Energy stored in glucose is released during respiration. Glucose molecules are broken down and their chemical bond energy is released.

11 Some of this energy is given off as heat, some is stored as ATP for use in cellular activities.

Homework Questions

1   In one sense Robert Hooke discovered cells, in another he did not. Discuss this statement.

2   State the two principles of the cell theory.

3   What are the main features that distinguish animal cells from plant cells?

4   Distinguish between permeable and selectively permeable membranes.

5   What is diffusion? What is the name for the balance that results from diffusion?

6   State the external factors that influence diffusion rates.

7   Define osmosis.

8   Distinguish between active and passive transport.

9   What is the biological importance of respiration?

10 Describe the two types of anaerobic respiration.

In-Depth Questions

1   In what respect is the cell the basic unit of life?

2   Describe what might happen to a cell if the membrane were permeable to all molecules.

3   What factors determine whether or not a particle will pass through a cell membrane?

4   Describe how cells obtain their usable energy.

2 Nutrition

By the end of this chapter, you should be able to understand:

- photosynthesis in terms of reactants and products;
- the factors which limit photosynthesis;
- how the products of photosynthesis are utilised by organisms;
- the functions and sources of food;
- the use of water by organisms;
- a variety of methods by which animals obtain food;
- the structure and function of the parts of the digestive system.

Energy is released from fuel and is one of the basic needs of all living things. Energy, contained in food, is released and used to maintain the living organism. Living things can be classified into three main groups according to their method of obtaining food.

1 **Autotrophs** – including plants which contain chlorophyll and make their own food by photosynthesis.

2 **Heterotrophs** – animals, parasites and saprophytes which obtain their food by eating animals and plants.

3 **Chemotrophs** – including certain bacteria which can use the energy from chemical reactions in order to make their own food e.g. nitrifying bacteria in the nitrogen cycle (see p. 248).

Photosynthesis

Autotrophs can turn a variety of simple chemicals into the complex molecules of food which may be used by heterotrophs. How do they do it? There are various ways of answering this question through investigations. Some important experiments were carried out hundreds of years ago which give us a basis to work on. From these experiments we can now state that the following three factors are the most important.

- light
- carbon dioxide
- chlorophyll

Separate investigations can be carried out to demonstrate the importance of each factor.

Coursework Activities

To show that there is food (starch) stored in a leaf

A RISK ASSESSMENT IS NEEDED. YOU WILL BE USING ETHANOL WHICH IS HIGHLY FLAMMABLE.

1. Wearing eye protection, remove a leaf from a plant which has been left in sunlight for several hours. Geraniums (*Pelargonium*) are most suitable because their leaves are soft with no thick cuticle.

2. Hold the leaf with forceps and kill it by putting it in boiling water in a beaker for at least 30 seconds.

3. Remove the chlorophyll by soaking the leaf in warm ethanol. Use a water bath to heat the ethanol. Do not expose ethanol to a direct flame.

4. When the leaf is colourless or pale yellow, wash it with cold water for a few seconds in a Petri dish.

5. Pour away the water and, making sure you are wearing eye protection, replace it with iodine in potassium iodide solution.

6. Observe any colour change. A blue-black colour indicates the presence of starch.

To show that light and carbon dioxide are needed for photosynthesis

- Destarch a plant by leaving it in the dark for 48 hours. During this time any starch present in the leaves will have been converted to sugar and removed from the leaves to the stem or roots.
- Test a leaf from the plant for starch before you begin the experiment.

a) Carbon dioxide

1. Select two leaves of approximately the same size.

2. Experimental leaf – wearing eye protection, surround one leaf with a 250 cm³ conical flask containing 25 cm³ of 0.4 M sodium hydroxide or potassium hydroxide, as shown in the diagram. Both chemicals will remove the carbon dioxide. A cotton wool plug soaked in limewater will prevent carbon dioxide entering the flask.

3. Control leaf – set up the second leaf in the same way as the experimental leaf but this time use 25 cm³ water, instead of the sodium/potassium hydroxide. Plug the flask with cotton wool soaked in water.

b) Light

1. Select two leaves of approximately the same size.

2. Cover the experimental leaf with a black card as shown in the diagram.

3. Test the leaves for starch after several hours in the light.

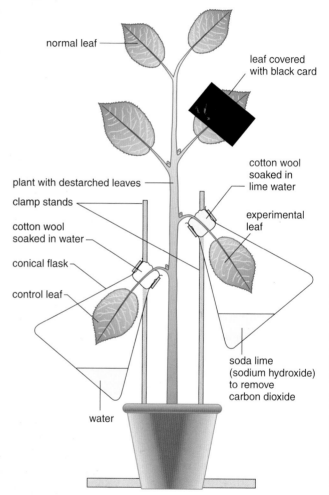

normal leaf

leaf covered with black card

plant with destarched leaves

clamp stands

cotton wool soaked in water

conical flask

control leaf

cotton wool soaked in lime water

experimental leaf

soda lime (sodium hydroxide) to remove carbon dioxide

water

Figure 2.1 *Apparatus used to show that light and carbon dioxide are needed for photosynthesis*

4. Record your observations in a table using the headings given overleaf.

5. Explain the observations.

Condition	Leaf	Observation after the starch test
With carbon dioxide	Experimental	
No carbon dioxide	Control	
With light	Experimental	
No light	Control	

To show that chlorophyll is needed for photosynthesis

The easiest way to do this is to use a variegated leaf of *Pelargonium* in which only the green parts have chlorophyll.

1 Destarch the plant by leaving it in the dark for 48 hours.

2 Leave the plant in bright light for several hours.

3 Test a leaf from the plant for starch as described previously.

4 Record the results.

5 Explain the results.

Figure 2.2 *Variegated leaves of* Pelargonium

Energy trapping

The Sun is the source of energy for all living things but up to 50% of its energy is reflected back into space and never reaches Earth. The relatively small amount that eventually reaches the surface of the Earth is in the form of light and heat. Light is trapped by the green pigment **chlorophyll** which is found in the leaves and stems of plants. Some plants do not appear to be green but can still capture light energy, for example red and brown seaweeds and ornamental plants with coloured leaves. These contain chlorophyll but it is hidden by the presence of other coloured pigments.

Visible white light consists of the seven colours of the spectrum but unless we see a rainbow, we are not usually aware of this. However, in a laboratory, we can split light into its seven colours using a prism. Green plants will absorb red and blue light and reflect the rest – particularly the green. This is why plants look green. The light that plants absorb provides the energy necessary to build up complex molecules of food from small molecules of carbon dioxide and water.

Where does the trapping of energy occur?

Chlorophyll plays a vital role in photosynthesis along with other pigments found in the leaves and stems of plants. Chlorophyll is packaged in chloroplasts (see p. 9). The leaves of plants are very well adapted for the purpose of trapping energy and acting as a centre for photosynthesis. Imagine that you had the ability to make a leaf. What features would you give it in order to make it good at its job? Here are some suggestions:

1 Large surface area to enable the leaf to trap the maximum amount of light energy and absorb the maximum amount of carbon dioxide.

2 Very thin structure so that no cell is far from the light source.

3 Cells which allow light to penetrate them (translucent).

4 Chlorophyll distributed in chloroplasts near the upper surface of the leaf.

5 Leaves positioned in such a way that each leaf receives the maximum amount of light without overshadowing.

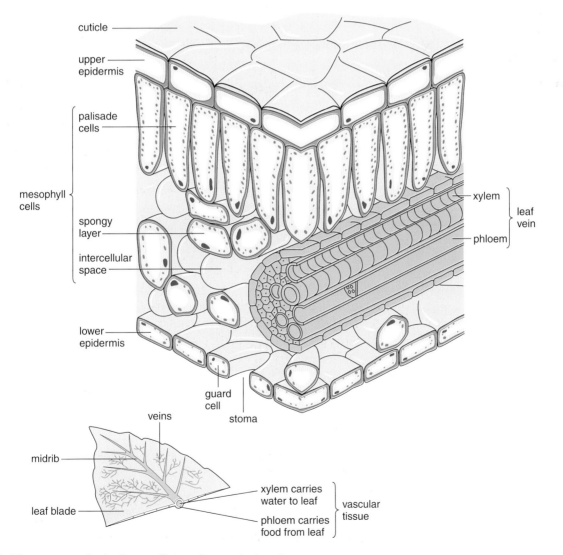

Figure 2.3 *The structure of a leaf – an efficient photosynthetic unit*

6 Holes in the leaf to allow for the exchange of gases.

7 Spaces between cells to allow the movement of gases.

8 Well-developed supply system to carry water and salts to the cells.

9 Distribution system to export manufactured food from the leaf.

If we examine the leaf of a plant in microscopic detail (as in Figure 2.3), we can see these specifications.

The raw materials

The elements needed for photosynthesis are carbon from carbon dioxide and hydrogen from water. These are discussed in greater detail below.

● Carbon dioxide reaches the plant from two possible sources: from the waste products of respiration within the plant or from the atmosphere, which contains about 0.04% carbon dioxide. The gas diffuses from the air into the leaf through holes called **stomata**. The movement of carbon dioxide into the leaf down a diffusion gradient continues as long as the chlorophyll continues to use it.

● Water reaches the plant from the soil via the roots. It is then transported to the leaves through the xylem vessels (see p. 71). The word equation for the process of photosynthesis is:

$$\text{Carbon dioxide} \; + \; \text{Water} \; \xrightarrow[Chlorophyll]{Light} \; \text{Glucose} \; + \; \text{Oxygen}$$

The complex chemistry involved is simplified below:

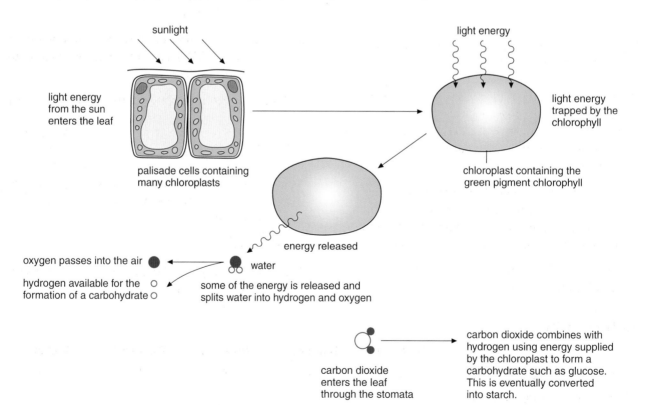

sunlight

light energy

light energy from the sun enters the leaf

light energy trapped by the chlorophyll

palisade cells containing many chloroplasts

chloroplast containing the green pigment chlorophyll

energy released

oxygen passes into the air

water

hydrogen available for the formation of a carbohydrate

some of the energy is released and splits water into hydrogen and oxygen

carbon dioxide enters the leaf through the stomata

carbon dioxide combines with hydrogen using energy supplied by the chloroplast to form a carbohydrate such as glucose. This is eventually converted into starch.

Figure 2.4 *The energy trap*

Coursework Activities

To demonstrate oxygen production during photosynthesis

Rusting of metals only occurs in the presence of oxygen. Providing that an oxygen-free environment is present at the start of this experiment, you can apply this principle to demonstrate that oxygen is produced as a result of photosynthesis.

1 Set up two specimen tubes A and B as shown in Figure 2.5.

2 Fill them with boiled, cooled water containing 2 g of sodium hydrogen carbonate.

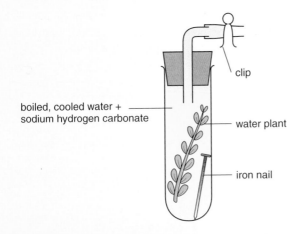

Figure 2.5 *Apparatus used to demonstrate the production of oxygen during photosynthesis*

3 Place equal sized pieces of Canadian pondweed (*Elodea*) into each specimen tube. The pondweed should have been left in the dark for 24 hours prior to the experiment. Wash your hands before continuing

4 Take some new iron nails, rub them with emery paper to remove the anti-rust coating, place one into each specimen tube and insert a bung. Ensure there is no air space at the top of the tubes.

5 Cover tube B with foil to prevent light from reaching the plant.

6 Leave the tubes in bright light for 1 hour and then observe the appearance of the nail in both tubes.

Questions

1 Explain your observations.

2 State why the water was boiled before the experiment.

3 State the purpose of the sodium hydrogen carbonate.

4 Why is it important to completely fill the tubes with boiled, cooled water?

To investigate the effect of light intensity on the rate of photosynthesis using *Spirogyra*

Spirogyra is a primitive plant (a type of alga) which normally lives in fresh water ponds. As an alga, it is not rooted into the bed of the pond.

1 Place some *Spirogyra* in a large beaker of water and leave it in the dark for 24 hours.

2 Place equal masses of *Spirogyra* in five beakers containing 100 cm³ distilled water and 0.5 g sodium hydrogen carbonate. Wash your hands after handling the *Spirogyra*.

3 Place the five beakers at increasing distances from a strong lamp (150 W). (Use the distances given in the table of results below.)

4 Record the time for *Spirogyra* to rise to the surface.

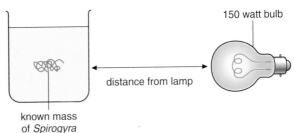

Figure 2.6 *Apparatus used to investigate the effect of light intensity on rate of photosynthesis*

Table of results

	Beaker 1	Beaker 2	Beaker 3	Beaker 4	Beaker 5
Distance from lamp/cm	5	25	50	75	100
Time taken for *Spirogyra* to rise					

Questions

1 Plot your results as a line graph. Draw a line of best fit.

2 Explain the results.

3 List any sources of error that could have caused the *Spirogyra* to rise more quickly than expected, particularly in beaker 1.

Coursework Activity

As oxygen is given off during photosynthesis, its rate of production can be used as a measure of photosynthetic activity. By counting the number of bubbles produced or measuring the volume of gas produced in a given time, the main limiting factors (see p. 24) of photosynthesis can be investigated. By using either of the sets of apparatus drawn below, investigate the effects of light intensity, carbon dioxide concentration and temperature on the rate of photosynthesis of the Canadian pondweed, *Elodea*.

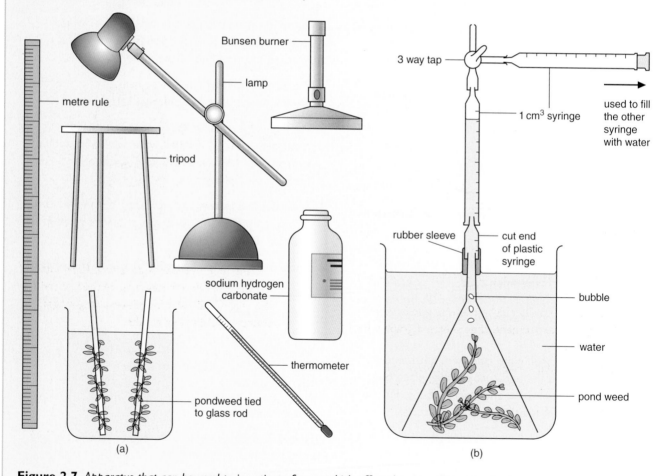

(a)   (b)

Figure 2.7 *Apparatus that can be used to investigate factors which affect the rate of photosynthesis*

Plot your results as graphs and evaluate them in terms of valid conclusions, possible sources of error and possible improvements. By using coloured filters or coloured cellophane stuck on the beakers, you could investigate the effect of different wavelengths of light on the rate of photosynthesis. Do different colours of light affect photosynthesis? How does acid rain affect photosynthesis?

To monitor photosynthesis – an alternative procedure using a computer

Oxygen production and carbon dioxide uptake can be monitored using sensors. Oxygen levels can be measured with an oxygen electrode, while changes in carbon dioxide level can be measured with a pH electrode. A data logger can collect the readings automatically over a few days.

To monitor oxygen production

1 Place an oxygen electrode in a flask with sodium hydrogen carbonate solution and fresh *Elodea*.

2 Place the flask and a light sensor near a window.

To monitor carbon dioxide uptake

1 Place a pH electrode in a flask with sodium hydrogen carbonate solution and fresh *Elodea*.

2 Clamp the electrode close to the plant where it will monitor small changes in pH.

3 Place a light sensor nearby and connect the sensor to a data logging system. You can now investigate the effect of light intensity on carbon dioxide uptake.

4 Start recording and continue for about 30 minutes.

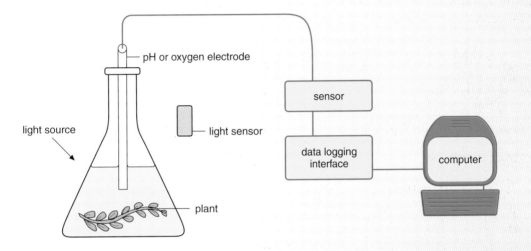

Figure 2.8 *Using a computer to monitor photosynthesis*

3 Connect the sensors to a data logging system and leave this to record for at least a day.

4 Think about how the light intensity will change during your experiment, then sketch a graph which shows this.

5 Next, think about how the oxygen level will change and add a sketch of a graph to show this.

6 Compare your predictions with your results.

5 For the first 10 minutes cover the flask with foil, for the next 10 minutes remove the foil and for the final 10 minutes, switch on a bright light source. Explain your results.

The Online Biology Book – Photosynthesis
http://gened.emc.maricopa.edu/

Photosynthesis
http://esg-www.mit.edu:8001/esgbio/ps/psdir.html
http://www.factmonster.com/science.html

Did you know?

An average person from a country in the developed world will eat about 30 tonnes of food in a lifetime. However, most of us manage to maintain a constant body weight, within 1%.

Animals and food

What is food?

Food is a collection of chemicals taken into an organism for the purposes of growth and energy release, and to maintain all the life processes. By this definition, water, minerals and vitamins are food as well as carbohydrates, fats and proteins.

The process of preparing the foods to reach the body tissues occurs in a 9-metre long tube, called the **alimentary canal**. Digestive enzymes break the carbohydrates, proteins and fats down into smaller molecules of glucose, amino acids, glycerol and fatty acids, respectively. These can then pass into the bloodstream.

The many uses of water

Water is an inorganic substance and gives no energy to the body tissues. It is, however, essential for all forms of life. Humans can survive for many weeks without food but will die very quickly without water.

If you weigh 50 kg, your body will contain between 30 and 35 kg of water. Much of this water is in the cytoplasm of your cells and in the spaces between cells. The fluid part of blood is up to 92% water. This water acts as a solvent for the transport of dissolved foods from the alimentary canal to the blood and dissolved waste materials which are carried to the skin and kidneys for excretion. Up to 2.5 litres of water pass through the kidneys each day.

The loss of water by sweating also helps in the regulation of heat loss from our bodies. Evaporation, the process by which liquids change to gases, requires heat. When your sweat evaporates from your skin, heat is lost from your body.

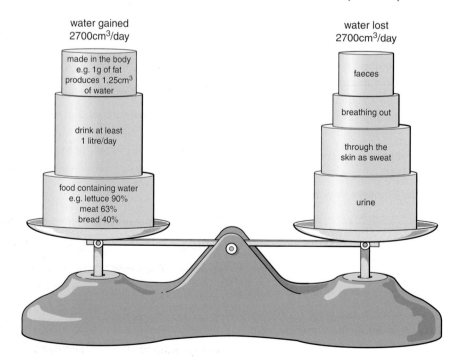

Figure 2.9 *Water balance in humans*

The water we lose in these ways must be replaced. We can take in water in three ways:

1 from the food we eat

2 as a by-product of chemical reactions in our cells

3 from drinking all types of liquids.

What happens if you do not drink enough water? First, you lose water from between your cells, then you lose it from the cells themselves. When this happens, the cytoplasm becomes affected. Eventually, the cells cannot function and they die as a result of dehydration.

Mineral salts in the body

Food supplies us directly with the mineral salts our bodies need. Two of the most important minerals are **calcium** and **phosphorus** which our bodies need in greater amounts than other minerals. Calcium is needed for proper functioning of cell membranes and for blood clotting (see p. 60), and together with magnesium, is essential for nerve and muscle action. Phosphorus is needed for making the complex chemical, DNA, found in our chromosomes (see p. 148) and also for ATP, our temporary store of energy, which is formed during respiration (see p. 19). Calcium phosphate is needed to form bones and teeth. Indeed, calcium and phosphorus make up about 5% of our tissue when combined with the other elements in proteins. Milk is a good source of these two elements along with wholegrain cereals, meat and fish.

Some more essential minerals are detailed below:

- **potassium** compounds are needed for growth and are abundant in meat and most vegetables.
- **iron** is needed for the formation of haemoglobin (see p. 59) and is found most commonly in meat, green vegetables and certain fruits such as plums, raisins and prunes.
- **iodine** salts are needed to form the hormone **thyroxine** (see p. 113) and are found in iodised table salt or any type of sea food.

Although minerals are vital to the body in many ways, our bodies can only use them as compounds. Eating chemically pure elements, such as sodium or chlorine, would kill you because of the damage they would inflict on your cells. As a compound, however, sodium chloride is essential.

Table 2.1 *A summary of some essential minerals*

Mineral	Essential for	Source
Calcium compounds	Bone and teeth development Nerve and muscle action Blood clotting	Milk, wholegrain cereals, meat, vegetables
Iron compounds	Haemoglobin formation	Liver, meat, spinach
Iodine compounds	Thyroxine formation (see p. 113)	Iodised table salt, sea food

Vitamins

In 1911, Dr Casimir Funk demonstrated that some substances, present in very small amounts in food, seemed to be essential for normal body growth and activity. They were not ordinary nutrients and without them, people suffered from deficiency diseases. Initially, when the chemistry of these essential substances was unknown, they were identified by means of letters – A, B, C etc. – instead of names. Today, the chemical nature of all vitamins is known and each has a given chemical name. We do, however, still use the letters for easy identification.

Vitamins are organic substances, but while they are essential to life, they are not sources of energy. They act by helping many of the enzymes which work inside your cells. Hundreds of years ago, when explorers went on long sea voyages they ate only preserved foods. Many became ill with **scurvy** and died from bleeding of the gums and internal organs. It was subsequently discovered that the eating of citrus fruits prevented scurvy because of the vitamin C found in them, and so ships began carrying barrels of limes on board. Unlike certain small mammals, such as rats and hamsters, humans cannot make this vitamin, so we must get it from our food.

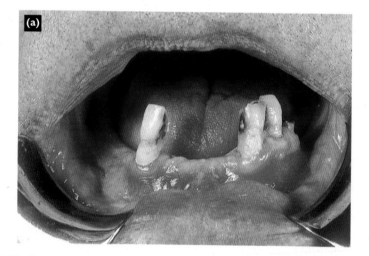
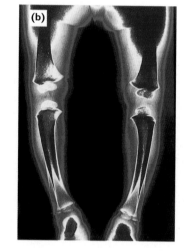

Figure 2.10 *Examples of two deficiency diseases: (a) scurvy and (b) rickets*

Table 2.2 *The functions and sources of vitamins A, C and D*

Vitamin	Best sources	Essential for	Symptoms of deficiency
A (fat-soluble)	Fish liver oils, liver and kidney, green and yellow vegetables, butter, egg yolk	Growth, good eyesight, healthy skin and mucous-membranes	Retarded growth, night blindness, viral infections
C (water-soluble)	Citrus fruit, vegetables, blackcurrants	Growth, maintaining strength of blood vessels, development of teeth and gums	Scurvy i.e. sore gums and bleeding around bones and from intestine
D (fat-soluble)	Fish liver oil, liver, milk, eggs	Growth, regulating use of calcium and phosphorus for making bones and teeth	Rickets i.e. soft bones and dental decay

We are able to store fat-soluble vitamins in our bodies, but those that are soluble in water cannot be stored and the excess is excreted in our urine. Vitamin D is unusual in that it can be made in our skin as a result of exposure to the Sun. We can get most vitamins from vitamin pills but a balanced diet should provide all the essential vitamins the body needs.

Coursework Activity

To investigate the level of vitamin C in fruit juice

Vitamin C, or ascorbic acid, is a powerful reducing agent and a dye, DCPIP, can be used to detect it. The vitamin causes the dark blue dye to be decolourised.

1 Pour 1 cm³ 0.1% DCPIP into a test tube.

2 Take a 1 cm³ syringe full of sample material, for example lemon juice.

3 Record the volume of sample material you need to add to the DCPIP to decolourise it.

4 Repeat the test with 1 cm³ of fresh 0.1% DCPIP using an ascorbic acid solution of known concentration.

5 Record the volume of this solution needed to decolourise the DCPIP solution.

Sample results

Volume of lemon juice used to decolourise 1 cm³ of DCPIP solution = 0.5 cm³

Volume of ascorbic acid of known concentration used to decolourise 1 cm³ of DCPIP solution = 0.4 cm³

Conclusion

The lemon juice was $\dfrac{0.4}{0.5}$ times as concentrated as the standard ascorbic acid solution. Therefore, if the standard ascorbic acid solution contained 1 mg ascorbic acid per cm³ water, the lemon juice must contain

$1 \times \dfrac{0.4}{0.5} = 0.8$ mg ascorbic acid per cm³ water.

Coursework Activity

Do canned fruits have the same vitamin C content as fresh fruits?

Organic nutrients

Carbohydrates, fats and proteins are called **organic nutrients** because they are formed by living cells and contain the element, carbon. Carbohydrates and fats are responsible for supplying most of our energy. The tissue-building value of foods can only be measured by observing the growth of animals when they are fed, but energy values of food can be measured in **calories** or **joules**. One calorie is defined as the amount of heat needed to raise the temperature of 1 g of water by 1°C. Though we commonly use the term calorie, the actual unit is called a **kilocalorie**. The international units scientists tend to use to measure heat energy are joules, where 1 kilocalorie = 4.2 kilojoules (kJ).

Here are some examples of the daily energy requirements of a variety of people:

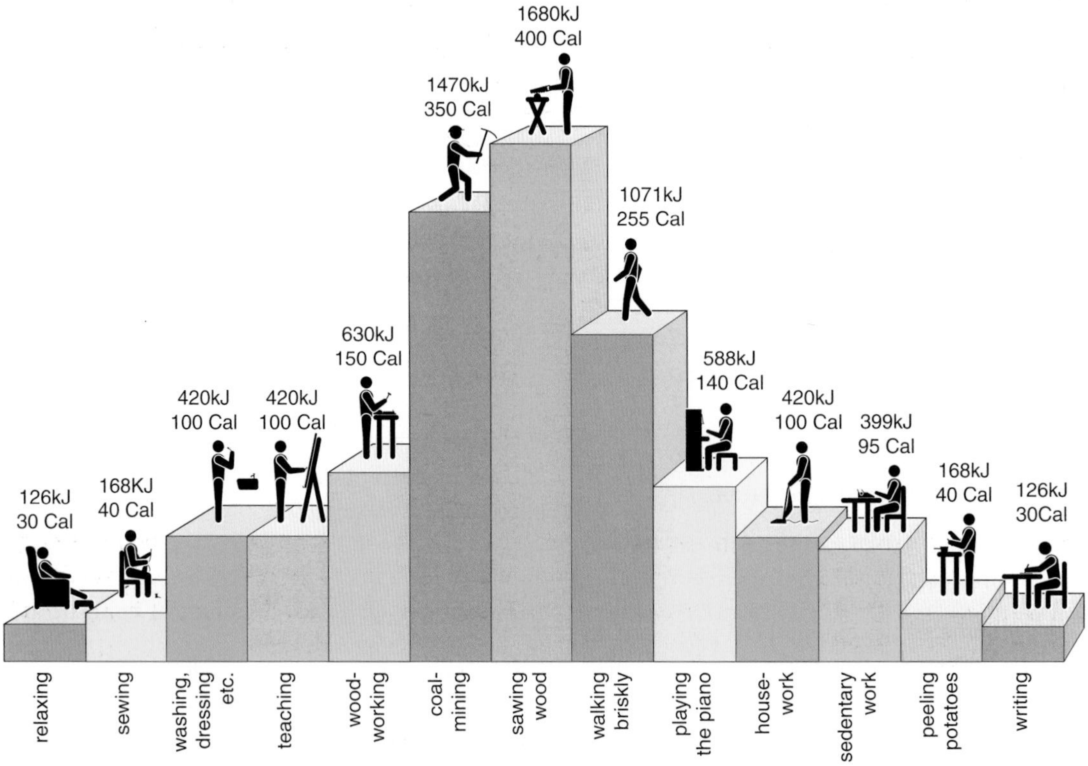

126kJ
30 Cal
relaxing
168KJ
40 Cal
sewing
420kJ
100 Cal
washing, dressing etc.
420kJ
100 Cal
teaching
630kJ
150 Cal
wood-working
1470kJ
350 Cal
coal-mining
1680kJ
400 Cal
sawing wood
1071kJ
255 Cal
walking briskly
588kJ
140 Cal
playing the piano
420kJ
100 Cal
house-work
399kJ
95 Cal
sedentary work
168kJ
40 Cal
peeling potatoes
126kJ
30Cal
writing

Figure 2.11 *Our energy needs per hour for a number of different activities*

Coursework Activity

To investigate the heat energy in a pasta shape

1. Weigh a pasta shape and mount it on a pin as shown in the diagram.
2. Place 20 cm^3 water in the boiling tube.
3. Note the temperature with a thermometer.
4. Set light to the pasta with a Bunsen burner and place the boiling tube over it to catch as much of the heat as possible. (Use safety goggles.)
5. Read the temperature as soon as the pasta has been completely burned.
6. Record the temperature increase.
7. Work out the number of joules of heat the water has received as follows:

   4.2 J raises 1 g water by 1 °C

   Temperature increase = Y°C, mass of pasta = X g, mass of water = 20 g

   Heat gained by water = 20 g × Y × 4.2 J

Heat produced by 1 g of sample

$$= \frac{20 \times Y\,g \times 4.2}{1000 \times X} \text{ kJ per g}$$

thermometer
cotton wool
boiling tube
tin can
20 cm³ water
pasta shape
pin on plasticine

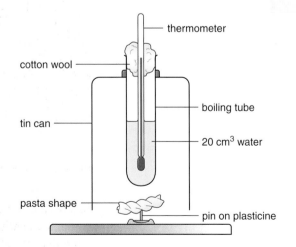

Figure 2.12 *Apparatus used to measure the heat energy in a pasta shape*

Note that the possible sources of error include:

- heat loss from around the sides of the boiling tube;
- heat used to raise the temperature of the thermometer and the glass of the boiling tube;
- incomplete burning of the pasta.

Heat loss could be minimised by insulating the apparatus.

Coursework Activity

Are all types of nuts equally fattening?

Did you know?

The average adult in Britain eats 43 kg of sugar every year. Sugar is a highly concentrated store of energy – 43 kg of it can keep you walking briskly for over 2000 miles. Do you walk 2000 miles in a year?

Even if you do, sugar is not the only energy-giving food that you eat. If present in excess in the diet, sugar is changed into fat which can result in a person becoming overweight. It also causes tooth decay.

Why are carbohydrates important?

Figure 2.13 *Foods rich in carbohydrates*

In a balanced diet, more than half of your food should be carbohydrate. Despite the large quantities in which it is eaten, stored carbohydrate never makes up more than 1% of your body weight because carbohydrates are mainly fuel which your cells use to release energy during **respiration** (see p. 19). You eat many different kinds of carbohydrates: some are digested easily and can travel to tissues with little chemical change; some have to be broken down before your tissues can use them; others are not digested at all. We need a certain amount of the indigestible types in our diets for bulk, or **roughage**. All digestible carbohydrates reach the body tissues as glucose.

There are many simple sugars in your food, such as glucose and fructose, which are immediate sources of energy and require no chemical change before the blood can absorb them from the digestive organs. Sucrose (cane sugar), lactose (milk sugar) and maltose (malt sugar) are larger molecules and have to undergo digestion in order to break them into small molecules before they can be absorbed.

A large proportion of the carbohydrate in most diets is starch. There is a lot of starch in potatoes and cereals. Starches are made up of long chains of glucose units. During digestion, starch is changed to maltose, which is then broken down to glucose. Glucose is absorbed by the blood and carried via the liver to the body's tissues. Much of the glucose that goes through the blood to the liver is turned into an animal starch called **glycogen** for temporary storage. Glycogen can be turned back into glucose when the body needs it (see p. 116).

Cellulose is a complex carbohydrate found in the walls of all plant cells. Although we cannot digest cellulose, it is a very important part of a balanced diet. Cellulose acts by stimulating muscle contractions throughout the alimentary canal and helping to pass the food along. Many herbivores, such as rabbits and horses, have microbes living in their digestive systems which are able to digest cellulose to produce sugars which the herbivore can use. This is an example of symbiosis where two different species live together for mutual benefit. How do you think the microbes benefit?

Fats as an energy store

Fats and oils give more than twice as much energy as carbohydrates. Common sources of fats and oils include butter, cream, cheese, margarine, vegetable oils and meats.

Figure 2.14 *Foods rich in fats and oils*

During digestion, enzymes slowly break down fats in three stages. The result is one molecule of glycerol and three molecules of fatty acid from each fat molecule digested.

Excess carbohydrates in the diet are converted into fats and stored under the skin and around the kidneys. Eating too much fat can be detrimental to health because it leads to obesity and cholesterol build-up (see p. 239). For this reason, it is important that you control how much carbohydrate and fat you eat. A balanced diet should consist of approximately 60% carbohydrate, 20% fat and 20% protein.

Proteins and their uses

Proteins are complex organic molecules made up of thousands of units called **amino acids**. They have to be broken down into these basic units during digestion so that they can be carried in the blood to tissues where they are built up again into human proteins. Proteins are used for growth and repair and as the basis for all enzymes and hormones.

When we take in more protein than our bodies need we cannot store it. After digestion, the excess amino acids are broken down into two parts in the liver by a process called **deamination**. One part (the amino part) contains nitrogen and is converted to **urea** and transported by the blood to the kidneys. From there it is excreted in the **urine** (see p. 93). The other part, containing carbon, is converted to glucose which can be used by the body. Some of the best sources of protein include lean meat, eggs, milk, cheese, whole wheat and beans.

Figure 2.15 *Foods rich in protein*

Coursework Activities

A RISK ASSESSMENT IS NEEDED FOR ALL CHEMICALS USED.

A test for starch

Wearing eye protection, add a few drops of iodine in potassium iodide solution (1 g iodine dissolved in 500 cm³ distilled water containing 7 g potassium iodide) to 2 cm³ of a suspension of the food under investigation.

If starch is present the suspension turns from its original colour to a dark blue-black.

A test for a simple reducing sugar

Add 2 cm³ Benedict's solution to 5 cm³ of a solution suspected to contain a simple reducing sugar. Wearing eye protection, boil the mixture in a water bath.

If a simple reducing sugar is present the mixture changes colour from light blue, through green, then yellow, to an orange-brown powder which settles as a precipitate.

The reducing sugar has reduced the copper salts in the Benedict's solution to copper oxide, the orange-brown precipitate.

A test for a soluble protein

Add a few drops of Biuret reagent to 2 cm³ of a solution suspected to contain protein. (If the Biuret reaction is to be carried out in two stages, 0.4 M sodium hydroxide solution is sufficient for solution A.)

If protein is present a violet colour is seen in the mixture.

A test for fat

Rub a sample of the suspected fat on a piece of paper.

If fat is present a translucent patch is seen on the paper which remains when it is dried.

Types of feeders   TRIPLE AWARD ONLY

Animals can be classified into three main groups according to their method of feeding:

- fluid feeders
- filter feeders
- large particle feeders

Fluid feeders

Some fluid feeders can absorb materials directly into their bodies without having to digest it. One example of such a fluid feeder is the tapeworm which inhabits the intestines of animals, absorbing food which has already been digested.

Other fluid feeders have special mouthparts that allow them to suck fluids into their digestive systems. Examples include butterflies and bees, which feed on nectar, and lice and ticks, which suck blood from their victims. Perhaps the most frightening example of this type of feeder is the vampire bat which attacks warm-blooded animals and has razor sharp teeth to penetrate the skin.

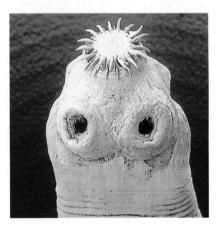

Figure 2.16 *A tapeworm*

Figure 2.17 *Two examples of fluid feeders (a) a butterfly, (b) a vampire bat*

Filter feeders

Filter feeders occur in almost every major group of animals. They rely on water to bring small particles to them and then filter the water with hair-like structures which may be microscopically small cilia in cockles and mussels to large, comb-like structures in the largest animal in the world, the blue whale.

Large particle feeders

Figure 2.18 *Two examples of filter feeders (a) a mussel, (b) a whale*

Large particle feeders break down particles of food which are large in proportion to themselves. Most use mechanical and chemical means, but some simple types, like single-celled animals, surround and engulf organisms before digesting them.

Mechanical digestion relies on the presence of teeth and a chewing action, both of which are modified according to the diet of the animals involved. The difference between the methods in plant eaters (herbivores) and meat eaters (carnivores) can be illustrated by a sheep and a dog.

Herbivores have large flat teeth to cut and grind their food, while carnivores have sharp pointed teeth for capturing and tearing their mobile prey before swallowing it. The jaw movements are also different: the side-to-side movements of the herbivore jaw ensure grinding of the food while an up-and-down movement of the jaw of a carnivore ensures shearing and tearing, with little chewing before swallowing.

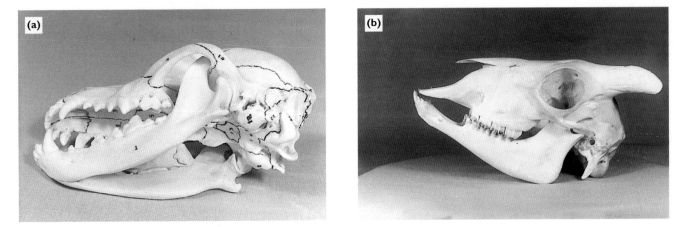

Figure 2.19 *The skull of (a) a dog and (b) a sheep to illustrate the differences between the teeth and jaws of a carnivore and a herbivore*

The stages of digestion

Did you know?

After you have finished eating, your meal is technically still on the outside of your body, or at least *on* one of your body surfaces. For all practical purposes your digestive system is nothing more than a tube.

Before the food can begin to satisfy your needs for protein, carbohydrate, fat, minerals and vitamins, your meal has to get inside your cells.

Why can't your body's tissues use foods in the form in which you eat them? There are two reasons:

1 Many foods will not dissolve in water which means that they could not get through cell membranes even if they could reach them.

2 The foods you eat are chemically complex so cells cannot use them either to release energy or to make proteins.

Digestion solves both these problems. During digestion, complex foods are broken down into small, water-soluble molecules which can be absorbed and used by your cells.

Digestion occurs in two stages, the first of which is **mechanical**. Your teeth chew the food which breaks it down into small enough pieces to be swallowed. The muscular movements of the wall of the digestive system then churn and mix it with various juices. All of this aids the second stage of digestion which is **chemical**. At this stage, digestive enzymes secreted by the digestive glands complete the job.

The digestive system comprises both those organs that form the alimentary canal which receive the undigested food and those that deliver secretions into the alimentary canal through tubes called ducts.

The digestive system

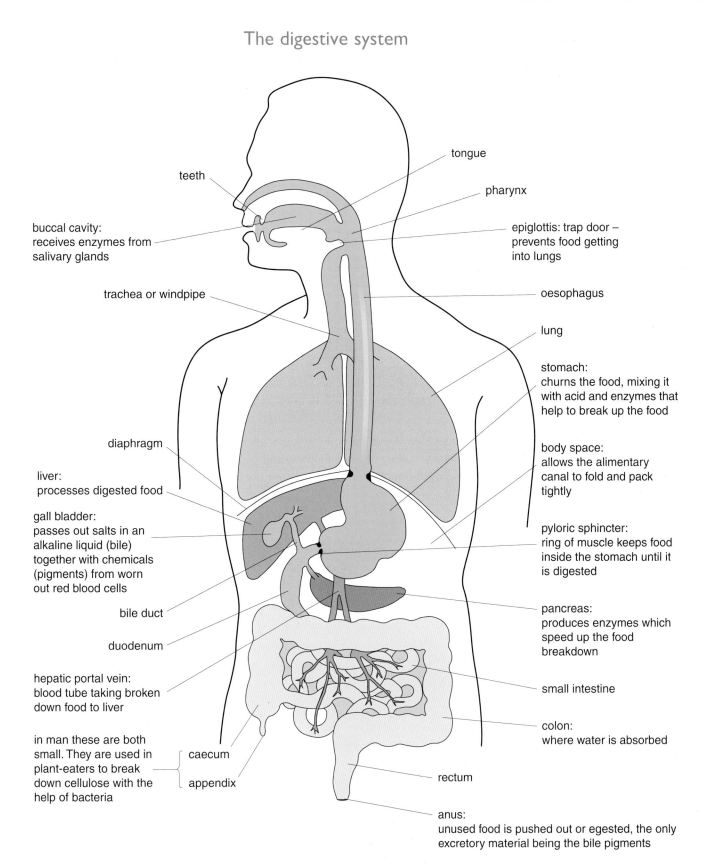

teeth

tongue

pharynx

buccal cavity:
receives enzymes from
salivary glands

epiglottis: trap door –
prevents food getting
into lungs

trachea or windpipe

oesophagus

lung

stomach:
churns the food, mixing it
with acid and enzymes that
help to break up the food

diaphragm

liver:
processes digested food

body space:
allows the alimentary
canal to fold and pack
tightly

gall bladder:
passes out salts in an
alkaline liquid (bile)
together with chemicals
(pigments) from worn
out red blood cells

pyloric sphincter:
ring of muscle keeps food
inside the stomach until it
is digested

bile duct

pancreas:
produces enzymes which
speed up the food
breakdown

duodenum

hepatic portal vein:
blood tube taking broken
down food to liver

small intestine

colon:
where water is absorbed

in man these are both
small. They are used in
plant-eaters to break
down cellulose with the
help of bacteria

caecum

appendix

rectum

anus:
unused food is pushed out or egested, the only
excretory material being the bile pigments

Figure 2.20 *The human digestive system*

The mouth

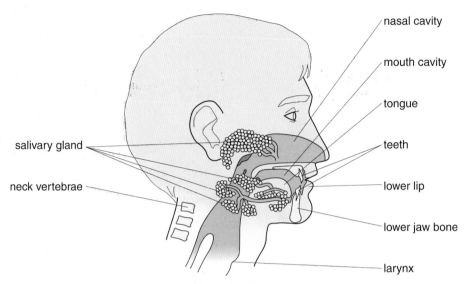

Figure 2.21 *The location of the salivary glands*

The chief job of the mouth is to prepare food for digestion. Salivary glands secrete **saliva** into the mouth through ducts located opposite your upper back (molar) teeth and also in the floor of the mouth, under the tongue.

When your mouth 'waters', it is as a result of these glands secreting saliva. This happens when you taste food or simply when you smell or see it. If you are hungry, the thought of food can start the secretion of saliva.

The types of teeth

We have two sets of teeth during our lives, the milk teeth and the permanent teeth. Milk teeth appear first and are not as strong as our final permanent teeth.

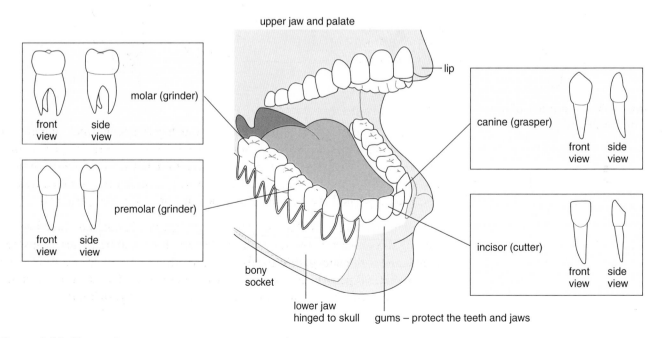

Figure 2.22 *Human dentition*

They also lack wisdom teeth (third molars). The permanent teeth are arranged in the same way in both the top and bottom jaw.

The two flat front teeth are called **incisors**. They have sharp edges for cutting food. Next to the incisors, at the corner of your lips on either side, is a large cone-shaped tooth called the canine. Behind the canine tooth are the two **premolars**. Next are the **molars**. You have three of these on either side if you have your complete set, though they may not appear until you are in your twenties. Premolars and molars have flat surfaces which are good for grinding and crushing. Many jaws are too small to hold the third molars, or wisdom teeth. In such cases wisdom teeth often grow crooked or remain impacted in the gums.

The structure of a tooth

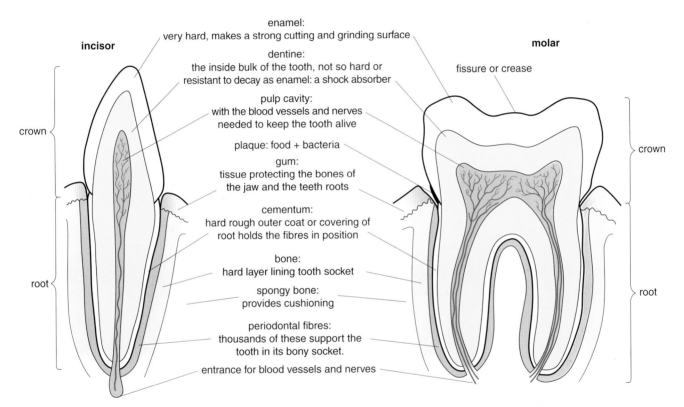

incisor

enamel:
very hard, makes a strong cutting and grinding surface

dentine:
the inside bulk of the tooth, not so hard or resistant to decay as enamel: a shock absorber

pulp cavity:
with the blood vessels and nerves needed to keep the tooth alive

plaque: food + bacteria

gum:
tissue protecting the bones of the jaw and the teeth roots

cementum:
hard rough outer coat or covering of root holds the fibres in position

bone:
hard layer lining tooth socket

spongy bone:
provides cushioning

periodontal fibres:
thousands of these support the tooth in its bony socket.

entrance for blood vessels and nerves

molar

fissure or crease

crown

root

crown

root

Figure 2.23 *The structure of two types of human tooth*

The oesophagus and stomach

When food is swallowed, it passes into the **oesophagus**, a tube which connects the mouth to the stomach. Two layers of muscle line the wall of the oesophagus and help the food to move to the stomach. One layer is circular and squeezes inwards, the other layer runs lengthwise and contracts in a wave that travels downwards. The food is pushed ahead of the contraction in a process called **peristalsis**.

The stomach has layers of muscle fibres which contract in different directions causing the stomach to twist, squeeze and churn. It is lined by a thick, wrinkled membrane with many **gastric glands**. There are three kinds of gastric glands: one kind secretes digestive enzymes; another secretes hydrochloric acid; and a third secretes mucus. The mixture of these secretions is called **gastric juice**.

Before swallowing

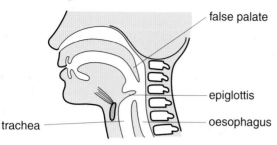

false palate

epiglottis

oesophagus

trachea

Swallowing

1 Tongue moves up and back pushing food into the throat.

3 False palate pushed back blocking the airway from the nose.

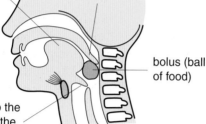

bolus (ball of food)

2 Muscles pull up the larynx and make the epiglottis drop down.

longitudinal muscle

circular muscle contracts behind bolus forcing it along

bolus

rubber tube

marble

Figure 2.24 *The mechanisms of swallowing and peristalsis*

Food usually stays in the stomach for 2 to 3 hours. Rhythmic muscular contractions churn the food back and forth in a circular path. This churning separates food particles and mixes them thoroughly with the gastric juice. When the stomach has finished digesting the food, a ring of muscle called the **pyloric sphincter** relaxes, allowing food into the **small intestine**. When the stomach is finally empty, it rests for a while. After several hours without food, the stomach starts contracting again, making you feel hungry.

The small intestine

The small intestine is a tube about 3 cm in diameter and 7 m in length. The first 25 cm is called the **duodenum**. This part of the tube curves upward, then back to the right, beneath the liver. Beyond the duodenum is the much longer **ileum** which is about 5 m long and coils through the abdominal cavity. The end of the ileum joins the **large intestine**.

The mucous lining of the small intestine contains many tiny intestinal glands which secrete **intestinal fluid** into the small intestine. This fluid contains enzymes used in digestion.

The liver

The liver weighs about 1½ kg. It is a dark chocolate colour and lies in the upper right area of your abdomen. The liver secretes **bile**, a brownish-green fluid which passes through a series of **bile ducts** to the **gall bladder** where it is stored. Here bile is concentrated by removal of part of its water content. The larger **common bile duct** carries bile from the gall bladder to the duodenum. In some people this bile duct becomes clogged by **gallstones**. When this happens the bile enters the blood stream and causes **jaundice** which turns the eyes and skin a yellowish colour.

The pancreas and pancreatic juice

The pancreas looks similar to a salivary gland in that it is white with many lobes. It lies behind the stomach against the back wall of the abdominal cavity. The pancreas performs two very different functions:

- it secretes **pancreatic juice** into the small intestine through the **pancreatic duct**. This duct leads to a common opening with the bile duct in the wall of the duodenum.
- it produces the hormones, **insulin** and **glucagon** (see p. 115).

The large intestine

The end of the small intestine connects with the **colon** in the lower right part of the abdominal cavity. The **caecum** is located at the point where they meet. Leading from the caecum is the finger-like **appendix** which may become infected, causing **appendicitis**. In herbivores the caecum and appendix contain microbes that help in the digestion of cellulose – a substance which cannot be digested by the digestive juices of the herbivores alone. The colon is about 7 cm in diameter and 1½ m long and forms an upside-down U-shaped structure in the abdominal cavity. At the end of the colon is the **rectum** which leads to the anal opening. A ring-like sphincter muscle in the lower end of the rectum controls the elimination of intestinal waste, or **faeces**.

The chemical stages of digestion

As foods move along the alimentary canal, they go through a series of chemical changes. By a step-by-step process, large, insoluble molecules are broken down into smaller, soluble molecules. At every stage, a specific digestive enzyme is used, each of which is responsible for splitting a specific kind of molecule. The digestive enzymes in the alimentary canal act outside the cells and are therefore responsible for **extracellular digestion**. In contrast, single-celled animals, such as *Amoeba*, have **intracellular digestion**.

Digestion in the mouth

Chemical digestion begins in the mouth. Here, a salivary enzyme begins the digestion of starch. Saliva is about 95% water but also contains mineral salts to regulate pH, lubricating mucus and the enzyme, **amylase** (a type of **carbohydrase**). Amylase converts cooked starch into maltose sugar. Starchy foods, like potatoes, should always be cooked before eating as this bursts their cellulose cell walls and allows the amylase to reach the starch grains. As food is only in the mouth for a short time, starch digestion is seldom finished when the food is swallowed.

Did you know?

Some of the earliest investigations into chemical digestion inside a living person became possible only when an 18-year old boy, Alexis St Martin, was accidentally shot by a blast from a shot gun in 1822. He survived and the wound healed, apart from a 2 inch hole which led directly into his stomach. Alexis experienced a normal, active life but the wound was a peep hole through which digestion could be observed by doctors. He was paid to be a 'guinea pig' and lived to be 76.

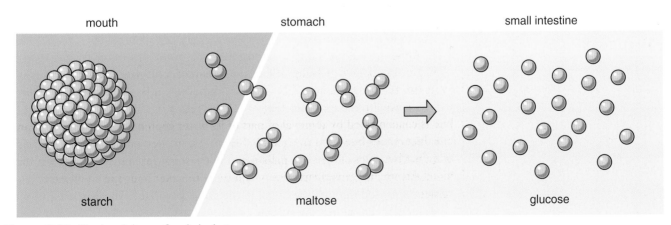

Figure 2.25 *The breakdown of carbohydrate*

mouth · stomach · small intestine

starch · maltose · glucose

Gastric juice at work

The main enzyme in gastric juice is **pepsin** (a type of protease). This enzyme works on protein, splitting the complex molecules into simpler groups of amino acids called **polypeptides**. This splitting is the first in a series of chemical changes involved in protein digestion.

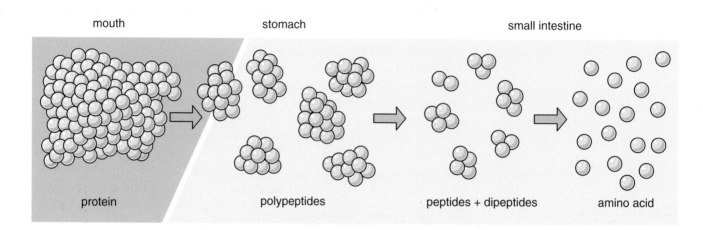

mouth   stomach   small intestine

protein   polypeptides   peptides + dipeptides   amino acid

Figure 2.26 *The breakdown of protein*

Hydrochloric acid is produced in the stomach. It helps pepsin to work efficiently and kills any bacteria which may enter the stomach with food. The food that passes from the stomach to the small intestine contains:

- fats, unchanged
- the sugars, sucrose, glucose and lactose unchanged
- maltose sugar, formed by the action of amylase on starch
- any starches not yet changed by amylase
- peptones and proteoses formed by pepsin acting on protein
- any proteins not yet acted on.

The liver and the bile

The liver has many functions. Some of the more important ones are listed below:

- It converts glucose from the blood into **glycogen** which it stores as a reserve of carbohydrate.
- It changes excess amino acids to urea. The liver can therefore be considered an organ of excretion.
- It secretes bile which has many important characteristics:
  - It contains materials from used, dead red blood cells so can be thought of in part as a waste substance.
  - Although it is *not* a digestive enzyme it helps the process of fat digestion by breaking down globules of fat into an emulsion. **Lipase** from the pancreas can act on fats more easily in this form because a larger surface area of fat is exposed to the enzyme.
  - It neutralises acid from the stomach so that pancreatic enzymes can function efficiently.
- It releases a lot of heat because of all the chemical reactions taking place there. In this way it helps the body to maintain a constant temperature because the heat is carried through the blood in the same way that heat is carried in the water of a central heating system.

● It stores many useful materials such as iron (used to make red blood cells in the bone marrow) and vitamins A and D.

The pancreas and digestion

Pancreatic juice contains enzymes which act on all three of the main classes of food. The enzymes are:

● **trypsin** which continues the process of protein breakdown that began in the stomach. It changes peptones and proteoses into simpler molecules called **dipeptides**.
● **pancreatic amylase** which changes any remaining starch to maltose sugar.
● **lipase** which splits fats into fatty acids and glycerol.

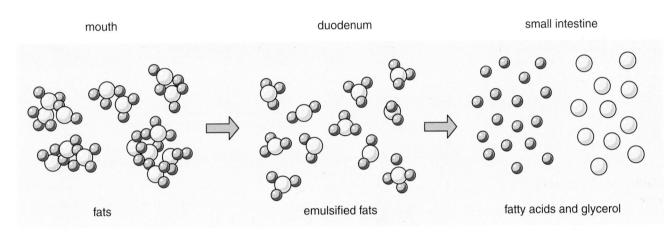

mouth   duodenum   small intestine

fats   emulsified fats   fatty acids and glycerol

Figure 2.27 *The breakdown of fat*

The small intestine and digestion

Table 2.3 *Summary of digestion*

Place of digestion	Glands	Secretion	Enzymes	Digestive action
mouth	salivary	saliva	amylase	starch to maltose
stomach	gastric	gastric juice	pepsin	proteins to polypeptides
		hydrochloric acid		activates pepsin; kills bacteria
small intestine	liver	bile		emulsifies fats
	pancreas	pancreatic juice	trypsin	proteins to polypeptides
			amylase	starch to maltose
			lipase	fats to fatty acids and glycerol
	intestinal	intestinal juice	peptidase	peptides to amino acids
			maltase	maltose to glucose
			lactase	lactose to glucose and galactose
			sucrase	sucrose to glucose and fructose
			lipase	fats to fatty acids and glycerol

Digestion is completed in the small intestine by the action of at least five enzymes:

1 Peptidase completes the digestion of protein to amino acids.

2 Lipase completes the digestion of fats to glycerol and fatty acids.

3 **Maltase** breaks maltose into glucose.

4 **Sucrase** breaks sucrose (sugar from sugar cane and sugar beet) into glucose and fructose.

5 **Lactase** breaks lactose (milk sugar) into glucose and **galactose**.

The products of digestion are now soluble and are ready to leave the alimentary canal by absorption so that they can be transported to where they are needed in the body.

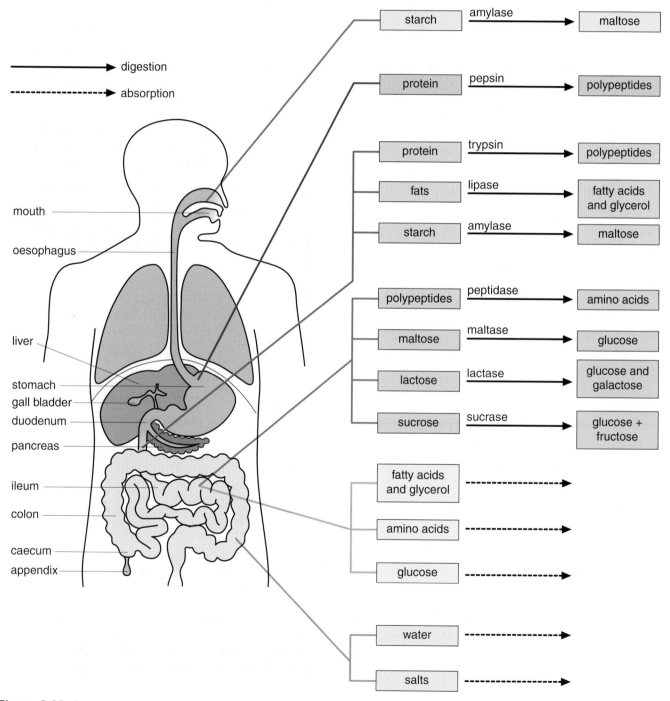

Figure 2.28 *A summary of enzymes in the alimentary canal*

Coursework Activities

To investigate the action of amylase on starch

Note: For this experiment it is important that bacterial amylase is not used, as it may not give the required results. Saliva can be used as an alternative, but care must be taken to sterilise equipment after use.

1 Label three test tubes 1, 2 and 3. Add 1% starch suspension to each.

2 Wearing eye protection, boil 2 cm^3 of 1% amylase in a water bath for 1 minute and add it to test tube 1.

3 Add 2 cm^3 of distilled water to test tube 2.

4 Add 2 cm^3 of unboiled 1% amylase to test tube 3.

5 Use a teat pipette to withdraw one drop of mixture from each of the test tubes 1, 2 and 3.

6 Wearing eye protection, add the drops to iodine in potassium iodide solution on a white tile as shown.

7 Record your observations in a table.

8 Place the three test tubes in a water bath at 35°C.

9 Test one drop of each mixture at 2 minute intervals for 20 minutes.

10 Record your observations.

11 Plan and carry out an investigation to determine the nature of the substance produced as a result of the reaction in test tube 3.

12 Carry out the original investigation at varying temperatures.

To investigate the action of pepsin on egg white

1 Take the white (albumen) of an egg and draw it into five pieces of capillary tubing, each 2 cm long.

2 Wearing eye protection, put the capillary tubes into a beaker of boiling water and leave them for 2 minutes.

3 After this time the capillary tubes will contain hard boiled egg white. Remove the tubes with tongs and measure the lengths of the egg white in each.

4 Place the capillary tubes in test tubes as shown in the diagram.

5 Place these test tubes in a water bath at 35°C for 30 minutes then measure the lengths of egg white in each tube again.

6 Record your results.

7 State your conclusion and evaluate the procedure.

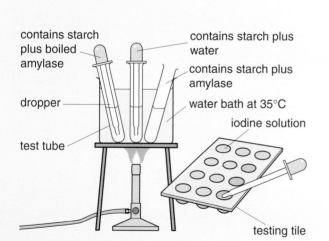

Figure 2.29 *Apparatus used to test the action of amylase on starch*

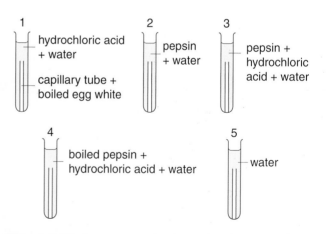

Figure 2.30 *Apparatus used to investigate the action of pepsin on egg white*

Safety note: Be careful not to rub your eyes when working with enzymes as this may cause contamination. Similarly, wash any splashes of enzyme solution off the skin as soon as possible.

Coursework Activities

What factors affect digestion in the mouth?
Does the digestion of starch stop in the stomach?
Will bile help the digestion of fats?

IT

To measure amylase activity – an alternative procedure using a computer

A light sensor can measure the light transmitted through a mixture of starch, amylase and iodine in potassium iodide solution. As the starch is digested, the mixture changes from blue-black to yellowish-brown. The light sensor monitors the colour change which can be plotted as a graph.

As the protein is digested, the mixture changes from cloudy to clear. The change can then be plotted as a graph.

1 Add 1 cm³ 1% fresh pepsin and 5 cm³ egg albumen to a cuvette.

2 Wearing eye protection, add a few drops of 1 M hydrochloric acid until the pH is 5 – this helps the pepsin to work.

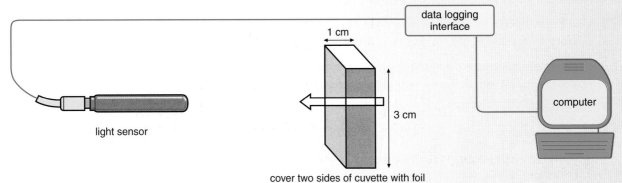

light sensor

data logging interface

1 cm

3 cm

computer

cover two sides of cuvette with foil

Figure 2.31 *The apparatus needed to monitor amylase activity or protein digestion using a computer*

1 Wearing eye protection, add 1 cm³ 1% fresh amylase, 5 cm³ 0.1% starch solution and three drops of iodine in potassium iodide solution to a cuvette.

2 Arrange the cuvette as shown and connect a light sensor to a data logging system. You may need to record for up to 15 minutes before a change is seen.

3 Look at the graph and label the points at which starch digestion appears to start and finish.

4 Repeat your experiment using a different starch concentration and compare your two graphs.

To measure pepsin activity – an alternative procedure using a computer

Exactly the same principle can be used to trace the digestion of egg albumen by pepsin. A light sensor measures the light transmitted through a mixture.

3 Arrange the cuvette as shown in Figure 2.31 and connect a light sensor to a data logging system.

4 Start recording.

5 Look at the graph and label the points at which digestion appears to start and finish.

To measure lipase activity – an alternative procedure using a computer

A pH sensor can monitor the digestion of fat by lipase. The lipase digests the fat to form fatty acids which then cause a decrease in the pH of the solution.

1 Add 5 cm³ of fresh UHT milk to a boiling tube in a water bath set at 35°C.

2 Place a pH electrode in the milk and connect the sensor to a data logging system.

3 Wearing eye protection, add a few drops of 1 M sodium carbonate solution to make the

milk sample alkaline at pH 9. This prevents the solution from becoming too acidic too quickly and provides the correct pH for the lipase to work.

4 Start recording, add 5 cm³ of 2% lipase solution and measure the pH for about 40 minutes.

5 Look at the graph and label the points at which digestion appears to start and finish. Suggest how you could use the graph to measure the rate of the reaction.

You can also investigate whether emulsifying the fat changes the rate of the reaction. Repeat your experiment exactly as before, but this time add a few drops of bile salts (washing up liquid can be used as a substitute) to the milk. Before you see the results, predict how the graph might appear this time. How do your graphs show that one reaction is faster than the other? Suggest why your two graphs should start and end at the same pH.

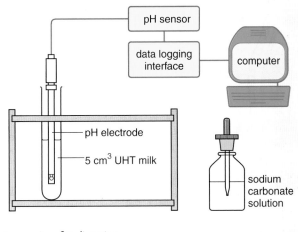

Figure 2.32 *Using a computer to monitor fat digestion*

Absorption

The small intestine has many finger-shaped projections in its irregular lining. These projections are called **villi**. There are so many of them that they give the intestinal wall a velvety appearance and vastly increase the total surface area in contact with the digested food. As a result, absorption into the transport system of the body is maximised. The small intestine is remarkably well adapted for its two important functions which are:

● the completion of digestion
● absorption.

Digestion is aided by the presence of intestinal glands which secrete intestinal juice, while absorption is maximised by:

1 millions of **villi** which increase the surface area;

2 a rich blood capillary supply to carry away glucose and amino acids. The capillaries join up to form the **hepatic portal vein** which carries blood directly to the liver;

3 **lacteals** which carry away glycerol and fatty acids;

Homework Questions

1   What are the functions of the main classes of foods?

2   Explain why the body must have water.

3   Explain why photosynthesis is essential to almost all forms of life.

4   Define photosynthesis using a word equation.

5   In what two general ways must food be changed during digestion?

6   List the divisions of the alimentary canal in order. What digestive processes occur in each?

7   Name the parts of a tooth.

8   Why is it especially important that you chew bread and potatoes thoroughly?

9   Suppose that you had a glass of milk and a sandwich made of bread, butter and chicken. Describe what would happen to each of these foods as digestion occurred.

10 Name an important function of the large intestine.

In-Depth Questions

1   Explain how a vitamin deficiency is possible even if an adequate amount of all the vitamins is taken daily.

2   Give an account of the conditions that affect photosynthesis.

3   Why is it an advantage to have acid conditions in the stomach and alkaline conditions in the small intestine?

4   What is the advantage of peristalsis?

5   Why is it easier to digest sour milk than fresh milk?

Transport of Materials in Animals and Plants

By the end of this chapter you should be able to understand:

● the composition and function of blood;

● the structure and function of the human circulatory system;

● how plants take up water and transpire;

● the importance of water to plants;

● that substances required for growth and reproduction are transported within plants.

A fluid tissue

The fluid that carries all the substances your body needs is called **blood**. An average person has about 6 litres of blood which makes up about 9% of your body mass. Blood is a type of connective tissue which is made of two different parts: a non-living fluid part called **plasma** and living blood cells which float in the plasma.

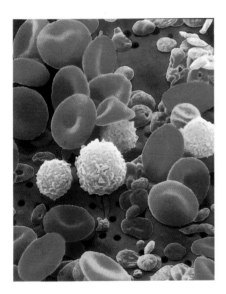

Figure 3.1 *The different cell types in blood – red cells, white cells (appear yellow) and platelets (small pink cells)*

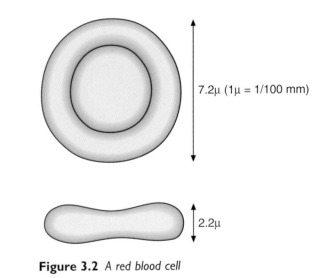

7.2μ (1μ = 1/100 mm)

2.2μ

Figure 3.2 *A red blood cell*

Plasma is a sticky, straw-coloured liquid, 90% of which is water. Proteins in the plasma make it sticky – this is essential to enable the blood to maintain the correct pressure in the blood vessels. One of the most important proteins is called **fibrinogen**, which is involved in blood clotting. Plasma also contains an enzyme called **prothrombin** which is produced in the liver in the presence of vitamin K and which also functions during blood clotting.

The other materials in plasma are chemicals dissolved in water. These compounds include:

- carbonates, chlorides and phosphates of the elements calcium, sodium, magnesium and potassium. These compounds are necessary for the normal functioning of your body tissues. Without calcium compounds, for example, your blood would not clot in a wound.
- digested foods in the form of glucose, fatty acids, glycerol and amino acids. These are carried to body tissues, the liver and other storage areas.
- nitrogenous wastes from protein metabolism in the tissues. One of these wastes is urea which is made in the liver during the breakdown of unwanted amino acids. These nitrogenous wastes travel in the plasma to the organs of excretion (see p. 90).

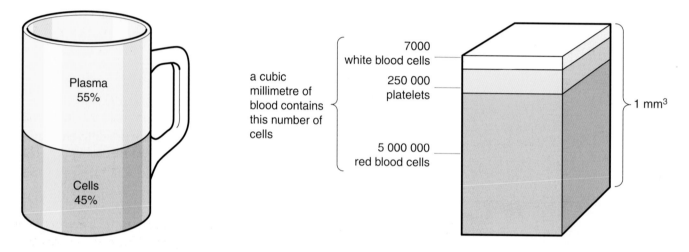

Plasma 55%

Cells 45%

a cubic millimetre of blood contains this number of cells

7000 white blood cells

250 000 platelets

5 000 000 red blood cells

1 mm³

Figure 3.3 *The percentage composition of the various components of blood*

The blood cells

There are three solid components of blood: red blood cells which are shaped like biconcave discs, white blood cells, and platelets which, unlike the red and white cells, are not complete cells.

Did you know?

Ten million red blood cells could be spread out in about 6 cm². A normal person has about 5.5 million red cells per mm³ of blood. If you laid the cells side by side, they would go around the world four times!

Figure 3.4 *If laid end to end, your red blood cells could circle the Earth four times*

The red cells are produced in the red bone marrow at the ends of such bones as the ribs, vertebrae and skull. In children, the ends of the long limb bones can also make these cells. Developing red cells are large, colourless and have big nuclei.

Usually, they have lost the nuclei by the time they enter the bloodstream from the bone marrow. They have also made the red pigment, a protein called **haemoglobin**, by this time, which remains functional for between 20 and 120 days. When red cells die, they are broken down by the liver or the spleen. At this time, these organs recycle valuable substances from the red cells such as iron from the old haemoglobin which is used to make new haemoglobin.

What do red blood cells do?

Haemoglobin is a complex protein which fills the red blood cells. Its ability to carry oxygen results from the fact that it contains iron. You have probably seen iron turn red with rust when it is oxidised. This means that iron has combined with oxygen in the air. The iron in haemoglobin combines with oxygen in your lungs. Rusty iron does not give up its oxygen easily but the iron of haemoglobin does. In fact, haemoglobin releases oxygen at exactly the right time and place in the body. The red cells are bright red when haemoglobin is combined with oxygen (**oxyhaemoglobin**). The oxygen is carried to tissues that need it and is given up. The red cells also play a part in carbon dioxide transport.

The white blood cells

White cells differ from red cells in four ways:

1 they tend to be larger than red cells

2 they have nuclei

3 they have no haemoglobin

4 they are almost colourless.

The ratio of red blood cells to white blood cells is about 600:1. White blood cells are formed in red bone marrow and in the lymph glands. There are on average about 8000 white blood cells in 1mm³ of blood.

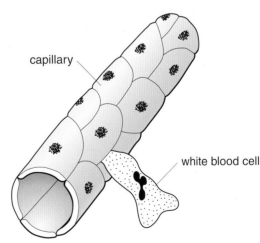

capillary

white blood cell

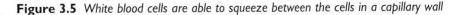

Figure 3.5 *White blood cells are able to squeeze between the cells in a capillary wall*

Some white blood cells move about on their own – they can squeeze through capillary walls into the tissue spaces. Here, they engulf solid particles and bacteria. Thus, white blood cells are important in defending your body against infection. Whenever you develop an infection, your white-cell count increases. It may rise from 8000 to more than 25000 per mm³. These cells collect in an infected area and proceed to ingest and destroy bacteria.

The platelets

Platelets are much smaller than red blood cells, they are irregularly shaped and are colourless. They are formed in the red bone marrow and are essential in the process of blood clotting.

Clotting results from chemical and physical changes in the blood. When a blood vessel is cut, the platelets are broken down in the blood which leaves the cut vessel. It is thought that platelets are destroyed by tissue fluids at the wound site. In the process, they release **thromboplastin** which reacts with **prothrombin** in the presence of calcium to form **thrombin**. Thrombin converts **fibrinogen**, a blood protein, to **fibrin**. Fibrin is made of numerous tiny threads which form a network to trap the blood cells. At this time, a clot forms to stop any more blood from escaping. The trapped blood cells dry out to form a scab.

Summary of clotting

1 thromboplastin + calcium + prothrombin → thrombin

2 thrombin + fibrinogen → fibrin

If any of these substances are missing, blood will not clot.

Table 3.1 *Summary of the composition of the blood*

Plasma	Solids
water	red cells
fibrinogen	white cells
serum albumin	platelets
globulin	
digested foods (glucose, fatty acids, glycerol, amino acids)	
mineral salts	
vitamins	
cell wastes (urea, carbon dioxide)	
hormones	

Table 3.2 *Blood as a transport medium*

Substance transported	From	To	Reason
digested food	alimentary canal and liver	tissues	growth and energy release
cell wastes	tissues	lungs, skin, kidneys	excretion
water	alimentary canal	kidneys, skin	excretion and to balance concentration of body fluids
oxygen	lungs	tissues	respiration
heat	tissues	skin	regulation of body temperature
hormones	ductless glands	tissues	regulation of body activities

The circulatory system

The Valentine Connection

Even in the 21st century we do not pretend to know all of the reasons for heart failure. However, we have come a long way since people began to understand the circulation of blood. Although attributed to William Harvey (1578–1657), the first sensible ideas on the mechanism of blood circulation were probably developed earlier, by Andrea Cesalpino (1519–1603). He envisaged a blood circulatory system at the time when he was physician to Pope Clement VIII. Until then, the ideas of Galen (129–200) ruled. Galen believed that the blood was formed in the liver and mixed with 'vital spirits' in the heart before flowing to the brain where it was converted into 'animal spirits'. In fact, Galen never dissected a human body; his knowledge of human anatomy was based on the dissection of a Barbary ape! His ideas were firmly believed right up until the 16th century.

Undoubtedly, William Harvey was one of the greatest English physicians in the history of medicine. He is regarded as one of the founders of anatomy and a major contributor to medical theory. Born in Folkestone, Harvey studied at Cambridge and then at the University of Padua. On returning to England, Harvey was appointed as a physician at St Bartholomew's hospital and lecturer to the Royal College of Physicians. In the years between 1612 and 1628, he undertook a remarkably detailed study of the human heart and blood system. This culminated in his major work *De motu cordis* in which he announced the theory, heretical at the time, of blood circulation.

Figure 3.6 *William Harvey*

Harvey's conclusions were classic in their simplicity. They lacked only one element to complete the account of circulation. He did not demonstrate the existence of capillaries, the observation of which required a more sophisticated microscope than was available to Harvey. Shortly after Harvey's death, the Italian anatomist, Marcello Malpighi (1628–1694) was able to complete the story of circulation by observing blood cells trickling, almost one at a time, through capillaries. He published his observations in 1661 in his classic study of the lungs, *De Pulmonibus*.

The heart

The heart is a pear-shaped muscular organ, enclosed within a sac called the **pericardium**, located under your breastbone and between your lungs. It is divided into two sides – right and left. These two halves are separated by a wall called the **septum**. Each half comprises two chambers: a thin-walled chamber called the **atrium** and a thick muscular **ventricle**. The two atria are reservoirs for the blood entering the heart. They contract at the same time, thus increasing the pressure and forcing the blood into the two ventricles.

(a)

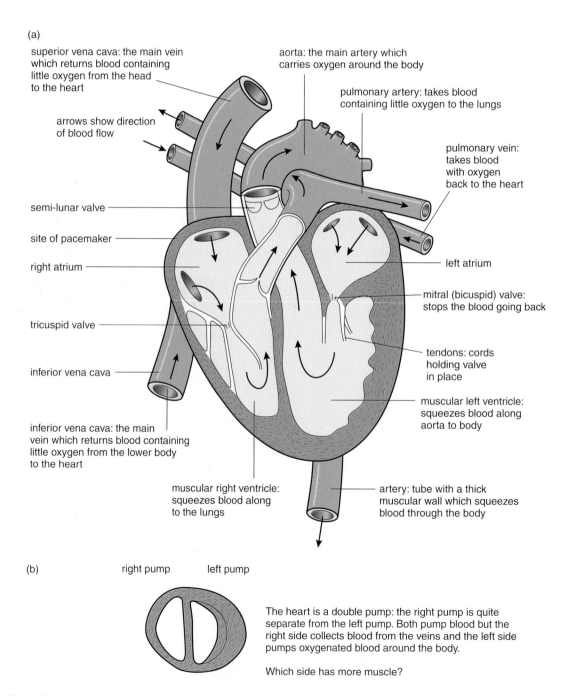

superior vena cava: the main vein which returns blood containing little oxygen from the head to the heart

arrows show direction of blood flow

aorta: the main artery which carries oxygen around the body

pulmonary artery: takes blood containing little oxygen to the lungs

pulmonary vein: takes blood with oxygen back to the heart

semi-lunar valve

site of pacemaker

right atrium

left atrium

mitral (bicuspid) valve: stops the blood going back

tricuspid valve

tendons: cords holding valve in place

inferior vena cava

muscular left ventricle: squeezes blood along aorta to body

inferior vena cava: the main vein which returns blood containing little oxygen from the lower body to the heart

muscular right ventricle: squeezes blood along to the lungs

artery: tube with a thick muscular wall which squeezes blood through the body

(b)   right pump   left pump

The heart is a double pump: the right pump is quite separate from the left pump. Both pump blood but the right side collects blood from the veins and the left side pumps oxygenated blood around the body.

Which side has more muscle?

Figure 3.7 *(a) The passage of blood through the heart. (b) A cross section through the ventricles of the heart*

When the muscular walls of the ventricles contract, the resultant increase in pressure forces the blood out through the main arteries.

The heart has two sets of one-way valves which control the flow of blood through the chambers. The valves between the atria and ventricles are called **atrio-ventricular valves** (the A-V valves). These are like flaps and are anchored to the floor of the ventricles by tendon-like strands. Blood passes freely through the A-V valves into the ventricles. As these valves cannot be opened from the lower side because of the anchorage of the tendons, blood is prevented from flowing backwards into the atria when the ventricles contract. The other valves are called the **semi-lunar valves** (S-L valves). These are cup-shaped and are located at the openings of the arteries. The force of blood passing from the ventricles into the arteries opens the S-L valves. When the ventricles relax, the S-L valves close, thus preventing blood from moving back into the ventricles.

See the heart and circulation in action!
http://www.innerbody.com/

An online exporation of the heart
http://sln2.fi.edu/biosci/heart.html

The passage of blood through the heart

One of the best ways to learn about the various parts of the heart is to trace the path of blood as it passes through it. Blood which has given up most of its oxygen, having been around the body, enters the right atrium from two different directions: through the **superior vena cava**, from the head and upper parts of the body, and through the **inferior vena cava** from the lower parts of the body. From the right atrium, the blood passes through the right A-V valve into the right ventricle. When the right ventricle contracts, blood is forced through a set of S-L valves into the **pulmonary artery** which takes the blood to the lungs. After the blood has picked up oxygen in the lungs it is carried by the **pulmonary veins** to the left atrium.

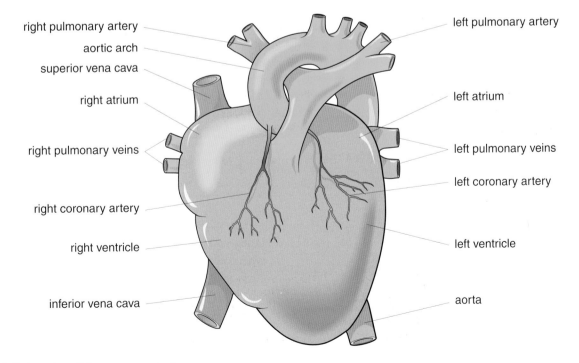

right pulmonary artery

aortic arch

superior vena cava

right atrium

right pulmonary veins

right coronary artery

right ventricle

inferior vena cava

left pulmonary artery

left atrium

left pulmonary veins

left coronary artery

left ventricle

aorta

Figure 3.8 *Location of the coronary arteries*

From there, the blood passes through the left A-V valve into the left ventricle and finally passes out through the **aorta**, from where it is carried to all parts of the body, apart from the lungs, under pressure.

The heart's muscle cells are supplied with blood by special arteries called **coronary arteries**. The right and left coronary arteries curve downward around each side of the heart and branch to smaller vessels that penetrate the heart's muscle tissue.

The heart as a highly effective pump

A complete cycle of heart activity is called a **beat** and has two phases. In the first phase, or **systole**, the ventricles contract and force blood into the arteries. In the second phase, or **diastole**, the ventricles relax and take in blood from the atria.

A normal heart beat makes 'lub' and 'dup' sounds, repeated over and over in perfect rhythm. The 'lub' is the systole phase and is the sound of the contraction of the ventricles' muscles and the closing of the A-V valves. The 'dup' is the diastole phase and is the sound of the closing of the semi-lunar valves.

The heart of an average resting adult beats about 70 times per minute. During physical exercise, the heart rate may be as high as 180 beats per minute.

www

How Your Heart Works
http://www.howstuffworks.com

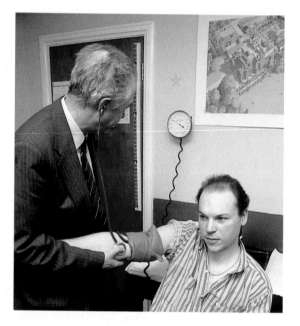

Figure 3.9 *This person is having his blood pressure taken*

Coursework Activity

To investigate the effect of exercise on pulse rate

Note: If you have any medical condition which may limit your ability to carry out this investigation, please take the necessary precautions and proceed carefully.

1 Using your fingertip, find your pulse at the point where an artery passes over a bone near to the surface of the skin in your wrist (see above diagram). Do not use your thumb because there is a pulse in it which might confuse your results.

2 Count the number of times you feel your pulse in 15 seconds and record the results.

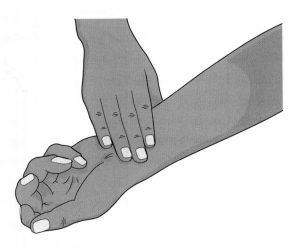

Figure 3.10 *How to measure your pulse rate*

3 Repeat three times and calculate the average. Multiply this figure by four to find your pulse rate per minute.

4 Exercise for 5 minutes by stepping up and down using a step or platform. Really put yourself to the test but not for more than 5 minutes.

5 Sit down and find your pulse again.

6 Record your pulse every 15 seconds until it returns to normal.

7 Plot your pulse rate per minute against time after exercise in seconds on a graph.

8 From your observations deduce

   a) your resting pulse rate per minute

   b) the length of time taken for your pulse to return to normal.

9 Suggest why your pulse rate did not return to normal as soon as you stopped exercising.

To measure your pulse using a computer

Not only can you measure your pulse by finger pressure, but you can also use one of many electronic devices such as wristwatches and sensors to do this. For example, you can use a sound sensor pressed close to your heart against your clothing. Connect this to a data logging system attached to the computer and watch the trace appear as a series of peaks. If you change the scale of the graph, you can count the number of beats in a minute and also 'see' the heart sounds.

As before, measure your pulse at rest and after some exercise.

Alternatively you can use a special pulse sensor which attaches to your chest, ear lobe or finger. When connected to the computer, it will count your heart beats and display them on a graph. Use the graph to show how long it takes for your pulse to return to normal after exercise. Are there other ways in which the graph shows how fit you might be? Label and print your graph to describe what you did in this investigation.

The blood vessels

Blood is carried around the body in a series of tubes of different sizes.

- **Arteries** and **arterioles** carry blood away from the heart.
- **Veins** and **venules** carry blood towards the heart.
- **Capillaries** are very small, thin-walled vessels.

The aorta branches into several smaller arteries which further branch and become arterioles. The arterioles branch into capillaries which can only be seen using a microscope. The tiny capillaries pass through tissues and come together to form venules. These join to become larger and larger veins, eventually leading to the venae cavae which enter the right atrium.

The **coronary circulation** supplies the heart muscle with food and oxygen. A blood clot in a coronary artery may prevent the flow of blood to the heart muscle and cause a 'heart attack'.

The **renal circulation** supplies the kidneys with blood containing urea which is filtered out to form urine (see p. 92).

The **portal circulation** is an extensive system of veins which lead from the small intestine and stomach. These join to form the **hepatic portal vein** which takes digested food to the liver.

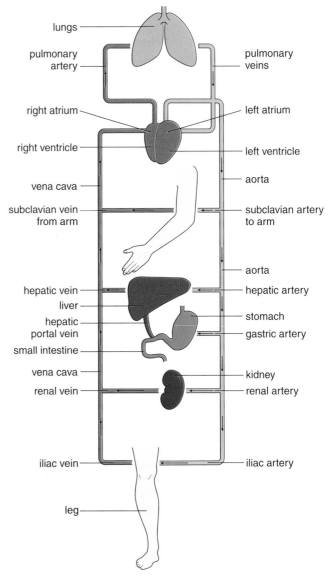

Figure 3.12 *The location of the main blood vessels in the human body*

Transport and circulation in plants
DOUBLE & TRIPLE AWARD ONLY

At least 75% of the mass of a plant is composed of water, and over 90% of the water taken in by the roots passes right through the stem and out through the leaves as water vapour. The plant uses water for transport and to maintain a high enough water pressure within its cells to support itself.

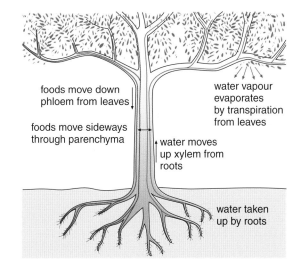

Figure 3.13 *The circulation of materials in a plant*

foods move down
phloem from leaves

foods move sideways
through parenchyma

water vapour
evaporates
by transpiration
from leaves

water moves
up xylem from
roots

water taken
up by roots

How does water pass into or out of plant cells?

The passage of water into or out of a cell is determined by the difference in concentration of water molecules between the inside and outside of the cell, and the selectively permeable membrane (see p. 12). Water will move into a cell if the concentration of water molecules outside the cell is higher. Similarly, water will move out of the cell if there is a lower concentration of water outside the cell. Figure 3.14 shows that as water passes in, the cell becomes firm or **turgid**. This can be likened to the pumping up of a tyre – as more air is pumped in, it pushes harder against the rubber wall until no more air can be forced in and it is fully turgid.

(see p. 12)

Did you know?

A hectare of sweetcorn needs about 5 million litres of water from the time it germinates until the time it is harvested.

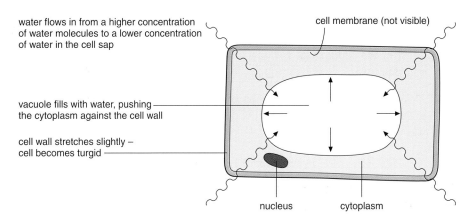

water flows in from a higher concentration
of water molecules to a lower concentration
of water in the cell sap

cell membrane (not visible)

vacuole fills with water, pushing
the cytoplasm against the cell wall

cell wall stretches slightly –
cell becomes turgid

nucleus   cytoplasm

Figure 3.14 *The passage of water in a plant cell surrounded by pure water*

Most cells within a healthy plant will be in a turgid state. This is very important in all plants, but is particularly important in young seedlings where it is the only means of support. If plants do not get enough water they will wilt. This can clearly be seen on a hot day. Wilting occurs when the water lost from a plant by evaporation is greater than the amount of water the plant can absorb from the soil. As you can see from the following diagram, water is drawn out of a cell.

water flows from a higher concentration of water molecules in the cell sap to a lower concentration

cell membrane pulls away from cell wall as the vacuole loses water

cell wall becomes soft – cell becomes flaccid

Figure 3.15 *The passage of water in a plant cell surrounded by a solution with a lower concentration of water molecules*

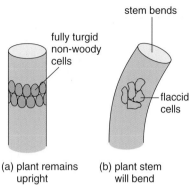

stem bends

fully turgid non-woody cells

flaccid cells

(a) plant remains upright

(b) plant stem will bend

Figure 3.16 *The effect of plasmolysis on a plant stem*

Water will be lost from a cell if neighbouring cells are losing water. If a lot of water is lost, the cell membrane pulls away from the cell wall. The effects of water loss are called **plasmolysis** and cells in this state are said to be **plasmolysed**. Cells in such a state are **flaccid** (the opposite of turgid). If the plant is young with little woody tissue, flaccid cells will cause it to droop or wilt (see Figure 3.16).

Did you know?

If you add too much fertiliser to a plant it can kill it. This is because it causes cells in the plant to lose water to osmosis. Gardeners will sometimes talk about roots as being 'burnt' by the addition of too much fertiliser.

Coursework Activity

To observe plasmolysis

1 Peel away a small piece of epidermis (outer layer of cells) of the red area of a rhubarb stalk or from a red onion set.

2 Place it on a slide and add a drop of solution X (15 g urea in 100 cm³ distilled water). Cover with a cover slip.

3 Observe the contents of the cells carefully under a microscope, first under low power, then under high power. Draw two or three cells.

4 Place a few drops of solution Y (0.17 g sodium hydrogen carbonate + 1 g magnesium sulphate + 100 cm³ water) at one edge of the cover slip.

5 Draw this solution under the cover slip by placing a piece of filter paper on the opposite side.

6 Observe the change that now takes place.

7 Draw two or three cells.

8 Explain your observations of the reaction of the cells in solutions X and Y.

Observe plasmolysis on this website!
http://www.cells.de/index_e. htm

The passage of water through a plant

The starting point of water's journey through the plant is the soil. The water enters the roots by osmosis from around soil particles where the concentration of water molecules is greater than that in the cell vacuole. Water can enter freely through the cell membrane which is selectively permeable. The cell wall is completely permeable and thus creates no barrier to the passage of water. Almost all the water taken in by the plant enters through the younger parts of the root.

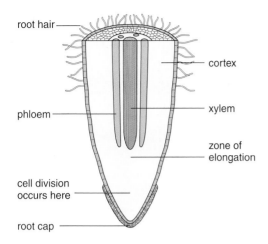

Figure 3.17 *Longitudinal section through a root tip*

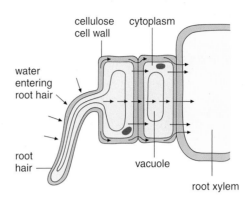

Figure 3.18 *The path taken by water molecules from the soil to the xylem vessels*

Little water is absorbed by the root tip, but several millimetres beyond the tip there are **root hairs** which increase the surface area of the root and are thus the site of maximal absorption.

As the water passes into root hair cells, the number of water molecules inside these cells increases compared with the neighbouring cells of the root cortex, thus setting up a concentration gradient of water within the root itself. As a result, water passes by osmosis into the neighbouring cells. These will now contain a greater number of water molecules than the cells next to them so water will pass on to the next ones and so on across the cortex of the root.

In fact, the water may pass along three different pathways. Most of it passes along the cellulose cell walls (see Figure 3.18) by being soaked up in the same way that a paper towel mops up spilled liquid. (If you have ever delivered newspapers on a rainy day you will know that when one newspaper in a delivery sack gets wet, the water moves to all the rest very quickly! The principle is the same when water passes from one cell wall to the next.) Some water travels through the cytoplasm of the cells, and the rest passes from vacuole to vacuole. Eventually the water reaches the xylem cells through which water is transported from the root, up the stem to the leaves.

It is important to appreciate how water gets from the roots to the leaves at the top of a plant. While this may not be too much of a problem for a daisy, it is a different matter for the giant redwood tree – the largest living organism – which can grow to over 100 metres tall!

There are two possible explanations for this phenomenon. The water can either be:

- pushed from the bottom or
- pulled from the top.

Pushing and pulling both occur, but one of these factors has a far greater effect than the other.

The push from the bottom is known as **root pressure** and is the result of the uptake of water by osmosis into the xylem vessels.

Figure 3.19 *The giant redwood tree – the largest living organism*

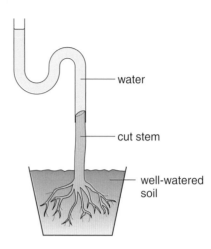

Figure 3.20 *A demonstration of root pressure*

Under certain environmental conditions, root pressure forces water through special water pores around the edge of leaves by a process called **guttation**. The water produced is not dew because it actually comes from *inside* the plant. In spring, it is possible to demonstrate root pressure with the apparatus shown.

The water will rise several centimetres up the tube. It is important to remember that root pressure only occurs at certain times of the year, under certain conditions and in certain plants.

The pull from the top is the main force responsible for movement against gravity. We know that we can pull water up by suction as we do when we drink through a straw, but what can explain the pulling force at the top of a giant redwood tree – a force great enough to raise tonnes of water?

The answer is dependent upon the properties of water and not the properties of the plant. Water has a tremendous power of **cohesion** – each molecule clings firmly to several neighbouring molecules. When the water molecules are pulled up through the xylem vessels, they pull others along with them, so the water molecules are in a continuous row. As one molecule moves up, it pulls the row behind it. What causes the row of water molecules to move upwards? Think about the main function of the leaf – photosynthesis. This process generally requires a leaf with a large surface area which is exposed to sunlight. This, together with the open pores (stomata), will lead to evaporation of water from the surface of the leaves by a process known as **transpiration**. Water is lost from the cells near the stomata which then draws water from adjacent cells by osmosis and so on down the chain, eventually taking water from the xylem vessels. The movement results in the **transpiration stream**.

www

The Online Biology Book – Plant Structure
http://gened.emc.maricopa.edu/

Ohio State University – Transpiration
http://www.hcs.ohio-state.edu/hcs300/pstrans.htm

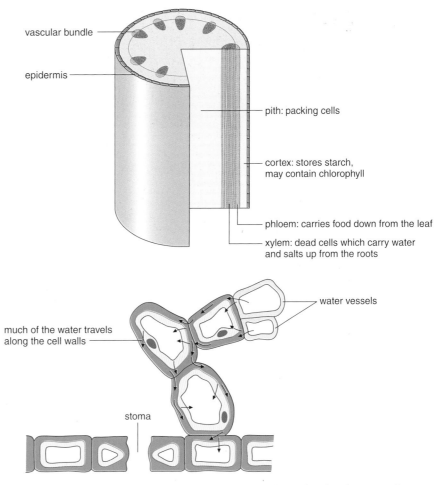

vascular bundle

epidermis

pith: packing cells

cortex: stores starch,
may contain chlorophyll

phloem: carries food down from the leaf

xylem: dead cells which carry water
and salts up from the roots

water vessels

much of the water travels
along the cell walls

stoma

Figure 3.21 *Section through a leaf and stem to show the path taken by water during transpiration*

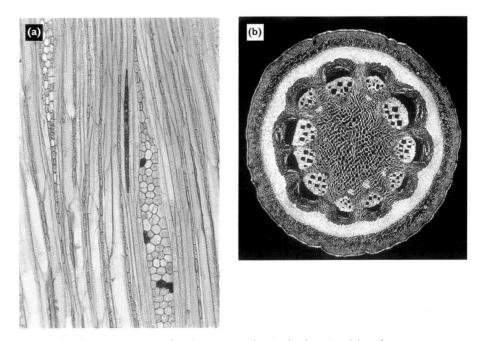

Figure 3.22 *The structure of a plant stem in longitudinal section (a) and transverse section (b)*

Coursework Activity

To trace the pathway of water through a plant

1 Take any suitable available plant, for example celery, busy lizzie or daffodil.

2 Place a length of stem in a small beaker containing a small amount of coloured ink.

3 Allow the tissue to stand for about 15–20 minutes.

4 Remove the stem from the beaker and cut some very thin sections from the end. Be very careful with the scalpel.

5 Take the thinnest section you can cut and place it on a microscope slide.

6 View it through a microscope.

7 Note the distribution of the ink. Which tissue is dyed most?

Factors affecting the transpiration stream

As water vapour is lost from the air spaces of the leaf, more water evaporates from the leaf cells. The factors that affect the rate of water loss from the leaf are essentially the same as those that affect the rate of drying of clothes on a washing line.

- *Temperature.* Warmer air increases the rate of transpiration because the heat energy gives the water molecules more energy for movement.
- *Wind.* In still air, the water vapour remains close to the surface of the leaf so the rate of transpiration is low. Wind carries the water molecules away and increases the rate at which they are lost to the air.
- *Humidity.* In conditions of high humidity, water molecules in the air prevent more water molecules escaping from the stomata of the leaves. Low humidity therefore increases transpiration.
- *Light intensity.* As light intensity increases, more stomata open and more transpiration takes place. At night, stomata close and so the rate of transpiration decreases.

Coursework Activity

To demonstrate transpiration

1 Remove a thin woody shoot from a tree or shrub and, in the laboratory, cut off the bottom inch under water so that no air gets into the shoot.

2 Fit the shoot to the capillary tube with a plastic tube as shown in the diagram.

3 Introduce an air bubble into the capillary tube by lifting the capillary tube out of the water and squeezing the rubber tube connector to remove one drop of water.

4 Replace the capillary tube in the beaker and leave the apparatus on a bench for 5 minutes.

5 Measure the distance travelled by the bubble.

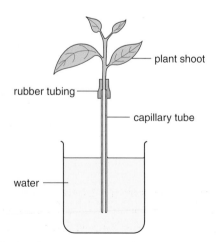

Figure 3.23 *A simple bubble potometer*

Coursework Activity

Using the same principle described, investigate the effect of temperature, humidity and wind on the rate of transpiration.

Think of ways of simulating these conditions in the laboratory. Record your results as graphs and evaluate the data obtained.

Can plants control their water loss?

Water loss is one of the greatest problems affecting land-living plants. If transpiration takes place at a greater rate than the absorption of water by the roots, the plant will wilt and die. Plants control water loss in two ways: via the stomata or via the leaf structure.

Stomata

In general there are more stomata on the lower surface of a leaf than on the upper surface. Exceptions to this rule include those plants with stomata only on the lower surface of their leaves, for example laurel, and those with equal numbers on both sides, such as grasses. How will the number and distribution of stomata determine the rate of water loss?

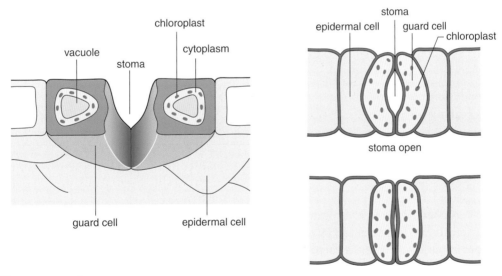

Figure 3.24 *The structure of a stoma*

Stomata consist of two guard cells surrounding a pore. Their opening or closing depends on the shape of the guard cells which, in turn, depends on the presence or absence of sugar in the cells.

Did you know?

The word stoma comes from the Greek word for mouth. Stomata can open and close like little mouths on the surface of the leaf. High summer temperatures and an increase of carbon dioxide in the atmosphere due to global warming (see p. 219) cause stomata to close.

This reduces transpiration, which in turn, prevents the recycling of water. There has been a reduction of transpiration by around 3–4% since 1950 and this could be enough to influence the weather by making it drier.

How stomata open and close

The guard cells are the only cells of the epidermis, the outermost layer of cells of the leaf, that have chloroplasts. They also have thicker inner cell walls than outer cell walls. In daylight, photosynthesis takes place in the guard cells and sugar is made. As the concentration of sugar molecules will be higher in the guard cells than the neighbouring cells (which cannot photosynthesise), the guard cells will take up water from these adjacent cells by osmosis (see p. 69) and swell. Because of the shape of the cell wall, they swell away from the pore and open like little mouths. At night, photosynthesis cannot take place, so they lose water pressure and close.

Leaf structure

Plants which live in dry conditions tend to have three characteristic features to reduce water loss:

1 a small surface area – to reduce evaporation

2 a thick waxy cuticle over the surface of the leaf – to act like a waterproof coat

3 sunken stomata.

Coursework Activity

To examine the distribution of stomata on the surfaces of leaves

1 Paint a thin layer of clear nail varnish on the upper and lower epidermis of any leaf which has a smooth surface.

2 When dry, peel off the strip and place it on a glass slide. Cover this with a cover slip.

3 Examine under low power and then high power of a microscope.

4 Count the number of stomata in the field of view under low power on the lower and upper surface.

5 Collect the results of other groups of students and calculate the averages.

Coursework Activities

Use the procedure described above to investigate the distribution of stomata on the upper and lower surfaces of two types of variegated leaf – a narrow-leaved plant like a spider plant and a flat-leaved plant like ivy.

Explain the data with reference to the numbers on the green and white parts. Consider the types of plants you are using and the distribution on both surfaces. Explain your observations and evaluate your procedure.

www

Ohio State University – Leaf structure and function
http://www.hcs.ohio-state.edu/hcs300/anat.3.htm

Bioweb – The Structure of Living Things
http://atschool.edweb.co.uk/middlecroft/KS4.htm

Summary

1 Your circulatory system transports blood through your body.

2 Blood is a fluid tissue. It is made up of liquid plasma and solid components.

3 Plasma contains water, blood proteins, prothrombin, inorganic substances, digested foods and cell wastes.

4 Blood has three solid parts: red cells, white cells and platelets.

5 Red cells transport oxygen to the cells and carbon dioxide from the cells as a waste product.

6 White cells help fight disease-causing bacteria.

7 Platelets are important in the process of blood clotting.

8 The heart is a pump that sends blood to all parts of your circulatory system. It has two atria and two ventricles – the atria receive blood from veins while the ventricles force blood through the arteries by contraction.

9 Arteries carry blood from the heart to the tissues. Veins return it to the heart. The arterial and venous systems are connected by networks of tiny capillaries. The real interaction of blood and cells takes place in these capillaries.

10 Flowering plants circulate materials by means of two tissues: phloem which carries dissolved foods from the leaves, where they are made, to the rest of the plant, and xylem which transports water and mineral salts from the roots to the leaves.

11 Circulation in plants depends on the evaporation of water from the surface of the leaves and stems. The evaporation of water in this way causes the materials from the roots to be sucked up in a transpiration stream.

12 Transpiration can be controlled by the opening and closing of stomata in the leaves and stem.

13 Water passes into the roots by osmosis. Mineral salts pass in by active transport.

Homework Questions

1   What are the functions of blood?

2   Where are the various blood cells made in the body?

3   What conditions might cause the white blood cell count to go up?

4   What are the stages in the clotting of blood?

5   Why is plasma more quickly and easily used in a transfusion than whole blood?

6   Trace the path of a drop of blood from the right atrium to the aorta.

7   Why can you feel the pulse in an artery and not in a vein?

8   Name two functions of the veins of a leaf.

9   What is the function of the cuticle of a leaf?

10 Describe the changes that occur in stomata during a 24-hour period.

11 How are succulent leaves an adaptation for life in a dry environment?

12 What process is used by root cells to absorb minerals?

In-Depth Questions

1   What is the reason for the saying that 'we are as young as our arteries'?

2   Alcohol dilates the arteries in the skin. What would be its effect on the temperature control of the body?

3   How is recycling of resources by the body shown by the manufacture of red blood cells?

4   Cells in the mesophyll of a leaf are thin-walled and loosely-arranged. Why is this important in the activities of the leaf?

5   Discuss the difference between the transport of sap and the transport of water in a plant.

6   Compare root pressure, capillarity and the transpiration pull as factors in the movement of water through xylem.

4 Breathing

Learning objectives By the end of this chapter you should be able to understand:

- the meaning of the term breathing;
- the functions of the parts of the breathing system;
- the mechanism of gas exchange in the lungs;
- the meaning of oxygen debt and the fact that it might occur in muscles during vigorous exercise;
- the importance of healthy lungs.

The two phases of breathing

Breathing is the mechanical process that allows air in and out of the lungs to enable oxygen to diffuse into the blood and carbon dioxide and water to diffuse out. The organs involved in breathing can be divided into two groups. The first group includes the passages through which air travels to get into the bloodstream – the nostrils, nasal passages, throat, trachea, bronchi, bronchioles and air sacs. The second includes those organs involved in the mechanics of breathing – including the ribs, rib muscles, diaphragm and abdominal muscles.

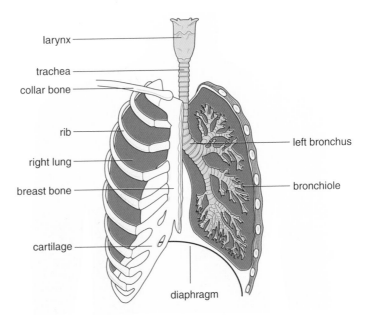

Figure 4.1 *The breathing system*

The breathing system

The nose and nasal passages

The air enters the nose in two streams through the two **nostrils**. From the nostrils, air enters the nasal passages which lie above the mouth cavity. Before air enters the nasal passages, hairs and mucous membranes filter out the dirt. A wafer-thin network of bones warms up the air by friction as the molecules of gas pass through the nasal passages. These advantages are lost when you breathe in through your mouth.

The trachea

From the nasal passages, air goes through the **throat (pharynx)** and down the **windpipe (trachea)**. The upper end of the trachea is protected by a flap of cartilage called the **epiglottis**. This closes over the trachea when you swallow to prevent food from getting into the lungs. The upper end of the trachea holds the **voice box (larynx)**. Within the larynx are the vocal cords which we use to make sounds by vibration. By learning to control these vibrations, we learn to talk.

Horseshoe-shaped bands of cartilage support the walls of the trachea, keeping it open for the passage of air. The trachea and its branches are lined with tiny, constantly moving, hair-like cilia which carry inhaled dirt and other foreign particles upward toward the mouth. This dirt is removed when you cough, sneeze or swallow.

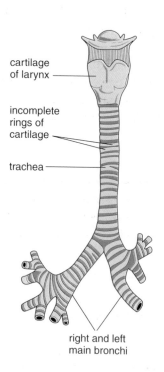

cartilage of larynx

incomplete rings of cartilage

trachea

right and left main bronchi

Figure 4.2 *The trachea*

Figure 4.3 *Ciliated epithelium of the bronchi*

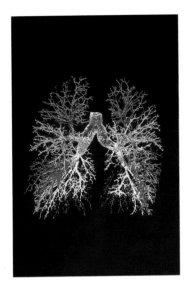

Figure 4.4 *The respiratory tree*

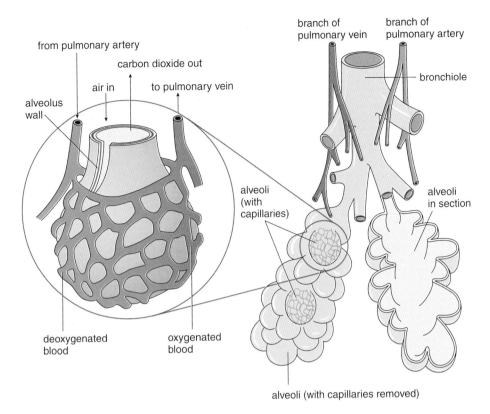

Figure 4.5 *The structure of the bronchioles and air sacs*

The bronchi and air sacs

The trachea divides at its lower end into two branches called **bronchi**. One bronchus extends to each lung and then divides to many smaller **bronchioles**, ending in clusters of tiny air sacs called **alveoli**. The walls of the alveoli are very thin and elastic, enabling the exchange of gases. The oxygen in air cannot travel any further than the alveoli without the help of the blood system. Capillaries carry the blood to the alveoli so that oxygen can be collected and carbon dioxide unloaded. The numerous tiny alveoli provide an enormous surface area between the blood and the air for gaseous exchange. Thus the lungs provide oxygen for the blood to carry to the millions of cells that need it for respiration (see p. 19).

Did you know?

You breathe in and out approximately 5.3 million litres of air each year! The lungs have to have an enormous surface area in contact with the air that we breathe in. They have an area which is over 40 times the outside surface area of the body, or approximately the size of a tennis court! This enables us to have greater powers of endurance than many other animals and do lots of muscular exercise for prolonged periods. Other animals, like frogs, may be active for short periods but they cannot keep up rapid movements for long.

The lungs fill the chest cavity from a point under the shoulders down to the diaphragm – except for the space occupied by the heart, trachea, oesophagus and blood vessels. Lungs comprise bronchioles, air sacs and blood vessels held together by connective tissue. This structure makes the lungs spongy. Surrounding the lungs are the **pleural membranes** which secrete mucus for lubrication. This allows them to move freely in the chest during breathing.

Breathing movements

Did you know?

When you inhale, your chest bulges. You might think that this is because your lungs draw in air and expand. Actually, this is the opposite of what happens. The lungs, although elastic in nature, have no muscle so cannot expand or contract on their own – they are spongy, air-filled sacs in the chest cavity. The power to breathe comes from rib, diaphragm and abdominal muscles. It is these muscles which control the size and air pressure of the chest cavity.

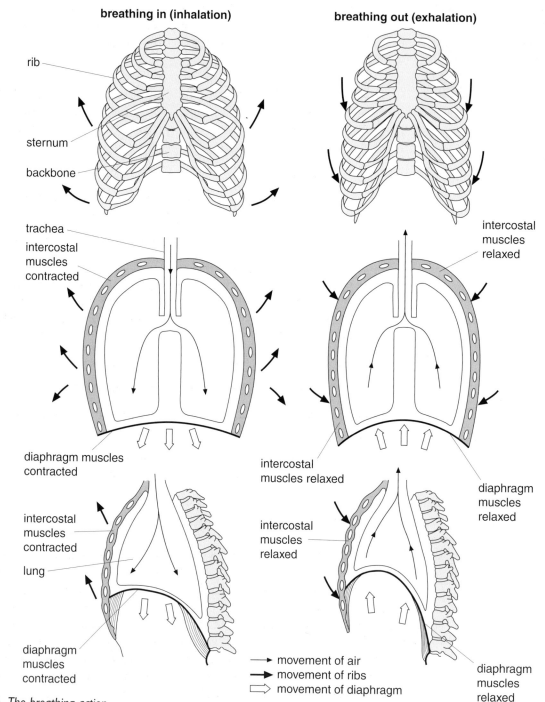

breathing in (inhalation)

rib

sternum

backbone

trachea
intercostal muscles contracted

diaphragm muscles contracted

intercostal muscles contracted

lung

diaphragm muscles contracted

breathing out (exhalation)

intercostal muscles relaxed

intercostal muscles relaxed

diaphragm muscles relaxed

intercostal muscles relaxed

diaphragm muscles relaxed

→ movement of air
➡ movement of ribs
⇨ movement of diaphragm

Figure 4.6 *The breathing action*

Use a CD-ROM encyclopaedia or a multimedia title about the human body to see your lungs and breathing muscles in action.

To measure your breathing using a computer

There are electronic devices which allow you to monitor your breathing movements automatically. For example, you can use a stethograph belt attached to a pressure sensor. When connected to a data logging system and computer, breathing movements appear as a series of peaks.

Measure your breathing rate at rest and after some exercise by counting the number of peaks in a minute. Look also for any change in the depth of breaths taken.
Alternatively you can use a special breathing sensor which attaches to your chest. When connected to the computer, it will show your breathing rate and display this on a graph. Use the graph to show how long it takes for your breathing rate to return to normal after exercise. Label and print your graph to describe what you did.

Animation of the lungs
http://www.innerbody.com

How your lungs work
http://www.howstuffworks.com

The intake of air, or **inspiration**, occurs when the chest cavity expands. When this happens, air pressure inside the sealed cavity decreases and air rushes into the lungs to equalise the pressure. The following movements are involved in expanding the chest cavity:

1　The rib muscles contract, pulling the ribs up and out.

2　The muscles of the dome-shaped diaphragm contract. This straightens and lowers the diaphragm, enlarging the chest cavity from below.

3　The abdominal muscles relax, allowing compression of the abdomen when the diaphragm lowers.

Expiration, or the forcing of air from the lungs, occurs when the chest cavity is reduced in size. This increases the air pressure inside the cavity, so to equalise internal and external air pressure, air is forced out of the lungs. The following movements are involved in expiration:

1　The rib muscles relax, allowing the ribs to spring back.

2　The diaphragm relaxes, rising to its original position.

3　The abdominal muscles contract, pushing the abdominal organs up against the diaphragm.

4　The elastic lung tissues, which were stretched when the lungs were full, recoil and force air out of the lungs.

The control of breathing

Nerves and chemicals are both involved in controlling the depth and rate of breathing. Nerves from the lungs, diaphragm and rib muscles lead to a control centre at the base of the brain (**the brain stem**). This controls the regular rhythm of breathing by detecting the amount of carbon dioxide in the blood. If the carbon dioxide concentration is high, the brain sends signals to the diaphragm and rib muscles to increase the breathing rate. This increased rate forces more carbon dioxide out through the lungs and lowers the concentration in the blood so breathing soon settles back to a normal rate. In humans, inspiration and expiration occur between 16 and 24 times a minute. The exact rate depends on physical activity, position, mood and age.

Coursework Activity

To investigate the effect of exercise on rate of breathing

1 While resting, place your hands on the lower part of your rib cage and count the number of inspirations over a period of 30 seconds. For this to be valid, you must breathe naturally – do not force your breathing. Repeat this four times so that you can calculate your average rate of breathing at rest.

2 Record the average reading and double it to find your breathing rate per minute.

Note: Students with medical conditions that affect breathing should proceed with caution.

3 Run on the spot vigorously for 1 minute, then stop and repeat the first procedure. Repeat four times as before to find an average reading for your rate of breathing after exercise.

4 Draw a bar chart to show the change in breathing rates of the students in a class after exercise.

Questions

What is your average breathing rate before and after exercise?

How close is your average to the average for the class?

The air capacity of the lungs

Only about 500 cm³ of air are involved each time we inhale and exhale. The air involved in normal, relaxed breathing is called **tidal air**. Forced breathing increases the amount of air movement. The effects of forced breathing can be demonstrated by the following method. Inhale normally without forcing – your lungs now contain about 2800 cm³ of air. Now exhale normally. You have moved 500 cm³ of tidal air from the lungs. Now, without inhaling again, force out all the air you can. You have now exhaled an additional 1100 cm³ of **supplemental air**. The lungs now contain about 1200 cm³ of **residual air**, which you cannot force out.

When you inhale normally again, you will replace the supplemental and tidal air. If you inhale with force, you can add about 3000 cm³ of **complemental air**. The maximum amount of air that you can move through your lungs is called the **vital capacity**. This is the total amount of air that moves through your lungs when you inhale and exhale as hard as you can. The vital capacity of an average person is about 4500 cm³. A well-trained athlete may have a vital capacity of 6500 cm³.

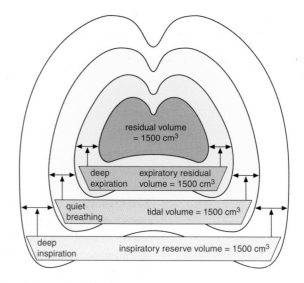

Figure 4.7 *The air capacity of the lungs*

Coursework Activities

To investigate the amount of air you breathe in during normal inspiration

1 Put a length of rubber tubing through the neck of a large container (a 5 dm³ polythene bottle is ideal) until it nearly reaches the bottom. (Use tubing with a wide internal diameter to minimise resistance.)

2 Invert the bottle and place it under water in a laboratory sink (see Figure 4.8).

3 Hold your nose and practise breathing in and out through your mouth.

4 Breathe in air from the inverted bottle. Repeat four times. If apparatus is to be shared between students, separate mouthpieces should be used.

5 After breathing in, quickly remove the rubber tubing, insert a stopper in the bottle neck and remove the bottle.

6 Measure the volume of water contained in the bottle using a measuring cylinder.

7 Repeat several times and take an average volume.

8 Record the volume of water. What does this volume represent?

To investigate how much you can breathe out in a single breath

1 Set up the apparatus as shown in Figure 4.9.

2 Practise deep breathing a few times, then blow out deeply through the mouth into the apparatus.

3 Collect the displaced water in the largest available container (at least 5 dm³ in volume).

4 Measure the volume of water collected in a measuring cylinder.

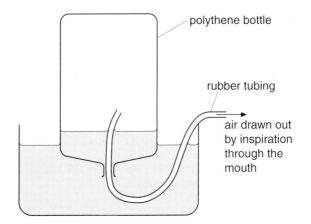

Figure 4.8 *Apparatus used to investigate inspiration*

5 Repeat several times and take your highest reading – this is your vital capacity.

6 Draw a bar chart for the vital capacities of all the students in your class.

7 Compare this with the bar chart made for the breathing rates and exercise.

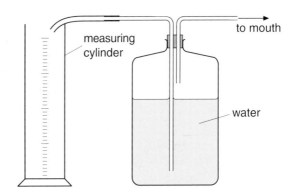

Figure 4.9 *Apparatus used to investigate exhalation*

Our source of oxygen

The main gases that make up air are nitrogen, oxygen and carbon dioxide. The gases have properties that are vital for life, one of which is the ability to diffuse through membranes. If there are different concentrations of oxygen on either side of a membrane, oxygen molecules will pass through the membrane from high to low concentration until the concentration of molecules is the same on both sides. The molecules will then move at the same rate in both directions.

Gases in air can also dissolve in water, which is why oxygen and carbon dioxide can be carried by the blood. The solubility of the gases depends on temperature – warm water dissolves much less oxygen than cold water. As water warms up, gases come out of solution as bubbles.

Table 4.1 *The composition of air (excluding rare gases e.g. argon, neon, radon)*

Gas	Inspired (%)	Expired (%)
Oxygen	21	16
Nitrogen	78	77
Carbon dioxide	0.04	4
Water vapour	Variable	Saturated

Gas exchange

The pulmonary artery (see p. 63) carries deoxygenated blood to the lungs where it branches into an extensive network of small capillaries which completely surround each air sac.

The air in the alveolus and the blood in the capillaries contain gases in different concentrations. Diffusion therefore occurs through the thin, moist membranes of both alveolus and capillary. Oxygen diffuses from the air into the blood and carbon dioxide diffuses in the opposite direction.

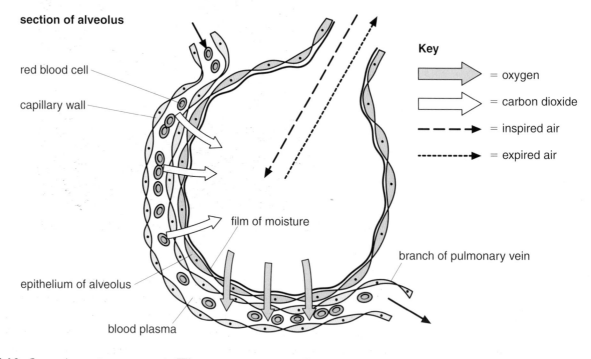

section of alveolus

red blood cell

capillary wall

film of moisture

epithelium of alveolus

blood plasma

branch of pulmonary vein

Key

= oxygen

= carbon dioxide

= inspired air

= expired air

Figure 4.10 *Gas exchange in an alveolus*

The transport of oxygen

Oxygen is not very soluble in the blood plasma. It is even less soluble at our body temperature of 37°C. The red cells contain **haemoglobin** which has such a strong chemical attraction for oxygen that blood can be up to 97% saturated with it.

Oxygen + Haemoglobin $\rightleftharpoons$ Oxyhaemoglobin

When blood reaches tissues which have a low concentration (**partial pressure**) of oxygen, the oxyhaemoglobin breaks down. The oxygen released diffuses into the tissue fluid, and from there, reaches the cells. The attraction of haemoglobin for oxygen decreases with increasing acidity. This is important because, during exercise, carbon dioxide, an acidic gas, is produced by the active muscle cells. Lactic acid may also be formed if the supply of oxygen to the cells is not sufficient. This increase in acidity causes the haemoglobin to release more of its oxygen just when it is needed.

The transport of carbon dioxide

Carbon dioxide is much more soluble in blood plasma than oxygen – it passes through membranes quickly and enters the bloodstream. In the blood, only about 15% of the carbon dioxide is dissolved in the plasma – the remainder is carried as sodium hydrogen carbonate to the lungs. Here, the carbon dioxide is released and diffuses through the membranes of the capillaries into the air sacs. From the air sacs it leaves your body in the expired air.

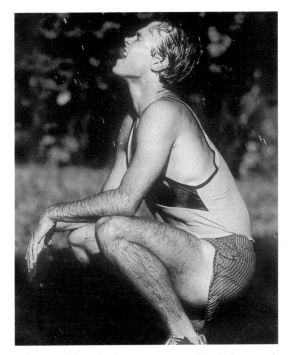

Figure 4.11 *This athlete will have built up an oxygen debt in his muscles*

Oxygen debt

During times of great muscular activity, the cells need more oxygen than the body can supply. The lungs cannot take in oxygen fast enough and the blood cannot deliver it fast enough. When this happens, the cells switch to **anaerobic respiration** (see p. 21). This means that oxygen is not used during respiration and **lactic acid**, a product of anaerobic respiration, collects in the tissues, causing a feeling of fatigue and even pain. The build up of lactic acid signals the brain's breathing centre to increase the breathing rate to supply the tissues with more oxygen. If the heavy exercise continues, lactic acid keeps building up and causes an **oxygen debt**. This will remain until the heavy exercise ends. Then, during a half-hour rest, some of the lactic acid is oxidised and some is converted to **glycogen**. The oxygen debt is paid and the body is ready for more exercise.

Carbon monoxide poisoning

Far too often, we read of people who have died as a result of carbon monoxide poisoning. The death is not actually caused by poisoning, but by tissue suffocation. Carbon monoxide will not support life, yet it combines with haemoglobin 250 times more readily than oxygen does. As a result, the blood becomes loaded with carbon monoxide and its oxygen-combining power decreases. The tissues suffer from oxygen starvation and paralysis soon occurs, followed by death.

Breathing at high altitudes

We live at the bottom of a large 'ocean' of air. As we move higher in it by, for example, climbing a mountain, the air pressure becomes less. Most of us have experienced the 'popping' of our ears during an altitude change, perhaps in an aeroplane. This is due to there being a reduction in air pressure. Our middle ear (see p. 104) has to equalise the air pressure.

Pressure is an important factor in determining how efficiently the oxygen combines with haemoglobin. This is why mountain climbers and aeroplane pilots have more difficulty in breathing as they move higher. Above 3500 m many people become tired easily. When an aeroplane approaches 6000 m, the pressure becomes so low that the pilot has difficulty in seeing and hearing. This condition results from oxygen starvation of the tissues and is avoided by having an extra supply of oxygen from an oxygen tank and mask.

Passengers in aeroplanes can fly at very high altitudes in the safety and comfort of pressurised cabins to counteract any natural pressure changes. In studying the problems of breathing at high altitudes, scientists observed Peruvian Indians.

These Indians inhabit very high mountains in South America and carry out normal activities at altitudes at which most people would simply become exhausted. The atmosphere at these altitudes has half the oxygen content of air at sea level. Scientists found that the Indians had a greater than average lung capacity and an abnormally high red blood cell count – they had adapted to the high altitude. It was also noted that similar adaptations can take place in anybody who spends time at high altitudes.

Figure 4.12 *Fighter pilots often wear oxygen masks at high altitude*

Figure 4.13 *Peruvians are used to low levels of oxygen and are adapted to working at high altitudes*

Summary

1 Breathing involves the exchange of gases between cells and their environment.

2 Breathing is a mechanical process that moves air in and out of the lungs due to expiration and inspiration.

3 During oxidation, foods break down and energy is released.

4 In lower animals, individual cells are in direct contact with the environment, but in higher animals, blood is the transporting medium.

5 Atmospheric pressure and the concentration of gases in the air both play important roles in the diffusion of gases through membranes.

6 Solubility in water is an important property of gases that we exchange in our lungs.

Homework Questions

1 What are the differences between respiration and breathing?

2 Describe the mechanism that controls breathing rate.

3 What properties of gases aid the body in respiration?

4 Describe gas exchange in the lungs. Name the structures involved and explain why the exchange takes place.

5 How do pressure changes within the chest cavity cause inspiration and expiration?

6 Why is haemoglobin vital to the respiratory processes of the cells in our bodies?

7 How is oxygen carried from the lungs to the tissues?

8 How is carbon dioxide carried from the tissues to the lungs?

9 How do you build up an oxygen debt? How is it repaid?

10 Explain carbon monoxide poisoning.

In-Depth Questions

1 What changes do you think would occur in the blood if you were to a) hold your breath for a period of time and b) breathe rapidly and deeply for a period of time?

2 Explain the decompression procedure used when divers come up from great depths.

3 What differences would you find in the blood of a person living at high altitudes compared to a person living at sea level?

4 Why is the fact that carbon dioxide is so soluble in water of vital importance to organisms?

5 Excretion

By the end of this chapter you should be able to understand:

- the functions of the parts of the kidney;
- that the kidney is an organ of excretion and regulation;
- how a nephron works;
- the principles of a kidney machine;
- the functions of the parts of the skin;
- that the skin is an organ of excretion;
- the functions of the skin in temperature regulation.

The removal of wastes of metabolism

Metabolism is the sum of the breaking-down processes (**catabolism**) and the building-up processes (**anabolism**) taking place in the body. During metabolism, many chemical reactions taking place in the body produce wastes which have to be removed to prevent them from poisoning our organ systems.

When the body oxidises fuel during respiration, it produces the waste products carbon dioxide and water. These are removed from the lungs during gaseous exchange (see p. 86) and so the lungs can be considered to have an excretory function. Single-celled animals excrete their wastes directly into the water-filled environment in which they live. Simple animals, like jellyfish and sponges, also do this, but the process is not so simple for complex organisms like ourselves which are made of millions of cells. In humans, each cell discharges its waste materials into the tissue fluid, which passes to the bloodstream. The blood then carries the wastes to the excretory organs – the lungs, kidneys and skin.

Kidneys – the main excretory organs

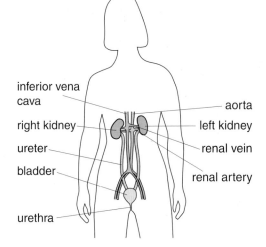

Figure 5.1 *The urinary system*

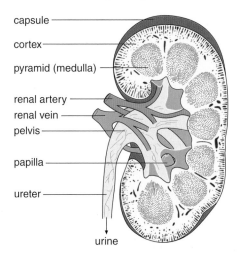

Figure 5.2 *Detailed structure of the kidney*

Did you know?

Each kidney has about a million tiny filters leading to tubules which, if laid together end-to-end, would measure more than 50 miles.

The kidneys are bean-shaped organs, about the size of your clenched fist. They lie on either side of the spine at the back of your abdominal cavity. Thick layers of fat cover and protect each kidney, and in order to see any details, you have to cut through a kidney lengthwise.

The firm outer part is the **cortex**, which is covered by a membrane, the **capsule**. The cortex makes up about one-third of the kidney tissue and surrounds the **medulla**. The medulla is filled with cone-shaped projections called **pyramids** which point to a sac-like cavity, the pelvis. From here, a long, narrow tube, the **ureter**, leads to the **bladder**. This is all you will be able to see by cutting through the kidney and looking at the surface with a hand lens. In order to see further detail, it is necessary to view thin sections of kidney tissue with a microscope.

All the filters work together, separating large molecules from small ones as blood is forced through them under pressure. These filters are called **nephrons** and control the chemical composition of the blood. They are responsible for the regulatory role performed by the kidneys.

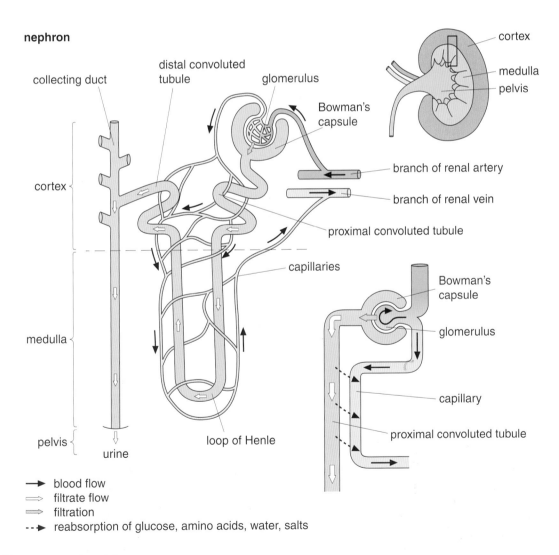

Figure 5.3 *The structure of a nephron*

www

How your kidneys work?
**http://www.howstuffworks.
com**

Body Quest – Excretory system
**http://library.thinkquest.org/
10348/home.html**

How does the nephron work?

Blood enters each kidney through a large **renal artery** which is a branch of the aorta. In the kidneys, each artery branches and rebranches into a mass of arterioles which eventually end in knots of blood capillaries called **glomeruli** (Latin for 'little balls'). Each glomerulus fills a cup-like **Bowman's capsule** and together, these form the actual filters of the kidneys.

Kidneys deal mainly with removal of urea which is formed in the liver (see p. 46). There are two stages to the removal of urea, excess water and minerals from the blood:

- filtration
- reabsorption.

The pressure of the blood is very high in the glomeruli. Note in Figure 5.3 that the diameter of the in-going arteriole is greater than that of the out-going arteriole. This increases the blood pressure which is very important, as high pressure is essential to efficient filtration by the kidneys. Water, urea, glucose, amino acids and minerals are forced by this **ultrafiltration** through the capillary walls of the glomerulus into the surrounding Bowman's capsule. The liquid that passes through (the **filtrate**) is like blood plasma but without blood proteins or cells. The filtrate does, however, contain materials which are essential for the correct balance of the body's fluids. For example, we cannot afford to lose glucose as it is our fuel, neither can we afford to lose water if we are in danger of dehydration, or minerals if they are not in excess. This is therefore corrected in the second stage of the process – reabsorption. After the filtrate leaves the Bowman's capsule, it moves through the tubule which is surrounded by a network of capillaries. These blood vessels reabsorb glucose, minerals and amino acids by active transport (see p. 16) and water follows passively by osmosis (see p. 14). For every litre of filtrate, up to 990 cm³ may be reabsorbed. The remainder passes through the tubules into the pelvis of the kidney as urine.

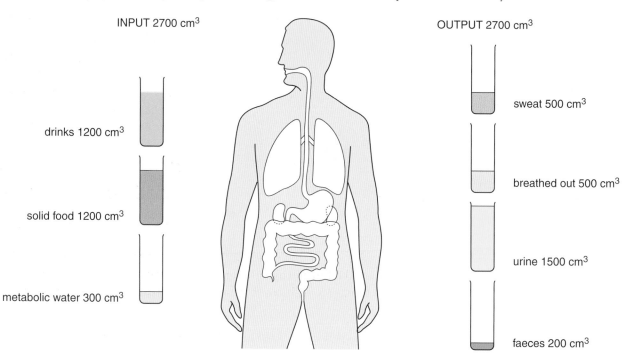

INPUT 2700 cm³

drinks 1200 cm³

solid food 1200 cm³

metabolic water 300 cm³

OUTPUT 2700 cm³

sweat 500 cm³

breathed out 500 cm³

urine 1500 cm³

faeces 200 cm³

Figure 5.4 *Daily input and output of water*

The regulation of water reabsorption is controlled by a hormone called **anti-diuretic hormone**, ADH. There is no direct link between the alimentary canal and the urinary system, yet the more we drink, the more we urinate. The explanation concerns the production of ADH. At times of water shortage, when we are thirsty, very little water is absorbed into the blood supply of the alimentary canal. Consequently, the blood becomes more 'concentrated', and when it reaches the brain, a gland called the **hypothalamus** responds to the high concentration by secreting ADH into the blood. The blood carries the ADH to the kidneys which results in changes in the cell membranes so that as much water as possible is reabsorbed into the blood capillaries surrounding the tubules. At times like this, we excrete small volumes of very concentrated urine.

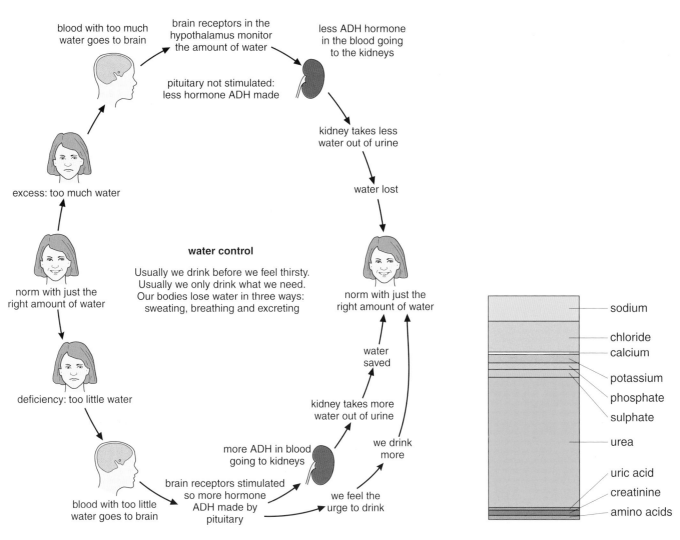

Figure 5.5 *Water regulation*

Figure 5.6 *The composition of urine*

After drinking lots of fluids, the concentration of our blood is decreased and the secretion of ADH by the hypothalamus is switched off. There is now nothing to cause the tubules to reabsorb more water so we excrete large volumes of very dilute urine.

The urine is made up mainly of water, urea and mineral salts.

Urine passes from the pelvis of the kidney to the ureters which transport it to the **bladder** by peristalsis. The filtered blood is now the purest in the body and leaves the kidneys in the **renal veins**. These lead to the inferior vena cava, which in turn carries the blood to the right atrium of the heart.

The bladder is a muscular sac which can expand to hold the urine until its contractions push urine through the **urethra**. Your kidneys have tremendous reserve power. If one has to be removed, the other will grow bigger and take over the job of both.

Living with kidney failure

Although it is possible to live a normal life with only one kidney, there are people in whom neither kidney can function properly. In such cases, the problem has to be remedied with either a kidney transplant or a kidney machine.

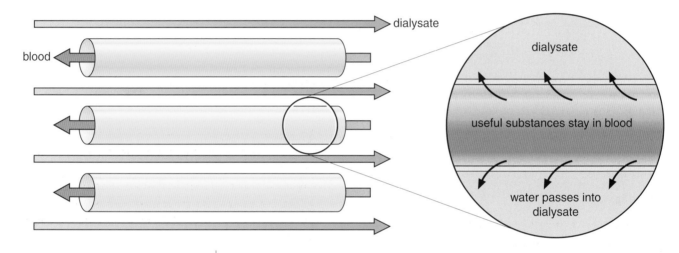

Figure 5.7 *Kidney dialysis*

Kidney machines work in some ways like real kidneys. The person's blood flows on one side of a very thin dialysing membrane. On the other side, a solution which resembles plasma without urea flows – this is called the **dialysate**. Waste products from the blood pass across the membrane into the dialysate in a process called **dialysis**. The dialysate contains dissolved sugar and salts just like plasma. If this were not the case, useful substances such as sugar and salts would also pass out of the blood, together with urea, by diffusion.

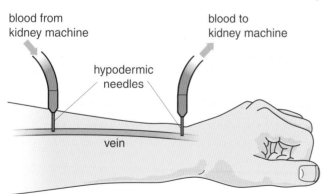

Figure 5.8 *Connecting a patient to a kidney machine*

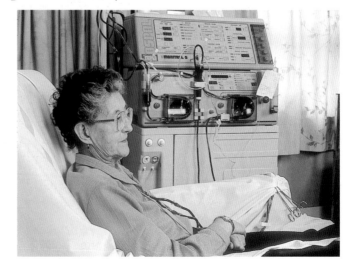

Figure 5.9 *This person is undergoing kidney dialysis*

A person must be connected to the machine for about 10 hours, two or three times a week. Blood is taken from a large vein which is surgically connected to an artery, usually in the arm or leg. It flows into the machine, is filtered by dialysis, and is pumped back into the same vein. The blood has to pass through the machine many times for complete filtration – this is why the person needs to be connected to the machine for so long.

Some people have their own kidney machine at home, others have to go into a hospital each time they need dialysis. Although kidney machines undoubtedly save many lives, they can bring problems. Normal life is restricted because dialysis is so time-consuming, and anaemia and infections can appear as side effects of the treatment. Also, a careful diet has to be followed to restrict those foods that would contain many mineral salts or produce a lot of urea.

Coursework Activities

What does a kidney filter out of the blood?

You are given four test tubes and asked to test the contents. You know that the tubes contain the following mixtures:

- egg albumen, distilled water, glucose and urea
- distilled water and urea
- distilled water, egg albumen and glucose.

You do not know which is which.

Carry out tests using the following materials to find which mixture represents

a) plasma from the renal artery

b) the filtrate from a kidney tubule

c) urine

d) plasma from the renal vein.

Materials to be used:

- Clinistix – changes yellow in the presence of glucose. (An alternative is Benedict's solution, see p. 40.)
- Albustix – changes red in the presence of protein. (An alternative is Biuret reagent, see p. 40.)
- Urease – acts on urea to form an alkali (ammonium carbonate)
- Indicator paper

Explain the results by relating your observation to the way in which a kidney functions.

The skin as an excretory organ

The skin excretes water, minerals and some urea when we sweat. This fluid has a useful role because it helps to regulate the body temperature. When liquid water is changed to water vapour by evaporation, heat is required. Thus, as water in sweat evaporates from the body surface, heat is withdrawn from the outer tissues. The skin acts like an automatic radiator – it is richly supplied with warm blood and heat is carried to the surface in this way. At the same time, production of sweat increases and bathes the skin which increases the rate of evaporation and the amount of heat loss.

Diabetes UK
http://www.diabetes.org.uk

What's Inside? – Learn about diabetes
http://www.bonus.com/bonus/intro/green.html

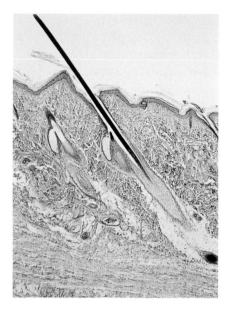

Figure 5.11 *A section through human skin*

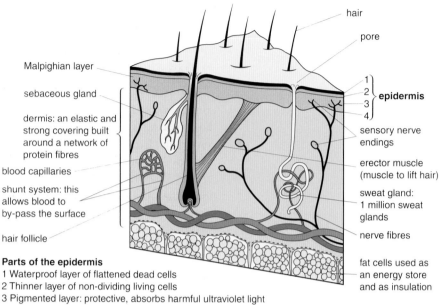

Malpighian layer

sebaceous gland

dermis: an elastic and
strong covering built
around a network of
protein fibres

blood capillaries

shunt system: this
allows blood to
by-pass the surface

hair follicle

hair

pore

1
2 **epidermis**
3
4

sensory nerve
endings

erector muscle
(muscle to lift hair)

sweat gland:
1 million sweat
glands

nerve fibres

fat cells used as
an energy store
and as insulation

Parts of the epidermis
1 Waterproof layer of flattened dead cells
2 Thinner layer of non-dividing living cells
3 Pigmented layer: protective, absorbs harmful ultraviolet light
4 Inner layer of dividing cells to replace those worn away

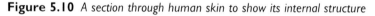

Figure 5.10 *A section through human skin to show its internal structure*

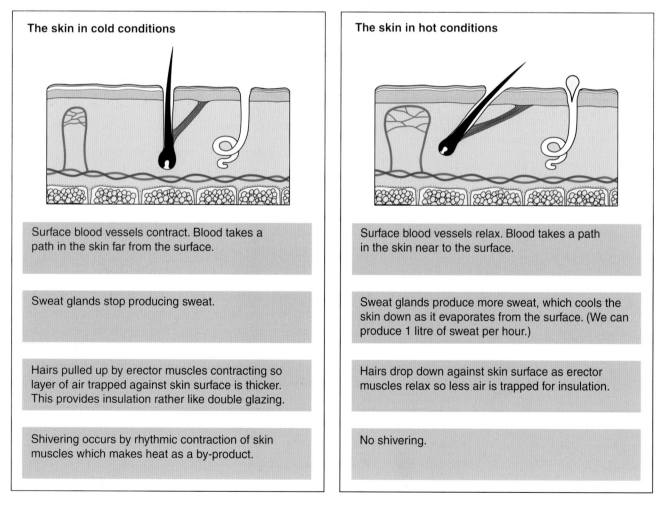

The skin in cold conditions

Surface blood vessels contract. Blood takes a
path in the skin far from the surface.

Sweat glands stop producing sweat.

Hairs pulled up by erector muscles contracting so
layer of air trapped against skin surface is thicker.
This provides insulation rather like double glazing.

Shivering occurs by rhythmic contraction of skin
muscles which makes heat as a by-product.

The skin in hot conditions

Surface blood vessels relax. Blood takes a path
in the skin near to the surface.

Sweat glands produce more sweat, which cools the
skin down as it evaporates from the surface. (We can
produce 1 litre of sweat per hour.)

Hairs drop down against skin surface as erector
muscles relax so less air is trapped for insulation.

No shivering.

Figure 5.12 *Temperature regulation*

Summary

I Various wastes result from the metabolism of protein, carbohydrate and fat.

2 They are removed from the body with the help of the kidneys, skin, lungs and liver.

3 The kidneys are the most important excretory organs.

4 They filter the majority of the urea from the blood.

5 The skin also excretes wastes in sweat.

6 Sweat helps to control your body temperature.

Homework Questions

I How do the kidneys regulate the contents of the blood?

2 What are the differences between the filtrate in the Bowman's capsule and urine?

3 What are the differences between the contents of the blood plasma of the renal artery and that of the renal vein?

In-Depth Questions

1 Why is increased salt intake recommended in hot weather?

2 How do the kidneys help to maintain the water balance of the body?

6 Body Controls

By the end of this chapter you should be able to understand:

- the path taken by impulses in response to a variety of stimuli, including touch, taste, smell, light, sound and balance;

- how the reflex arc involves a nerve impulse carried via neurons and across synapses so that a rapid, automatic, protective response is made to a stimulus;

- the structure and function of the eye and ear.

The nervous system

Animals have a nervous system to make them aware of changes in their surroundings (**stimuli**) and to help them co-ordinate a reaction to stimuli in such a way that it is to their advantage.

The nervous system is divided into three main parts:

1 the **central nervous system** – the **brain** and **spinal cord**

2 the **peripheral nervous system** – nerves connecting the central nervous system with all organs of the body

3 the **autonomic nervous system**, which regulates all the automatic actions of organs that carry out vital activities, such as the heart beat, breathing rate and peristalsis.

Nerve cells are called **neurons** and each acts as a link in the nervous system by virtue of its unique structure.

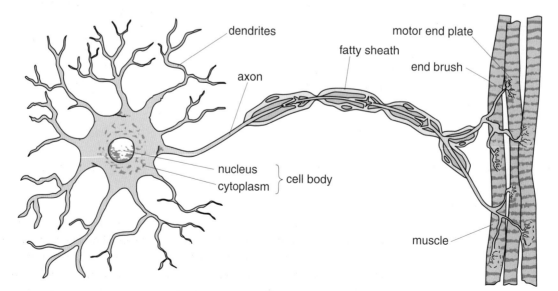

Figure 6.1 *A neuron*

Each neuron has a star-shaped cell body containing the nucleus and bulk of the cytoplasm.

Thread-like projections called **nerve fibres** extend outwards from the cell body and are used to conduct messages, called **impulses**, to their destinations.

We react to changes in our environment through our senses. When you stub your toe, the impulse travels to your central nervous system and is relayed very quickly back to the muscles in your foot. These contract to move your foot away. In the meantime, your brain has registered the feeling of pain and you are aware of the problem.

Nerve cell fibres run in bundles called **nerves**. They are similar in structure to an electrical cable, as they are made up of insulated wires bound together. In the peripheral nervous system, nerves which carry impulses that activate muscles are called **motor nerves**. In contrast, nerves which carry impulses away from sense organs towards the central nervous system are called **sensory nerves**. Nerve fibres of one neuron never touch those of a neighbouring neuron – there is always a tiny space between them. The spaces are called **synapses** and have to be crossed by impulses before a message can be sent from one neuron to another. Furthermore, an impulse never travels from one motor neuron to another or from one sensory neuron to another. Impulses bridge the synapse with the help of fast-acting chemical reactions in **transmitter substances** produced at the endings of neurons.

The brain

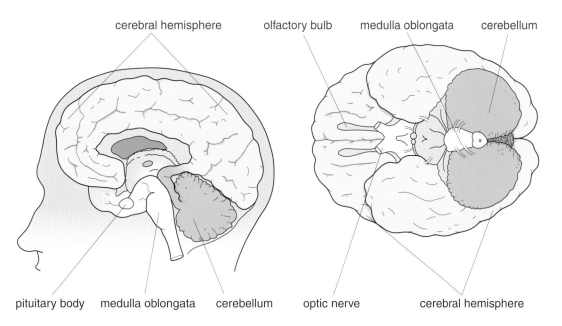

cerebral hemisphere   olfactory bulb   medulla oblongata   cerebellum

pituitary body   medulla oblongata   cerebellum   optic nerve   cerebral hemisphere

Figure 6.2 *Two views of the human brain*

The part of the brain called the **cerebrum** is proportionally larger in humans than in any other animal. It consists of two halves, the **cerebral hemispheres**, which have an outer surface called the **cortex** that is deeply folded into irregular wrinkles and furrows. These greatly increase the surface area so that countless numbers of neurons can develop in this region. Indeed, the vast numbers of neuron cell bodies that are found here give this tissue its name of **grey matter**.

The cerebrum below the cortex is called the **white matter** because it is formed from masses of nerve fibres surrounded by insulating white fatty sheaths of **myelin**. These fibres extend from the neurons of the cortex to other parts of the body.

Specific regions of the cerebrum control specific activities. Some areas of the cerebral cortex are called **motor areas** and these control voluntary movements. There are also **sensory areas** that interpret sensations. The cerebrum is responsible for storing information and for processes that we associate with complex activities, thinking and intelligence.

The **cerebellum** lies below the back of the cerebrum and both work together in the control of muscular activity. Nerve impulses do not originate in the cerebellum and you cannot control its activities. It is the cerebellum that co-ordinates the motor impulses sent from the cerebrum. Without the cerebellum, the cerebrum's impulses would produce unco-ordinated motions.

Another function of the cerebellum involves the maintenance of balance. Impulses from your eyes and inner ears (see p. 105) inform the cerebellum of your position relative to your surroundings. The cerebellum then controls the muscular contractions necessary to maintain balance.

The **brain stem (medulla oblongata)** is an enlargement at the base of the brain. It is where nerve fibres from the cerebrum and the cerebellum collect before leaving the brain. The brain stem controls the activity of the internal organs and also contains the respiratory control centre (see p. 83). All automatic activities are controlled here – the heart action, peristalsis, glandular secretion, diaphragm action, dilation of blood vessels.

www

Explore the human body
http://www.bbc.co.uk/science/humanbody

Explore the brain and spinal cord
http://facultywashington.edu/chudler/introb.html

IT

Use a CD-ROM encyclopaedia or a multimedia title about the human body to see how the nervous system and your senses work.

The spinal cord and spinal nerves

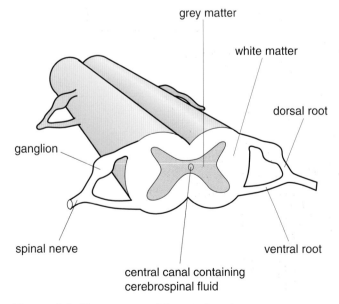

Figure 6.3 *The structure of the spinal cord*

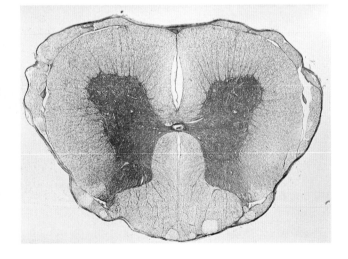

Figure 6.4 *The human spinal cord in transverse section showing the grey matter (the brown butterfly-shaped core) surrounded by the white matter*

The **spinal cord** extends down from the brain stem, passing through the protection of the **vertebrae** along the length of the spine. In the spinal cord, the positions of the grey and white matter are reversed with respect to the brain. In transverse section, the grey matter in the spinal cord takes on the shape of a butterfly with outspread wings (see Figure 6.4).

Thirty-one pairs of spinal nerves branch off the nerve cord, pass out between the vertebrae and divide again to make up the majority of the peripheral nervous system. Each spinal nerve divides just outside the cord. The sensory fibres that carry impulses from the sense organs to the cord go through the dorsal route and enter the grey matter. Cell bodies of the sensory fibres form a swelling called the **dorsal route ganglion** on this branch of the spinal nerve. The other branch at this junction is the **ventral route** and carries the motor fibres from the grey matter where their cell bodies are located. The motor fibres of this branch carry impulses from the spinal cord to muscles or glands of the body.

If your spinal cord were cut, serious problems would result. All the parts of your body controlled by nerves that leave the cord below the point of the cut would be totally paralysed. In addition you would lose all sense of feeling in many areas below the damaged spinal cord.

Reflex actions

The simplest kind of nervous reaction in humans is called a **reflex action**. It can involve only two or three nerves which link a receptor (sense organ) to an effector (muscle or gland) via the central nervous system (spinal cord or the brain).

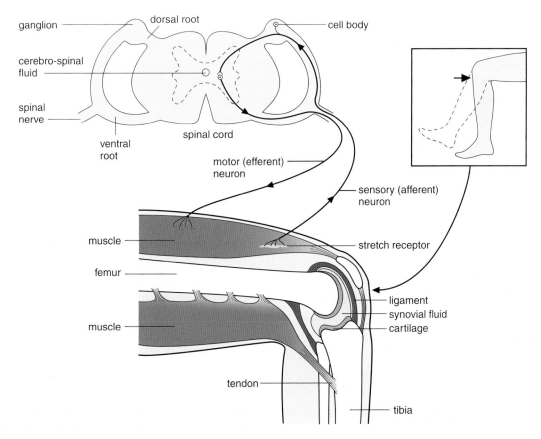

Figure 6.5 *The processes involved in the knee-jerk reflex*

Nerve-muscle connection
http://www.innerbody.com

A reflex action is a rapid, automatic reaction which does not involve conscious effort and may not involve the brain. The knee jerk is a good example of a simple reflex action. Sit on the edge of a table and let your knee swing freely. Tap the area just below the knee cap with a narrow object. Your lower leg will jerk upward because the tap has stimulated a sensory neuron in the lower leg. An impulse travels along the sensory neuron to a motor neuron via a synapse and the impulse travels to muscles in the leg which contract, causing the jerking movement. The entire reflex takes a split second.

Reflex actions have a protective function – for example, when you touch a hot object, your hand jerks away almost instantly. The reflex is complete even before your brain registers the pain. If the muscle response were delayed until the pain impulse was complete and interpreted, the effects of the burn would be much greater. Other reflexes include sneezing, coughing, blinking and the constriction or dilation of the pupil in the eye.

The skin as a sense organ

Specialised parts of sensory neurons make up the **receptors** found in the skin. They can be bare nerve endings or collected into one or more cells. Each receptor is adapted to receive only one type of stimulus. This stimulus will trigger an impulse which travels along a sensory neuron to the central nervous system. There are five distinct kinds of receptor in the skin which can be differentiated by the types of stimuli to which they respond. They are: pain, touch, pressure, heat or cold. The pain receptor, for example, is a bare ending of a neuron. If the stimulus is strong enough, a pain receptor will react to heat, mechanical, electrical or chemical stimuli. The sensation of pain is protective and signals a threat of injury to the body. It is, therefore, an advantage for pain receptors to be located throughout the skin.

The sensory nerves lie at different depths in the skin. For example, if you move the point of a pencil over your skin very lightly, you stimulate only the nerves of touch because the receptors for touch are close to the surface of the skin. The fingertips, the forehead and the tip of the tongue contain many receptors that respond to touch.

Receptors that respond to pressure lie deeper in the skin. If you press the pencil point against the skin, you feel both pressure and touch. Since the nerves are deeper, a pressure stimulus must be stronger than a touch stimulus.

Heat and cold stimulate different receptors – this is an interesting protective adaptation of the body. If both great heat and intense cold stimulated a single receptor, we would be unable to tell the difference between the two, and we would be unable to react to either. However, since some receptors are stimulated by heat and others by the absence of it, we can react to both conditions.

The sense of taste

Most animals have a preference for certain foods because of their ability to distinguish different chemicals. Like other senses, taste results from the stimulation of certain nerve endings. In this case, the stimulation is chemical and, in humans, the nerve endings for taste are located in flask-shaped taste buds on the tongue.

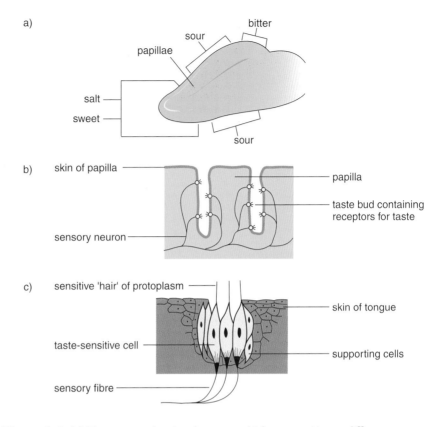

Figure 6.6 *(a) The tongue, showing the areas which are sensitive to different tastes. (b) A taste papilla from the back of the tongue. (c) A taste bud*

The taste buds lie on the front of the tongue, along its sides, and near the back. Bits of food, mixed with saliva, enter the taste buds through little pores at the top and stimulate hair-like nerve endings. The messages carried to the brain from these nerve endings are interpreted as a sense of taste.

Our sense of taste, like our sense of smell, is not very well developed. In fact, we can only taste four basic flavours: sour, sweet, salty and bitter. The taste buds for each of these flavours are located in different parts of the tongue. Those for sweetness are on the tip of the tongue – that is why chocolate tastes sweeter when you lick it than when you chew it. Salt-sensitive buds are also on the tongue's tip. Those for sour flavours lie along the sides of the tongue, and those for bitterness lie on the back of the tongue. That is why if you eat something both sweet and bitter, you taste the sweetness before the bitterness. Some foods, like pepper and other spices, have no distinct flavour. They taste the way they do because they irritate the entire tongue, causing a burning sensation.

Much of the sensation we call taste is really smell. When you chew some onion or apple, the vapours enter the inner openings of the nose, where they reach the nerve endings for smell. It is these nerve endings which can distinguish between the two flavours. You may have noticed the loss of what you thought was taste when you had a cold. When your nose is blocked up with mucus, few food vapours can get to the nerve endings for smell. That is why food does not taste very good when you have a head cold. In fact, under these conditions, the apple and the onion may even have the same sweet flavour.

Did you know?

Chewing food and adding saliva to it can release strong smells of food and increase the intensity of a flavour. The smell reaches the nose through the back of the mouth.

www

Our sense of smell
http://www.schoolscience.co.uk

The sense of smell

Like taste, smell results from the chemical stimulation of certain nerve endings. In smell, the chemical stimulator is in the form of gases which dissolve in mucus. These gases stimulate the nerve endings and cause impulses to be transported to the central nervous system where they are interpreted as smell. If the smell receptors are exposed to a particular odour for a long time, they stop reacting to it but will respond to other odours. If, for example, you go into a laboratory where a particularly smelly chemical is being made, the smell may be overpowering to start with but you soon fail to notice it. The part of the brain responsible for interpreting the impulse has become fatigued and does not respond.

The sense of hearing

Like all mammalian ears, human ears are very complex organs as can be seen in Figure 6.7.

The Eustachian tube which connects the middle ear with the throat is responsible for equalising the pressure in the middle ear with that of the outer atmosphere. When it becomes blocked by mucus from a cold, the inner and outer pressures do not equalise and, if the pressure difference becomes great enough, the eardrum may burst. For this reason, professional divers and aeroplane pilots do not work when they have colds. The outside pressure increases with increasing depth of water and if a diver had a blocked Eustachian tube, the middle ear pressure would not be equalised. The difference might be great enough to burst the eardrum. With the pilot, the situation would be reversed – the pressure would be less outside the middle ear than inside. That is why all commercial airlines have pressurised cabins.

We are able to hear because all noises are caused by vibrations. When an object vibrates in the air, it moves the air molecules mechanically. Some of them are squeezed together or compressed, others are spread apart or rarefied. The regular pattern that is produced by any vibrating object in the air, or any other medium, is called a **sound wave**. These waves pass more effectively through liquids and solids than they do through air because the molecules are more closely packed together in the more dense media.

When sound waves reach the ear, they pass through the **auditory canal** to the **eardrum**. The sound waves start the eardrum vibrating in the same pattern as the particular wave. The vibrating eardrum then causes the **hammer**, the **anvil** and the **stirrup** to vibrate. These in turn cause the **oval window** to vibrate which sets up vibrations in the fluid inside the **cochlea**. The vibrations of the fluid stimulate the nerve endings that line the cochlea which in turn transmit impulses via the auditory nerve to the cerebrum. The specific pattern of the impulses is determined by the pattern of the sound wave that started the whole chain of events. The cerebrum picks up the impulses and translates them into a perception of sound.

The sense of balance

The **semi-circular canals** are the structures responsible for our sense of balance. The canals contain many receptors and lie at right angles to each other on three different planes. They also contain a fluid similar to that inside the cochlea. When your head changes position, this fluid rocks and stimulates the receptors which then start impulses that go through a branch of the **auditory nerve** to the

passage of sound waves through the ear

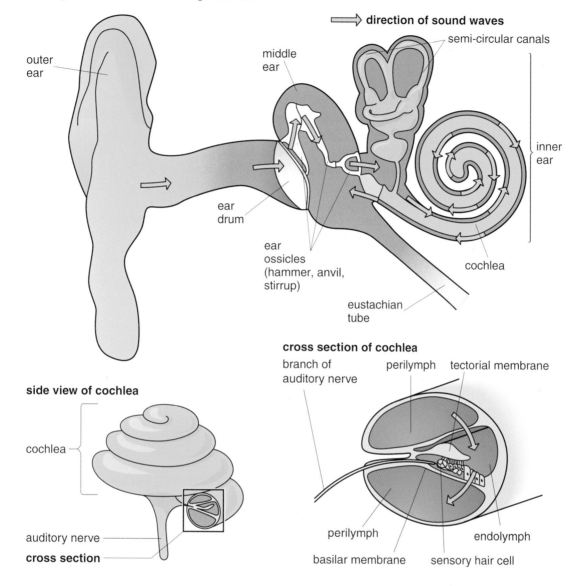

direction of sound waves

outer ear

middle ear

semi-circular canals

inner ear

ear drum

ear ossicles (hammer, anvil, stirrup)

cochlea

eustachian tube

cross section of cochlea

branch of auditory nerve

perilymph

tectorial membrane

side view of cochlea

cochlea

auditory nerve

cross section

perilymph

basilar membrane

sensory hair cell

endolymph

Figure 6.7 *How we hear*

cerebellum. The brain is thus made aware of changes in head position. The canals lie in three different planes so that any changes in the head's position will rock the fluid in one or more directions.

People get dizzy when they spin around and then suddenly stop. The spinning forces the fluid to the ends of the canals. When the spinning stops, the fluid rushes back, causing the sensation of spinning in the opposite direction. The sensory conflict causes a feeling of dizziness or nausea. In some people, regular rhythmic motions produce unpleasant sensations that involve the whole body. When this occurs in a ship, aeroplane or car, it is called **motion sickness**. If the semi-circular canals become diseased, temporary or permanent dizziness may result.

www

Animation of the ear
http://www.innerbody.com

The sense of sight

The function of the majority of structures in the eye is to focus light on the retina. The retina contains the receptors that are stimulated by light. The receptors are of two types – **rods** and **cones**. When they are stimulated, they start impulses which eventually pass through the **optic nerve**. There are no rods or cones at the spot where the optic nerve joins the retina. There can, therefore, be no vision at this point and consequently it is called the **blind spot**. The optic nerve from each eye leads to the vision centre of the brain in the cerebrum. The focusing mechanisms of the eye attempt to direct light rays onto the most sensitive part of the retina, the **yellow spot** or **fovea centralis**, which has more cones than other parts of the retina. The cones are more sensitive to bright light than the rods, and are responsible for colour vision. An image formed as a result of light rays focusing outside the fovea is less distinct. This explains why if you focus your eyes directly on an object, you see it clearly, while surrounding objects tend to lack detail.

In the dark, there is not enough light to stimulate the cones, but there may be enough to stimulate the rods. Since rods cannot distinguish colours, however, you do not see much colour in dim light. Human eyes contain fewer rods than those of many other animals and as a result, our night vision is relatively poor. Cats, deer and owls see well at night because they have many rods. The owl, however, lacks cones in its eyes and is therefore day-blind.

Automatic focusing is brought about by a process known as **accommodation**. The eye is remarkable in that it can focus on a very distant object and then suddenly focus equally sharply on words in a book held close to the eye. The younger you are, the quicker the process of accommodation occurs. Your lens changes shape from being thin when you focus on distant objects to becoming fatter when you focus on near objects. As you become older, the tissue of your lens becomes stiffer and does not alter shape so quickly. The process is summarised in Figure 6.8(b). Note that several automatic changes occur to other parts of the eye besides the lens.

www

The National Eye Institute
http://www.nei.nih.gov/publications/schintro.htm

Body Quest – Tour of the human body – the eye
http://library.thinkquest.org/10348/home.html

Examcentre – Biology – The Mammalian Eye
http://www.examcentre.com/

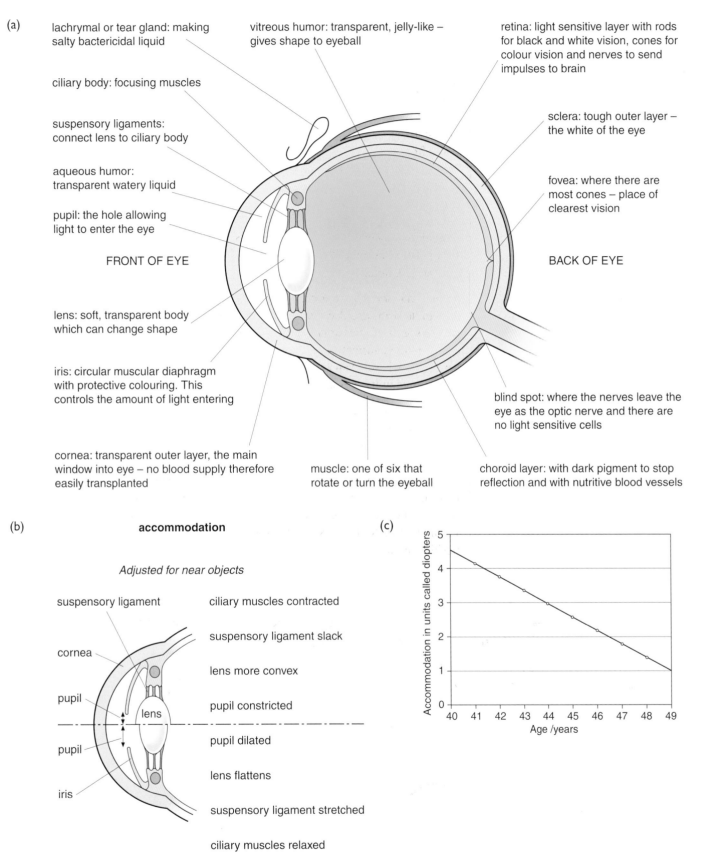

(a)

lachrymal or tear gland: making salty bactericidal liquid

vitreous humor: transparent, jelly-like – gives shape to eyeball

retina: light sensitive layer with rods for black and white vision, cones for colour vision and nerves to send impulses to brain

ciliary body: focusing muscles

suspensory ligaments: connect lens to ciliary body

sclera: tough outer layer – the white of the eye

aqueous humor: transparent watery liquid

fovea: where there are most cones – place of clearest vision

pupil: the hole allowing light to enter the eye

FRONT OF EYE

BACK OF EYE

lens: soft, transparent body which can change shape

iris: circular muscular diaphragm with protective colouring. This controls the amount of light entering

blind spot: where the nerves leave the eye as the optic nerve and there are no light sensitive cells

cornea: transparent outer layer, the main window into eye – no blood supply therefore easily transplanted

muscle: one of six that rotate or turn the eyeball

choroid layer: with dark pigment to stop reflection and with nutritive blood vessels

(b)

accommodation

Adjusted for near objects

suspensory ligament

ciliary muscles contracted

cornea

suspensory ligament slack

lens more convex

pupil

pupil constricted

lens

pupil dilated

pupil

lens flattens

iris

suspensory ligament stretched

ciliary muscles relaxed

Adjusted for distant objects

(c)

Accommodation in units called diopters (y-axis: 0 to 5)

Age /years (x-axis: 40 to 49)

Figure 6.8 *(a) The structure of a human eye. (b) The process of accommodation. (c) A graph of accommodation against age*

Summary

1 Humans have the most complex central nervous system of any animal. It comprises the brain and spinal cord and communicates with all parts of the body via the nerves.

2 The cerebrum controls conscious activities and is the centre of intelligence. The cerebellum co-ordinates impulses and controls movement and balance. The medulla oblongata controls the automatic actions of the body.

3 Sensory nerves carry impulses to the central nervous system from sense receptors which include those of the:

   a) skin, responsible for the sense of touch, pressure, pain, heat and cold

   b) tongue and nose, which respond to chemical stimuli

   c) cochlea of the inner ear, which respond to vibrations in the form of sound waves

   d) semi-circular canals, which detect the position of your head when balancing

   e) rods and cones of the retina in the eye which respond to light.

Homework Questions

1 Name the main division of the nervous system and state the functions of each.

2 Name the main parts of the brain and give brief functions of each.

3 Name the five sensations of the skin. In what ways are the receptors different?

4 Describe how sound waves in the air stimulate the receptors in the cochlea.

5 Why is our night vision relatively poor compared to the night vision of an owl?

In-Depth Questions

1 Account for the fact that we think we can distinguish more than the four tastes the tongue can detect.

2 How can an infection in the middle ear produce temporary deafness?

3 Describe the movements of the head that would be necessary to stimulate each semi-circular canal separately.

7 Chemical Regulators

Learning objectives

By the end of this chapter you should be able to understand:

- how plants move towards or away from stimuli;
- the functions of plant hormones;
- the functions of the endocrine glands;
- how the endocrine glands work together in a balanced way.

Plant responses DOUBLE & TRIPLE AWARD ONLY

Most living plant cells respond to changes in their surroundings but in general, they do not respond to the same stimuli to which animals respond. Flowering plants respond by growing in a particular direction and respond to four kinds of stimuli: light, gravity, water and touch. These growth responses are called **tropisms**. If a shoot or root grows towards a stimulus it is said to be a **positive response**. If it grows away from a stimulus it is said to be a **negative response**.

A response to light – phototropism

Look at any plant that has been growing on a window sill for any length of time in the same position. The leaves and the stem of the plant will be bending towards the light. The plant has moved in this way to enable it to capture as much sunlight as possible for photosynthesis. It has shown **positive phototropism**.

Did you know?

Some of the earliest experiments on tropisms were carried out by one of the most famous scientists of all time – Charles Darwin. Along with his son Francis, Darwin published *The Power of Movement in Plants* in 1881. After noticing that plants tend to bend towards light, the Darwins investigated whether the plants were responding to some sort of signal from the tip of the stem. To do this, they covered some shoot tips and exposed them to light from one side. The plants did not grow towards the light. When they capped the tips with transparent glass, however, normal bending occurred.

In Figure 7.1 you can see what happens if you allow some cress seeds to grow in three different conditions.

What is it that is made in the shoot tip that causes this pattern of growth? The unknown substance that the Darwins suggested in 1881 is now known to be a plant hormone called **auxin** (from the Greek *auxein*, to increase). It works by softening the cell walls of plants, allowing water to swell the vacuoles of the cells. Thus the cells grow by enlarging rather than by dividing (see p. 144).

When a shoot is exposed to light from one side only, the cells on the shaded side grow more rapidly than those nearest the light source.

The unequal growth is due to a higher concentration of auxin on the shaded side.

Figure 7.5 *A plantation of oil palms produced by cloning*

Figure 7.4 *This plant cutting has been treated with rooting powder, containing a plant hormone*

Regulators in animals – the endocrine system

Some glands, for example the salivary glands, pour secretions into the digestive system through ducts or tubes. These are called **exocrine glands**. **Endocrine glands** are quite different because they are ductless, and their secretions go directly into the bloodstream which carries them to all parts of the body.

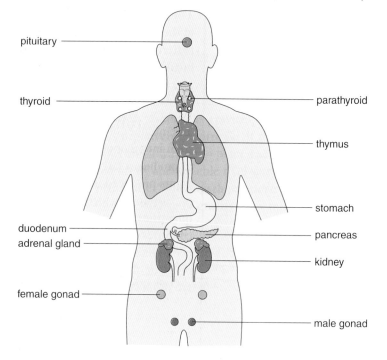

Figure 7.6 *The endocrine system*

The secretions of ductless glands are called **hormones** and they are responsible for regulating the activities of all the body processes.

The thyroid

The **thyroid gland** is in the neck, near the region where the lower part of the larynx meets the trachea. It consists of two lobes connected by a narrow bridge. The hormone produced by the thyroid is called **thyroxine** and contains the highest concentration of iodine found in any substance in the body. Purified thyroid extract from sheep is used to treat thyroid disturbances in humans. Although it is the least expensive of all commercial endocrine preparations, its supply can be increased by genetic engineering.

Thyroxine regulates certain metabolic processes, particularly those related to growth and respiration within cells. If the thyroid gland is overactive, it results in a condition called **hyperthyroidism**. If this happens, the rate of cellular respiration increases, the body temperature increases, and the heart rate goes up along with blood pressure. Sweating when the body should be cool is a common symptom, and the person often gets very nervous and irritable. Some people's eyes bulge slightly, and they develop a staring expression. Surgery used to be the only treatment for this condition, however, a drug called **thiouracil** has since been developed and doses of radioactive iodine can also be effective. The radiation works by destroying some of the thyroid tissue.

If the thyroid gland is underactive, the symptoms are the opposite of those given above. People with this condition are characteristically physically or mentally retarded. Their hearts enlarge and the rate of heartbeat slows down. The condition can be treated with thyroid extract.

Sometimes the thyroid does not function properly during infancy. This results in **cretinism** which is characterised by physical and mental retardation. Treatment must occur during the critical stages of development to be successful.

When iodine is deficient in the diet, the thyroid gland enlarges to form a **goitre**. People who eat seafood regularly rarely have this condition because of the iodine content. In areas where iodine is deficient in the soil, it can be added to the diet through additives in such foods as table salt.

The pituitary

The **pituitary** is a small gland, about the size of a pea, located at the base of the brain. It used to be called the 'master gland' because its secretions affect the activity of all other endocrine glands. It is now known that other glands, in turn, affect the pituitary.

Two lobes make up the pituitary gland – the anterior lobe and the posterior lobe. The anterior lobe secretes several different hormones, one of which is the growth hormone which controls the development of your skeleton – your whole body framework. This lobe also secretes the **gonadotropic hormones** which influence the development of your reproductive organs and also affect the hormone secretions of the ovaries and testes (see p. 117). Other hormones from the anterior lobe are responsible for stimulating milk production in the mammary glands, thyroxine in the thyroid and hormones in the adrenal glands.

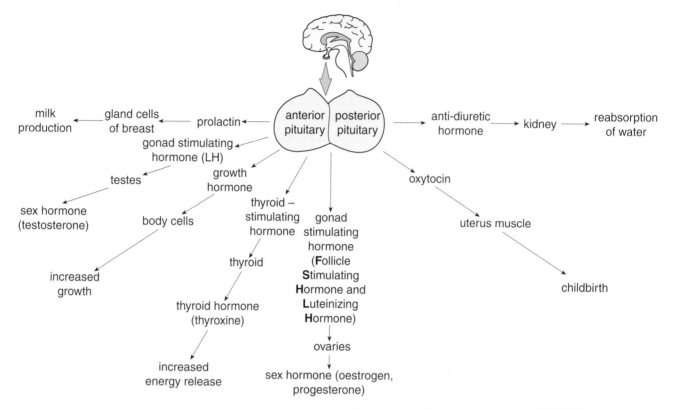

Figure 7.7 *The pituitary gland (below) and the effects of its hormones (above)*

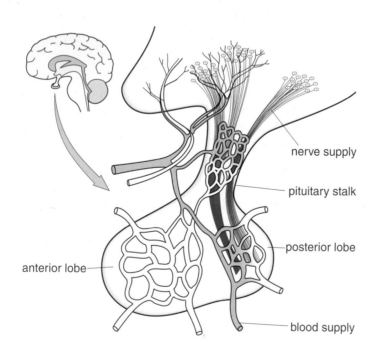

Figure 7.8 *The world's tallest person*

The posterior lobe of the pituitary releases two hormones:

- **oxytocin**, which helps regulate your blood pressure and stimulate your smooth muscles. During childbirth, oxytocin is secreted in large amounts to make the uterus contract.
- **anti-diuretic hormone** (ADH), which controls water reabsorption in the kidneys (see p. 93). A deficiency of this hormone causes **diabetes insipidus** which allows too much water to be lost in urine.

The most common disorder of the pituitary gland involves the **growth hormone**. If the pituitary secretes too much of this hormone during infancy, the bones and other tissues grow too fast and the person may grow to 2.5 m in height (see Figure 7.8).

This condition is known as **gigantism**. In contrast, deficiency of the growth hormone slows down the process of growth and results in the production of midgets who tend to be mentally retarded. These midgets are *not* the same as dwarfs who grow as a result of thyroid deficiency.

The adrenal glands – glands of emergency

On top of each kidney are the **adrenal glands**, also called supra-renal glands. These glands have an outer layer called the **cortex** and an inner part called the **medulla**. Unlike the adrenal medulla, the adrenal cortex is essential for life, as it secretes hormones called **corticoids** which control the metabolism of carbohydrates, fats and proteins. The corticoids also affect the balance of salt and water in your body. Other hormones produced in the adrenal cortex control the production of certain types of white blood cells and the structure of connective tissue. If the adrenal cortex is damaged or destroyed, a person develops **Addison's disease** with symptoms including tiredness, nausea and weight loss. Blood circulation is affected and the skin colour changes. Sufferers can be helped by treatment with a corticoid hormone called **cortisone**.

The medulla secretes a hormone called **adrenalin**. This hormone can cause sudden body changes during anger or fright. As a result, the adrenal glands are often called 'glands of emergency'. When a lot of adrenalin is produced, the following changes happen:

- you become pale, because of the constriction of blood vessels in your skin. If you have a skin wound, you will lose less blood because of its diversion from the skin. At the same time, more blood is supplied to your muscles, brain and heart.
- your blood pressure goes up, because the blood vessels in your skin have constricted.
- your heart beats faster and its stroke volume increases. The stroke volume is the volume of blood pumped out of the heart at each beat.
- your liver releases some of its stored carbohydrate. This is oxidised to release more energy during cellular respiration.

The pancreas

Besides producing pancreatic enzymes to aid digestion (see p. 47), the pancreas also has special cells which produce hormones. The cells are called **Islets of Langerhans** and the hormones produced are called **insulin** and **glucagon**.

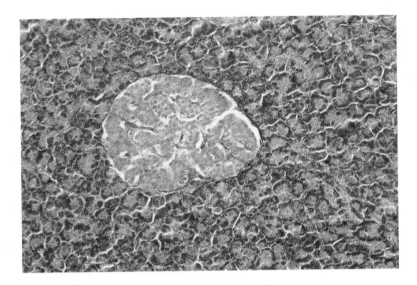

Figure 7.9 *A section through a human pancreas showing an Islet of Langerhans*

Insulin enables the liver to store glucose in the form of glycogen and speeds up the oxidation of glucose in cellular respiration. A person who cannot produce insulin is unable to store or oxidise carbohydrate properly. Consequently, tissues are deprived of fuel, leading to a build-up of glucose in the blood which can be dangerous. The normal concentration of glucose in the blood is 0.1 g per 100 cm^3 of blood. If it rises above this, the kidney tubules cannot cope when they try to re-absorb the glucose back into the blood (see p. 93). The tubule 'pumps' effectively break down. As a result, glucose passes right though the kidney tubules and is lost in urine. This condition is called **diabetes mellitus** and is caused by a combination of factors, not just the failure of the islet cells to produce insulin. The condition can also be affected by the activity of the pituitary, thyroid, adrenals and liver.

There are three main types of diabetes mellitus:

1 *Juvenile* – either insulin is not produced or the body does not react to insulin in the normal way. It is detected early in the life of the person.

2 *Maturity onset* – confined mainly to overweight, middle-aged women. It occurs when there is too little insulin to meet the demands of the body.

3 *Stress* – may occur during pregnancy or under physical or mental stress. The body fails to respond to insulin at its normal levels in the blood.

Treatment by regular injection of the correct amount of insulin normally allows people with diabetes mellitus to lead a normal life. They must, however, pay close attention to the carbohydrate intake in their diet.

If too much insulin is produced, the result is a condition called **hypoglycaemia**. This means 'low blood sugar level' and results in tiredness. The hormone called glucagon, produced in different islet cells, has the opposite effect to insulin. It encourages the change from glycogen to glucose when extra fuel is needed by the body's cells.

Teens Health – questions about puberty
http://teenshealth.org/

The ovaries and testes

Besides producing the body's sex cells, the ovaries and testes produce **sex hormones** which are used to regulate sexual cycles in the body. The ovaries secrete **oestrogen** and **progesterone** and the testes produce **testosterone**. Sex hormones affect the development of the secondary sexual characteristics which appear at the time of change from child to adult. They begin with the maturation of the ovaries and testes during puberty. Among animals, sex hormones result in the bright feathers of most male birds, and the antlers of stags. In boys, the voice breaks and becomes deeper, and a beard and pubic hair appears. These features are accompanied by a broadening and deepening of the chest and rapid bone growth. As a girl matures, her breasts develop and her hips become broader. Fat deposits form under the skin, pubic hair grows and menstruation begins. These physical changes cause both boys and girls to go through major mental and emotional changes.

Control mechanisms in gamete production

The production of gametes in both male and female occurs under the control of the endocrine system (see p.112). In the male, the pituitary gland at the base of the brain secretes **luteinising hormone** (LH) which travels to the testes in the bloodstream. Here, it causes the interstitial cells to produce the hormone testosterone which is responsible for the proper maturation of sperm. Very little LH is secreted before puberty, which takes place between the ages of 10 and 15 years. Once the secretion begins, it continues throughout a man's life.

The female system is far more complex and operates on a monthly cycle. In this cycle, one egg is released from one of the two ovaries approximately every 28 days (this time varies between individuals). The cycle begins when the pituitary gland secretes the **follicle-stimulating hormone** (FSH). This causes a number of ovarian follicles to secrete another hormone called **oestrogen**. The effect of oestrogen is to stimulate the repair and thickening of the lining of the uterus, the **endometrium**, after the previous menstrual period. When the concentration of oestrogen builds up in the blood, it stimulates the pituitary to release luteinising hormone. This reaches the ovaries via the bloodstream where it causes the mature follicle to rupture and release an egg. This process – **ovulation** – occurs about 14 days after the beginning of the previous menstrual period (see Figure 7.10).

Once the egg has been released, the now empty follicle collapses and, stimulated by luteinising hormone, changes in structure. At the same time, its colour changes from white to yellow. The follicle has now changed into a **corpus luteum** (yellow body). The cells of the corpus luteum continue to produce oestrogen along with a second hormone called **progesterone**, which helps to stimulate the build-up of the uterus lining. Meanwhile, the egg begins its journey towards the uterus in a fallopian tube. If the egg is not fertilised, the corpus luteum disintegrates. This occurs about 22 days after the beginning of the previous menstrual period and causes a decrease in levels of oestrogen and progesterone in the blood. By day 28, the level of these two hormones is not sufficient to keep the lining of the uterus growing, so it breaks down. The resulting menstrual blood flow usually lasts for about 5 days, at the end of which FSH is again secreted from the pituitary.

If the egg is fertilised, the corpus luteum continues to grow and produces higher concentrations of progesterone in the blood. The lining of the uterus becomes

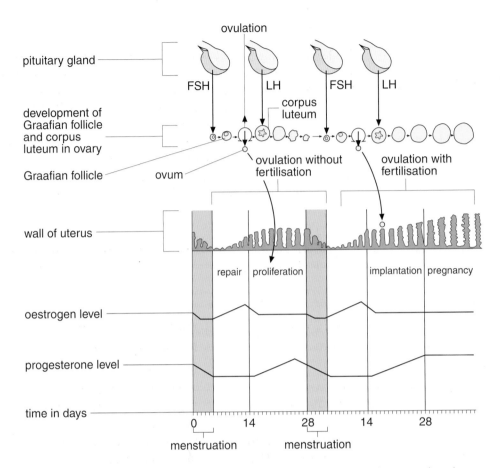

Figure 7.10 *The menstrual cycle. FSH = follicle stimulating hormone, LH = luteinising hormone*

progressively thicker and more spongy, ready to receive the zygote at implantation. The corpus luteum continues to produce progesterone long after the fertilised egg is implanted, and the uterine wall continues to thicken.

Puberty and hormones

The production of oestrogen and testosterone increases dramatically at the stage of growth called **puberty**. In girls this may occur at any time between 11 and 16 years, while in boys it usually occurs slightly later, between 13 and 17 years. The rise in hormone levels at this time of life is responsible for causing the development of the secondary sex characteristics. Important physiological changes also take place in both sexes at this time. The changes are summarised in Table 7.1 below.

Table 7.1

Male	Female
Hair grows on face, chest, in pubic regions and armpits	Hair grows in pubic regions and armpits
Larynx enlarges and voice deepens	Pelvis becomes broader, fat is deposited on hips and thighs
Body becomes more muscular	Breasts develop
The penis, scrotum and prostate become larger	Fallopian tubes, uterus and vagina enlarge, together with the linings of the uterus and vagina
Sperm formation begins	Ovulation and menstruation begin
Feelings and sexual drives associated with adulthood begin to develop	Feelings and sexual drives associated with adulthood begin to develop

The human body
**http://www.bbc.co.uk/science/
humanbody**

The hypothalamus

The **hypothalamus** is located at the base of the brain, just above the pituitary gland. It is vital in the maintenance of the internal environment of the body. Body temperature, ion and water balance, and release of pituitary hormones are some of the functions regulated by the hypothalamus. The pituitary is directed by the hypothalamus to release the required amount of a particular hormone. For example, if the level of water in the blood is low, it is detected by the hypothalamus which in turn directs the posterior pituitary to secrete more anti-diuretic hormone. This causes the kidney tubules to re-absorb more water in order to restore the water balance of the body (see p. 93).

IT Use a CD-ROM encyclopaedia or a multimedia title about the human body to see what the endocrine organs do.

Table 7.2 *A check list of the main ductless glands and their secretions*

Gland	Location	Hormone	Function of hormone
Thyroid	Neck, below larynx	Thyroxine	Accelerates the rate of metabolism
Pituitary – anterior lobe	Base of mid-brain	Growth hormone	Regulates growth of the skeleton
		Gonadotropic	Regulates the development of sex hormones in the ovaries and testes
		Adreno-corticotrophic hormone (ACTH)	Stimulates secretion of hormones by the adrenal cortex
		Lactogenic	Stimulates the secretion of milk by the mammary glands
		Thyrotropic	Stimulates activity of the thyroid gland
– posterior lobe		Oxytocin	Regulates blood pressure and stimulates smooth muscle
		ADH	Controls water re-absorption in the kidney
Adrenal cortex	Above kidneys	Cortin	Regulates metabolism, salt and water balance. Controls the production of certain white cells and the structure of connective tissue
Adrenal medulla		Adrenalin	Causes constriction of blood vessels, and increase in heart action and output
Pancreas (Islets of Langerhans)	Below and behind the stomach	Insulin	Enables the liver to store carbohydrate and regulates the oxidation of glucose
		Glucagon	Changes glycogen to glucose
Ovaries	Pelvis	Oestrogen	Produces female secondary sex characteristics
		Progesterone	Maintains growth of uterus during pregnancy
Testes	In scrotum	Testosterone	Produces male secondary sex characteristics

Summary

1   Hormones are the major internal factors in regulating the way a plant grows.

2   Plants respond to their surroundings by growing either toward a stimulus (positive tropism) or away from one (negative tropism).

3   There are many important groups of hormones and some are used commercially to destroy weeds or to promote the growth and ripening of fruits.

4   Ductless glands are called endocrine glands and secrete hormones directly into the bloodstream.

5   Many important hormones are produced by the thyroid, pituitary and adrenal glands.

6   The pancreas, ovaries and testes also secrete hormones essential for normal growth and body functions. Together, these hormones influence body metabolism, growth, mental ability and chemical balance in the body fluids.

7   Glands are controlled by their influence on each other, by feedback and by the nervous system.

Homework Questions

1   Name three tropisms and link each with an external stimulus.

2   How does the blood help in the work of the endocrine glands?

3   How does the thyroid gland control the rate of metabolism?

4   In what ways do the pituitary and thyroid glands affect growth?

5   In what ways are puberty and adolescence a result of glandular activity?

6   Why does sugar appear in the urine of a person with diabetes mellitus?

In-Depth Questions

1   How do auxins relate to tropisms?

2   Give an account of experimental evidence showing that auxin is secreted near the tip of a stem.

3   How do you account for the fact that the heartbeat of a footballer increases a great deal before the game as well as during the game?

4   Why is a study of the endocrine glands often carried out at the same time as a study of the nervous system?

8 Skeletons and Movement

Learning objectives

By the end of this chapter you should be able to understand:

- that there are different types of joints;
- the theory of muscle contraction;
- that there are three types of muscle;
- how muscles work in pairs to cause movement;
- that limb bones have the same basic structure in all air-breathing animals with backbones;
- how movement takes place in a variety of animals.

The skeletal system

Most of our support comes from a very efficient framework called an **endoskeleton**. It gives maximum support with the minimum of material and allows us to move freely. One disadvantage of having our skeleton on the inside of the body is that it does not offer the same protection to soft parts as an **exoskeleton** – a skeleton on the outside of the body. Many delicate parts are, however, protected, such as the brain, eyes and ears (by the skull), and the spinal cord (by the vertebrae).

Your skeleton carries out the following functions:

- support, for example the vertebral column
- provision of a surface for muscle attachment to enable movement to occur, for example limb bones, ribs, hip and shoulder girdles
- protection of some delicate organs, for example the skull and the rib cage
- storage of minerals, for example calcium is stored throughout the skeleton
- manufacture of blood cells, for example in the red bone marrow of the breast bone and ankle bones.

The joints of the body

The point at which two bones meet is called a **joint**. Several types of joint occur in the human skeleton.

1 **Hinge joints,** for example elbows and knees, which allow movement in one plane. When the biceps muscle of the upper arm, or humerus, contracts, the lower arm can be pulled upwards only. Such joints can provide great mechanical power because there is little danger of twisting them.

2 **Ball-and-socket joints** occur at your hips and shoulders. At your hip, the ball on the end of your thigh bone, or femur, fits into a socket in the hipbone, the pelvis. This kind of joint allows movement in any direction which the muscles around it will allow. The humerus fits into the shoulder, or pectoral girdle, in a similar way.

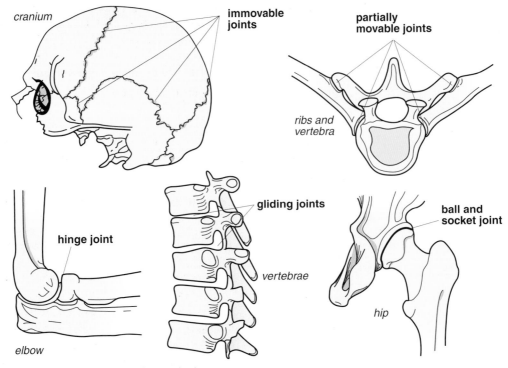

Figure 8.1 *Different types of joints in the human body*

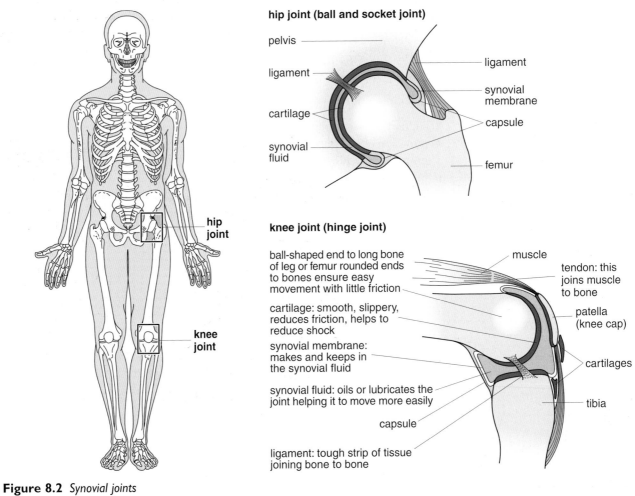

Figure 8.2 *Synovial joints*

3 **Partially-movable joints** attach your ribs to the vertebrae in your backbone. Together with the long strands of **cartilage**, which attach some ribs to the breast bone, they allow breathing movements (see p. 82).

4 **Immovable joints** occur in our skulls.

5 A **pivot joint** connects your head to your spine.

6 **Gliding joints** connect the vertebrae.

Tough strands of connective tissue, called **ligaments**, hold the bones in place at joints to prevent dislocation. Ligaments are elastic so can stretch to loosen a joint and let you move more easily.

All movable joints have inner surfaces lined by smooth, slippery cartilage and are lubricated by **synovial fluid**, secreted by the **synovial membrane**.

How muscles produce movement

The bones of the skeleton need muscles to make them move. Muscle cells are specialists at movement because they are able to contract. Every movement you make is caused by the contraction of bundles of muscle cells. Besides the obvious movements you make to lift things or walk, the muscles in your digestive system and in your heart are important for peristalsis (see p. 45) and blood circulation (see p. 61), respectively. In fact, muscle tissue makes up about half of your body weight.

Muscles which move the skeleton are made of bundles of long slender cells called **fibre**s. Each fibre contains many fine parallel threads called **fibrils** which run lengthwise in the fibre. Two proteins – **actin** and **myosin** – make up the bulk of the fibrils and are responsible for the actual process of contraction.

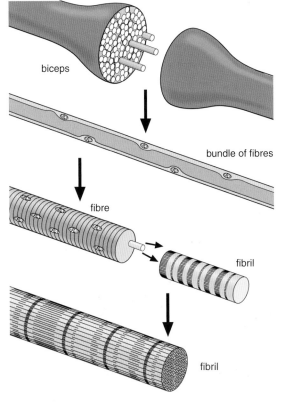

biceps

bundle of fibres

fibre

fibril

fibril

Figure 8.3 *Muscle structure*

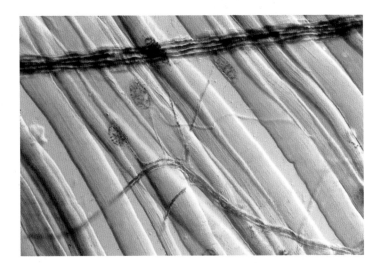

Figure 8.4 *A motor end plate, where the nerve cell endings meet the muscle*

When stimulated by a nervous impulse, each fibre contracts as tight as it can. The strength of each contraction is always the same – the strength of the movement depends on the number of muscle fibres called into action. The more fibres that contract, the greater the movement. In this way we can control both very precise movements and very forceful ones. Muscle fibres can also be stimulated by heat, chemicals, pressure and electricity.

Muscles which cause movement are made of bundles of fibres, with each fibre containing many nuclei. Most of these types of muscles are attached to bones by inelastic **tendons**. As these muscles can be controlled by conscious effort, they are called **voluntary**.

In order to cause movement, muscles must be attached to bones at two points and must contract across joints. The attachment to the stationary bone is the **point of origin**, while the attachment to the movable bone is the **point of insertion**. A simple example of this is shown in the movement of the forearm.

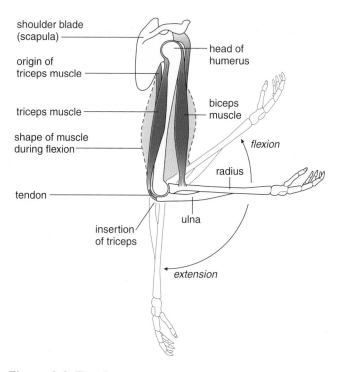

Figure 8.6 *The elbow joint – an example of a hinge joint. It shows flexion and extension, but not rotation*

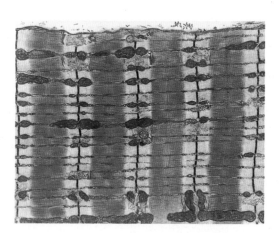

Figure 8.5 *The structure of human striated muscle*

IT Use a CD-ROM encyclopaedia or a multimedia title about the human body to see how joints and muscles work.

The diagram illustrates the antagonistic action of pairs of muscles. When the **biceps** (flexor) contracts, the **triceps** (extensor) relaxes and the forearm is raised. The opposite happens when the forearm is straightened. The same action occurs between the flexors and extensors in the leg.

Even when you are at rest, flexor and extensor muscles are slightly contracted. This is called **muscle tone** and the more you use your muscles, the larger they become and the more tone they have. Good posture is only possible if your muscle tone is good and your muscles have not become weak and flabby through under-use.

Coursework Activity

To investigate the strength of your arm

1 Place your arm on a flat surface as shown in the diagram and get someone to hold your upper arm in position X.

2 Fix a newtonmeter to a point which cannot move below the bench as shown.

3 Without moving the upper arm, pull on the newtonmeter and record the maximum force you can exert.

4 After resting the arm, repeat the procedure with the upper arm held in positions Y and Z.

Which is the best position to hold your arm when you lift things? Explain your answer.

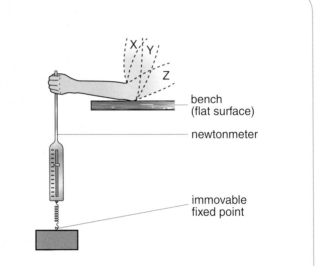

Figure 8.7 *Apparatus needed to measure the strength of your arm*

Movement without muscle TRIPLE AWARD ONLY

The simplest animals are made of single cells. They all live in water or body fluids and have no need for muscles or skeletons. Their size is limited because if they grew larger, it would be impossible for gases to diffuse in and out of their cytoplasm fast enough for energy release. They have special methods of movement. Most of them rely either on flowing along as moving blobs of jelly, for example *Amoeba*, paddling through the water with hair-like cilia (see p. 10), such as *Paramecium*, or using a longer whip-like flagellum to pull them along, for example *Euglena*.

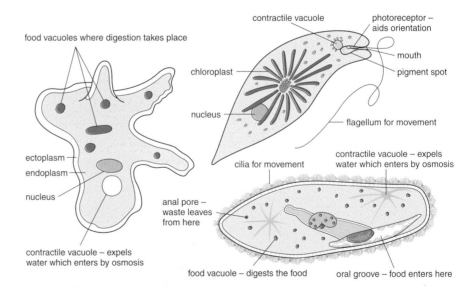

Figure 8.8 *(a) Amoeba, a simple single-celled animal. (b) Euglena, a single-celled plant with animal characteristics. (c) Paramecium*

Adaptations in vertebrates for locomotion

TRIPLE AWARD ONLY

Did you know?

A horse's hoof is equivalent in structure to the bones in your middle fingers and middle toes! Air-breathing animals with backbones all have forelimbs containing the same basic bones.

Sometimes the basic pattern has one or more bones missing, but a bone found in one forelimb can usually be identified in all air-breathing vertebrates. This suggests an evolutionary link between all animals with backbones.

Figure 8.9 shows the forelimbs of some **vertebrates** (animals with backbones). Although the limbs are specialised for flying, running or burrowing, the same bones are present, though they differ quite noticeably in shape and size.

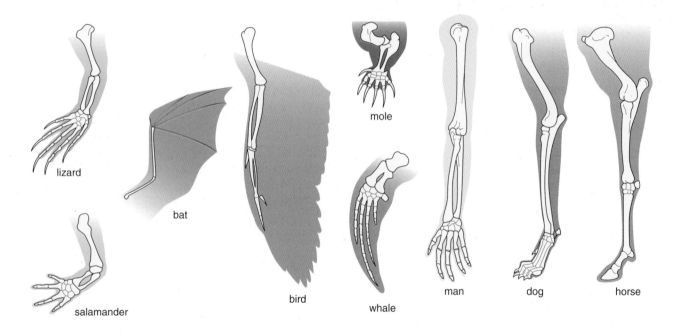

lizard

bat

salamander

mole

bird

whale

man

dog

horse

Figure 8.9 *The pentadactyl limb has been modified in all these different vertebrates*

Movement through the air

Birds are the masters of flight and, apart from bats, are the only vertebrates to flap their wings. Other 'flying' vertebrates include gliders, some fish and a few mammals. The birds are divided into two main groups – those that fly, i.e. the majority of birds, and those that are adapted to running, such as the ostrich and emu.

The main structural adaptations necessary for birds to be able to fly are given below:

- the forelimbs are modified as wings
- bones are lightweight, porous and sometimes filled with air
- the body is covered with feathers with interlocking barbs, providing lightness and a large surface area
- the skeleton has a large breast bone (**sternum**) with a keel like a yacht for the attachment of the powerful muscles which move the wings.

Figure 8.10 *A bat in flight*

Figure 8.11 *A bird in flight*

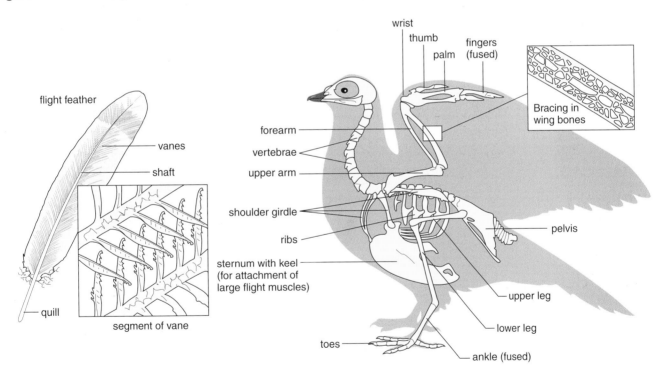

Figure 8.12 *The main features of the bird skeleton. The bones and feathers are shown in greater detail*

The movement of wings

When a bird flies, its wings move in a horizontal figure-of-eight motion. They go down and back, then up and forward. The downward stroke provides the power, while the upward stroke returns the wing for the next power stroke. Each movement uses a different set of muscles. The power stroke needs stronger muscles – these are located near the surface of the breast. The return stroke uses the weaker muscles underneath the power stroke muscles. You may have noticed these muscle layers on the breast of a chicken – they separate easily.

Movement through water

Fish are, by definition, cold-blooded vertebrates with paired fins, gills and biting jaws. They are ideally adapted for movement through water and have the following features to help them swim in practically every type of aquatic (water) environment.

- They can adjust their depths in the water using **swim bladders** which are thin-walled sacs lying in the upper part of the body between the gut and the backbone. The sacs can be inflated or deflated like ballast tanks in a submarine, but in fish, the gases are passed in and out of the sac from the blood system. The gas is a mixture of nitrogen, oxygen and carbon dioxide and enables the fish to remain at any depth without much effort. By adjusting the amount of gas in the swim bladder, the fish can move to different levels in the water. Sharks and their relatives have no swim bladders. These must keep swimming to be able to stay at a particular depth.
- They have a zig-zag arrangement of muscles, producing wave-like side-to-side swimming movements. These muscle blocks are obvious in slices of larger fish, like salmon and cod, as the flakes of flesh. They run along each side of the backbone from head to tail. It is the muscular tail that propels the fish through the water. The muscle action is co-ordinated so that when one block is contracting, the opposite block is relaxing.

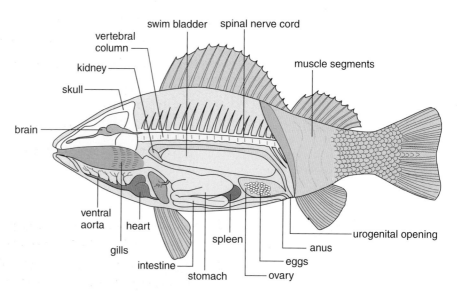

Figure 8.13 *The main features of a fish skeleton*

- They have pairs of **fins** which stabilise the fish or act like brakes. The **pectoral fins** are nearest the head and the **pelvic fins** are nearest the tail. These fins reduce pitching and allow upward and downward movement. The pelvic fins are also used when the fish moves backward. The **tail fin** is in two parts – upper and lower. It is the tail fin and the attached muscles that pushes the fish forward. The **dorsal fin** has a corresponding **anal** or **ventral fin**. These fins reduce yawing and rolling, and prevent the fish from falling over from side to side.

Summary

1 Unlike simple animals, humans have bony skeletons.

2 Our skeletons have several functions including support, movement, protection, blood cell production and mineral storage.

3 Muscles produce movement of the skeleton through attachment to bones and by acting across joints.

4 Single-celled animals do not use muscles for movement and may use cilia or whip-like flagella.

5 All air-breathing animals with backbones have limbs which are based on the same design but are adapted for movement in various environmental conditions.

6 Fish have a body plan which enables them to move in water by using the powerful tail muscles. They usually use their fins as stabilisers.

Homework Questions

1 What are the functions of the bones? Give an example of a bone serving each purpose.

2 Describe the tissues found in a joint and state their functions.

3 Describe the types of joints found in humans.

4 Explain antagonistic muscle action.

5 Describe how movement in single-celled animals differs from that seen in animals with backbones.

6 What is the function of the swim bladder found in fish?

7 Describe the features of birds that are adaptations for flight.

In-Depth Questions

1 Explain the importance of a highly-developed nervous system in an organism with an internal skeleton.

2 Suggest why the ankle bones of birds are fused together and why a common sports injury in humans is a sprained or dislocated ankle.

12 The diagram shows the mean daily input and output of water for an adult.

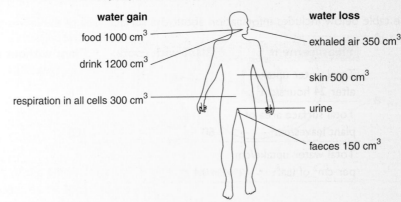

water gain
food 1000 cm³
drink 1200 cm³
respiration in all cells 300 cm³

water loss
exhaled air 350 cm³
skin 500 cm³
urine
faeces 150 cm³

(a) Respiration is a source of water. Complete the equation for respiration.

$$\text{sugar} + \quad ? \quad \rightarrow \text{water} + \quad ? \quad + \text{energy}$$

(2 marks)

(b) The kidneys keep the water content of the body constant by controlling the volume of water passed out in the urine.

 (i) Use the data from the diagram to calculate the mean daily output of water in urine. Show your working. *(2 marks)*

 (ii) Describe how the amount of water in the body is controlled by the kidneys. *(3 marks)*

(c) Sometimes kidneys fail. Two ways of treating kidney failure are the use of a dialysis machine and kidney transplants. Describe what happens to the composition of a patient's blood as it passes through a dialysis machine. *(3 marks)*

(d) In the treatment of kidney failure:

 (i) give two possible advantages of using a kidney transplant rather than a dialysis machine;

 (ii) give two possible disadvantages of using a kidney transplant rather than a dialysis machine. *(4 marks)*

AQA

13 The graphs below show the blood glucose levels of two people, A and B, after both ate 70 g of glucose and then rested. Person A was healthy, but person B suffered from a medical condition related to the control of blood glucose level.

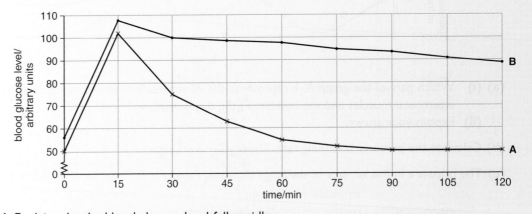

(a) Explain why the blood glucose level fell rapidly. *(3 marks)*

(b) Suggest why the blood glucose level of B fell only slowly. *(2 marks)*

(c) Control of blood glucose level is achieved by means of a negative feedback mechanism. Explain the meaning of the term negative feedback. *(2 marks)*

EDEXCEL

Summary

1 Unlike simple animals, humans have bony skeletons.

2 Our skeletons have several functions including support, movement, protection, blood cell production and mineral storage.

3 Muscles produce movement of the skeleton through attachment to bones and by acting across joints.

4 Single-celled animals do not use muscles for movement and may use cilia or whip-like flagella.

5 All air-breathing animals with backbones have limbs which are based on the same design but are adapted for movement in various environmental conditions.

6 Fish have a body plan which enables them to move in water by using the powerful tail muscles. They usually use their fins as stabilisers.

Homework Questions

1 What are the functions of the bones? Give an example of a bone serving each purpose.

2 Describe the tissues found in a joint and state their functions.

3 Describe the types of joints found in humans.

4 Explain antagonistic muscle action.

5 Describe how movement in single-celled animals differs from that seen in animals with backbones.

6 What is the function of the swim bladder found in fish?

7 Describe the features of birds that are adaptations for flight.

In-Depth Questions

1 Explain the importance of a highly-developed nervous system in an organism with an internal skeleton.

2 Suggest why the ankle bones of birds are fused together and why a common sports injury in humans is a sprained or dislocated ankle.

Theme 1 Exam questions

1 **(a)** The diagram shows part of a leaf.
Name cells A, B and C.

(3 marks)

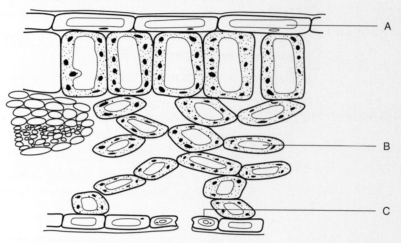

A

B

C

(b) The graph shows the amount of carbohydrate stored in the leaves and new potatoes of potato plants between June and September.

new potatoes

leaves

time/months

amount of carbohydrate/
arbitrary units

June   July   August   September

(i) Explain the differences in the carbohydrate levels of the leaves and new potatoes in June and September.

(4 marks)

(ii) In what form is carbohydrate stored in potato plants? *(1 mark)*

(iii) Give two uses, other than storage, for the carbohydrate made by photosynthesis. *(2 marks)*

(iv) Which tissue transports carbohydrate? *(1 mark)*

(c) The table shows the results of an experiment to measure the rate of photosynthesis under different conditions.

Carbon dioxide concentration in air %	Rate of photosynthesis/arbitrary units	
	Low light intensity	**High light intensity**
0.00	0	0
0.05	30	30
0.10	40	60
0.15	40	84
0.20	40	90
0.25	40	90

(i) Plot these results as two lines using the same axes.

(4 marks)

(ii) At what carbon dioxide concentration does light limit photosynthesis at low light intensity and high light intensity?

(2 marks)

(iii) Name one other factor which limits photosynthesis.

(1 mark)

(NICCEA)

2 Students investigated the rate at which a pond plant produced oxygen at different temperatures. They used the apparatus shown below.

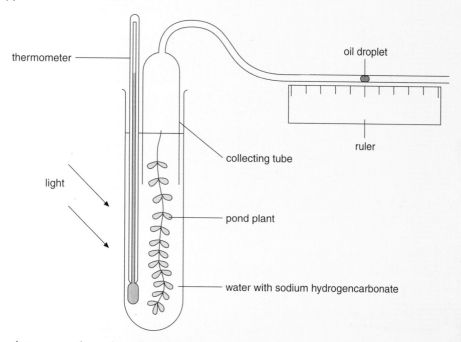

The oil droplet moves along the tube as the plant produces oxygen. The students measured the distance moved by the oil droplet in one hour. The experiment was repeated at six different temperatures. The results are shown in the table below.

Temperature/°C	Distance moved by oil droplet in one hour/cm
15	0.4
25	2.7
35	3.2
45	1.6
55	0.2
65	0.1

(a) Plot a graph of distance moved by oil droplet in one hour (cm) against temperature (°C)

(2 marks)

(b) The students said that the pond plant photosynthesised fastest at 35°C. Why could this conclusion be wrong?

(1 mark)

(c) Sodium hydrogencarbonate was added to the water to keep the amount of carbon dioxide constant. Explain why this was necessary.

(2 marks)

EDEXCEL

3 The diagram below shows an investigation into the action of a carbohydrase called amylase. The apparatus was left for 20 minutes.

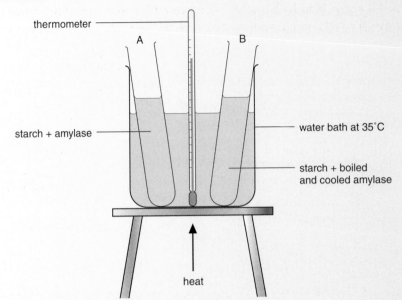

Iodine changes from yellow-brown to black if starch is present. When boiled with a reducing sugar, Benedict's solution changes from clear blue to brick red.

(a) After 20 minutes, what colour would you expect to see if the contents of tube A were added to
   (i) iodine? *(1 mark)*
   (ii) Benedict's reagent and boiled? *(1 mark)*

(b) What colour would you expect to see if the contents of tube B were added to
   (i) iodine? *(1 mark)*
   (ii) Benedict's reagent and boiled? *(1 mark)*

(c) What does this investigation tell you about the effect of temperature on enzyme action? *(1 mark)*

(d) Give a definition of an enzyme. *(2 marks)*

(e) What is meant by the optimum pH or temperature at which an enzyme works? *(1 mark)*
                   WJEC

4 The diagram shows five test tubes A–E and their contents. The contents of each test tube had a pH of 7. The test tubes were kept in water baths for half an hour at the temperatures indicated.

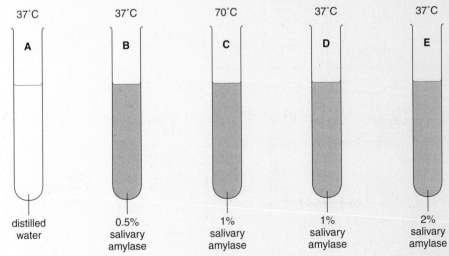

A pupil took a petri dish containing starch-agar (a set jelly in which starch has been dissolved). She cut five small holes in the jelly. She filled each hole with 1 cm³ of the fluid from a different test tube. She put distilled water in hole 1. The other holes were filled with one of the other solutions B, C, D, E. After one hour she flooded the dish with dilute iodine solution. The results are shown below:

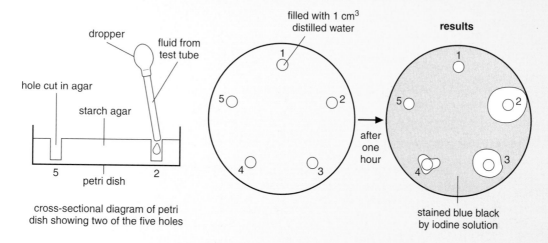

cross-sectional diagram of petri dish showing two of the five holes

stained blue black by iodine solution

Use the information shown in the diagrams to answer the following questions.

(a) Which hole (2, 3, 4 or 5) contained 1% salivary amylase solution which had been kept at 70°C? Explain your answer.

(4 marks)

(b) Explain the difference in the results obtained for holes 2 and 3.

(4 marks)

(c) Describe how you would test for the presence of reducing sugars in hole number 2.

(3 marks)

(d) Describe how you would adapt this experiment to investigate the pH at which salivary amylase works best. You may use diagrams if you wish.

(6 marks)

OCR

5 The diagrams A, B and C below show apparatus that is used to measure the rate of three important processes in biology. One is used for photosynthesis, another for respiration and a third for transpiration.

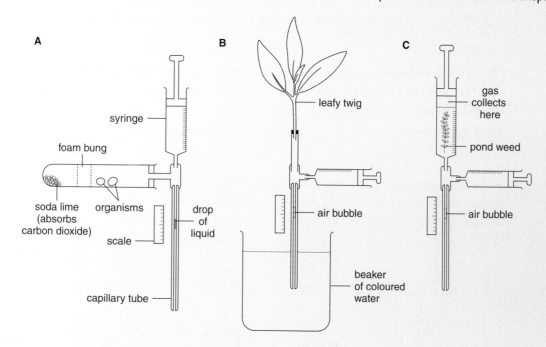

(a) Use letters from each of the diagrams of apparatus shown and match them with the correct process. Then write the gas produced by each process.

(5 marks)

Process	Apparatus letter	Gas produced by process
Photosynthesis		
Respiration		
Transpiration		

(b) Suggest one way in which transpiration is a disadvantage to plants.

(1 mark)

EDEXCEL

6 (a) What is the function of an artery?

(1 mark)

(b) The diagram below shows samples of artery taken from the hearts of two men. The samples were taken from the same area of each heart as indicated by the circle on the diagram.

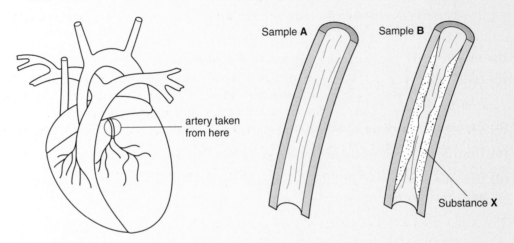

- Sample A is from the heart of a young man who was killed in a road accident.
- Sample B is from a 54-year-old man who died suddenly from a heart attack.

(i) Name the artery from which the sample was taken *(1 mark)*
(ii) Name substance X which is lining sample B. *(1 mark)*

(c) (i) A few weeks before his heart attack, the 54-year-old man's blood pressure was higher than normal. Explain the likely reason for this. *(2 mark)*
(ii) Explain how substance X probably helped to cause the heart attack. *(2 marks)*

(d) Suggest two ways in which a young man could help prevent X forming in his artery. *(2 marks)*

EDEXCEL

7 A person's heart rate was measured before, during and after an exercise. The person then trained for several weeks to improve fitness. After this training, the heart rate was again measured before, during and after an identical exercise. The results of this investigation are shown on the graph opposite.

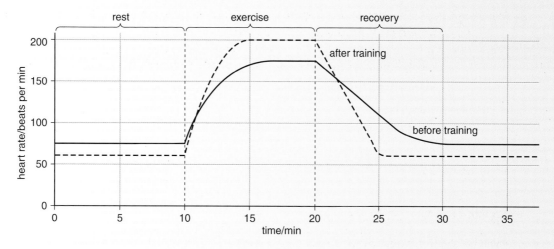

Use the information from the graph and your knowledge to answer the following questions.

(a) Describe and explain the effect that training had on the person's heart rate before, during and after the exercise.

(4 marks)

(b) After the period of training, the person's heart stroke volume increased to 100 cm³ per beat.
  (i) After the period of training, the heart rate at rest was 60 beats per minute. What volume of blood left the heart in one minute during this period? Show your working. *(2 marks)*
  (ii) Which chambers of the heart are responsible for producing the heart stroke volume? *(1 mark)*
  (iii) How is the blood forced out of these chambers? *(1 mark)*

(c) Give two advantages of regular exercise, other than improvements to the heart. *(2 marks)*

EDEXCEL

8 The drawings show the underside of two leaves, A and B.

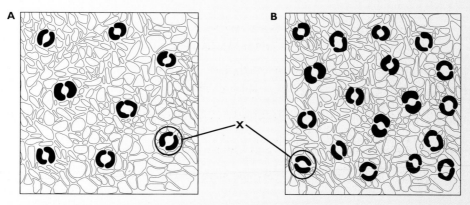

(a) Name structures X. *(1 mark)*

Water can be lost from a leaf by diffusing through these structures.

(b) (i) Name this process. *(1 mark)*
  (ii) Suggest one advantage to the plant of this process. *(1 mark)*

(c) (i) Count the structures X in each of the leaves and record the numbers in a table. *(2 marks)*
  (ii) Suggest which leaf is better adapted to living in dry conditions. Explain your answer.

(2 marks)

NICCEA

9 The diagram below shows a cross section of an artery, a vein and a capillary.

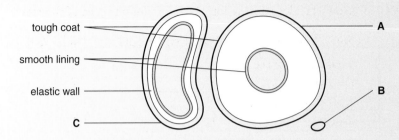

tough coat

smooth lining

elastic wall

A

B

C

(a) (i) Which of the blood vessels A, B or C is an artery?   (1 mark)
   (ii) Give one reason for your answer.   (1 mark)

(b) (i) In which of the blood vessels A, B or C does blood flow with a pulse?   (1 mark)
   (ii) Explain the cause of this pulse.   (1 mark)
   (iii) Describe how you would measure your pulse rate.   (3 marks)

EDEXCEL

10 An experiment was carried out to compare the uptake of water in plants with and without roots. The experiment was set up as shown in the diagram below. The volume of water in the measuring cylinders was recorded at the start of the experiment and again after 24 hours.

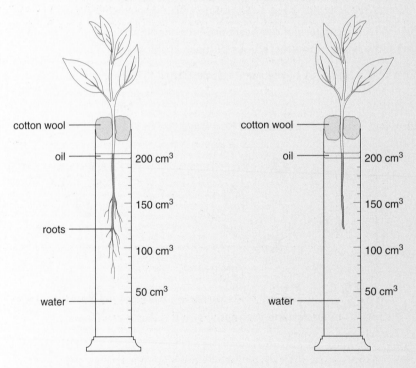

cotton wool

oil

200 cm³

150 cm³

roots

100 cm³

50 cm³

water

cotton wool

oil

200 cm³

150 cm³

100 cm³

50 cm³

water

The results of the experiment are shown below.

| Time/hours | Volume of water/cm³ | |
	Plants with roots	**Plants without roots**
0 (start)	200	200
24	194	194

(a) In what way are the results different from what you might expect? *(1 mark)*

(b) The table below includes information about the surface area of the leaves of each plant.

Measurement	Plant with roots	Plant without roots
Total water uptake after 24 hours/cm³		6
Total surface area of plant leaves/cm²	60	100
Total water uptake/cm³ per cm² of leaf	0.1	

   (i) Use the results of the experiment to fill in the empty boxes in the table. *(2 marks)*
   (ii) Does the information in this table support the idea that roots help plants to take up water? Give a reason for your answer. *(1 mark)*

(c) Suggest why oil was used in this experiment. *(1 mark)*

(d) Describe three ways in which you could make sure that this was a fair and reliable experiment. *(3 marks)*

EDEXCEL

11 The graphs below show the changing lung volume and the changing air pressure in a lung during a single inspiration and a single expiration when a person was breathing normally (at rest).

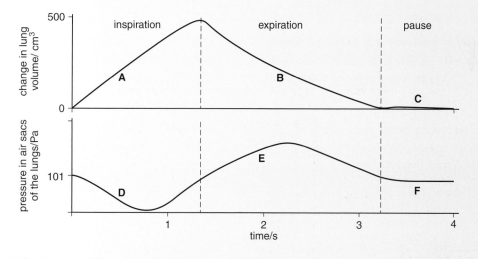

(a) (i) Which part of the graph A–F represents the direct result of the contraction of the external intercostal muscles and the muscles of the diaphragm? *(1 mark)*
   (ii) Explain your answer. *(3 marks)*

(b) Calculate the person's breathing rate. Show your working. *(1 mark)*

(c) The pressure in the air sacs of the lungs increases rapidly at E. Describe how this is brought about. *(3 marks)*

OCR

12 The diagram shows the mean daily input and output of water for an adult.

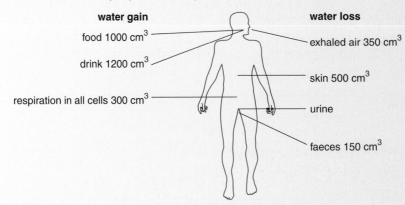

water gain
food 1000 cm³
drink 1200 cm³
respiration in all cells 300 cm³

water loss
exhaled air 350 cm³
skin 500 cm³
urine
faeces 150 cm³

(a) Respiration is a source of water. Complete the equation for respiration.

sugar + ? → water + ? + energy   *(2 marks)*

(b) The kidneys keep the water content of the body constant by controlling the volume of water passed out in the urine.

  (i) Use the data from the diagram to calculate the mean daily output of water in urine. Show your working.   *(2 marks)*

  (ii) Describe how the amount of water in the body is controlled by the kidneys.   *(3 marks)*

(c) Sometimes kidneys fail. Two ways of treating kidney failure are the use of a dialysis machine and kidney transplants. Describe what happens to the composition of a patient's blood as it passes through a dialysis machine.   *(3 marks)*

(d) In the treatment of kidney failure:

  (i) give two possible advantages of using a kidney transplant rather than a dialysis machine;

  (ii) give two possible disadvantages of using a kidney transplant rather than a dialysis machine. *(4 marks)*

AQA

13 The graphs below show the blood glucose levels of two people, A and B, after both ate 70 g of glucose and then rested. Person A was healthy, but person B suffered from a medical condition related to the control of blood glucose level.

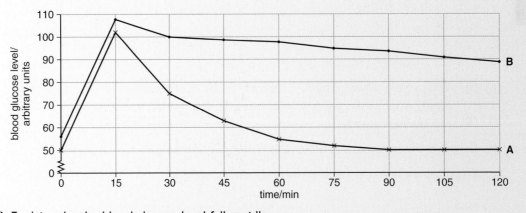

(a) Explain why the blood glucose level fell rapidly.   *(3 marks)*

(b) Suggest why the blood glucose level of B fell only slowly.   *(2 marks)*

(c) Control of blood glucose level is achieved by means of a negative feedback mechanism. Explain the meaning of the term negative feedback.   *(2 marks)*

EDEXCEL

14 Diagram A shows an investigation to show the effect of light on the growth of oat shoots (coleoptiles). B shows the results one day later. Shoot 2 had the tip cut off; the tip of shoot 3 was covered with a cap of aluminium foil.

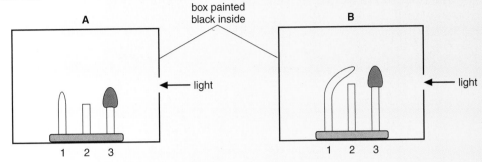

(a) Name the type of response shown in B. *(1 mark)*

(b) (i) Which part of the oat shoot is sensitive to light? *(1 mark)*

(ii) Give two reasons for your answer. *(2 marks)*

(c) (i) What substance is responsible for the changes shown in B? *(1 mark)*

(ii) Describe the effect of this substance on the shoots. *(1 mark)*

(iii) What is the effect of light on this substance? *(1 mark)*

(d) State the purpose of the treatments given to shoots 2 and 3. *(1 mark)*

WJEC

15 (a) Drawing A shows Rhian's eye before she went into a dimly lit room.

drawing A

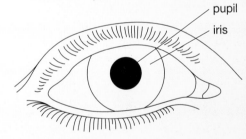

(i) Complete drawing B to show what Rhian's eye was like after 30 minutes in the dimly lit room. *(1 mark)*

drawing B

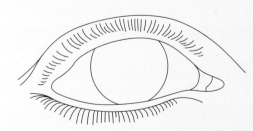

(ii) What type of action is responsible for the change? *(1 mark)*

(iii) In this action, name the following: *(4 marks)*
I the stimulus, II the receptor, III the co-ordinator, IV the effector

(iv) Which of the terms I to IV above is part of the central nervous system? *(1 mark)*

(b) In an investigation, Rhian's reaction time for blinking was measured when a light was flashed rapidly every second for 15 seconds.

The results were plotted on the graph.

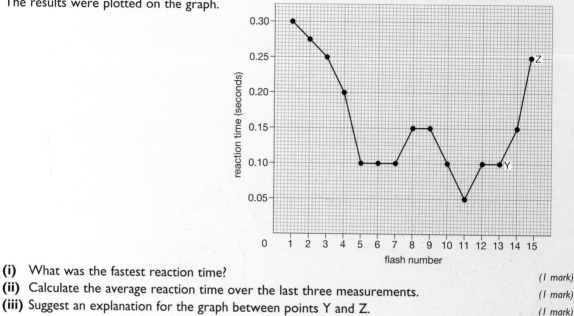

(i) What was the fastest reaction time? *(1 mark)*

(ii) Calculate the average reaction time over the last three measurements. *(1 mark)*

(iii) Suggest an explanation for the graph between points Y and Z. *(1 mark)*

WJEC

16 The graph shows the levels of the hormones oestrogen and progesterone in a woman's blood during a month when she becomes pregnant.

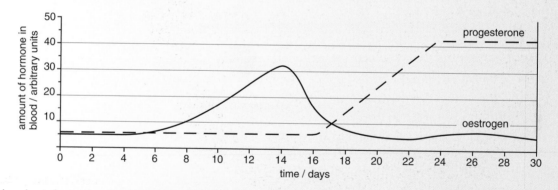

Use the information in the graph and your own knowledge to answer the questions below.

(a) When are the levels of oestrogen and progesterone equal? *(1 mark)*

(b) Which process occurred between day 0 and day 5? *(1 mark)*

(c) Give one function of each of these hormones
(i) oestrogen, **(ii)** progesterone. *(2 marks)*

(d) What evidence from the graph shows that an ovum was fertilised? *(1 mark)*

(e) What would be the probable level of progesterone between day 16 and day 30 if she had *not* become pregnant.

(2 marks)

(f) How does the lining of the uterus help in the development of a fertilised ovum? *(4 marks)*

EDEXCEL

The continuity of life

(2)

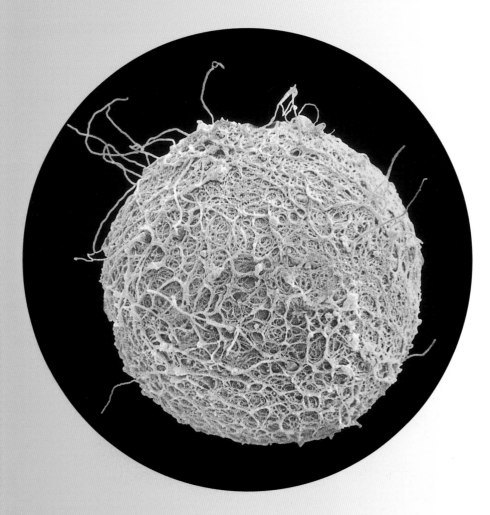

Sperm fertilising a human egg. Once fertilised, the egg begins its process of growth into a human embryo.

Chromosomes and Cell Division

By the end of this chapter you should be able to understand:

- the relationship between genes, chromosomes and the nucleus;

- the major stages in cell division and their significance;

- the role of DNA and RNA in protein synthesis;

- how Mendel's theories apply to the behaviour of chromosomes and genes;

- sex determination.

Sites of genetic material

In any study of biology we recognise variation and can explain it. However, we must consider its basic cause in more detail. It would be ideal if we could look down a microscope and see the cause of variation revealed. Alas this is not possible. Variations are handed down from one generation to the next through genetic material. Those cells which form a link between generations, the gametes, must contain genetic material and are therefore the best starting point for our study.

Figure 9.1 shows a male gamete, a sperm. In common with other cells, it has a nucleus and a cell membrane. Unlike the female gamete, the egg (Figure 9.2), it has very little cytoplasm. Male gametes contain all of the genetic material in the nucleus, which is in the so-called 'head' of the sperm. Sperms are motile (i.e. they can move) as they have a 'tail'. When fertilisation takes place, the nucleus enters the female gamete and fuses with the female nucleus (see Figure 9.3).

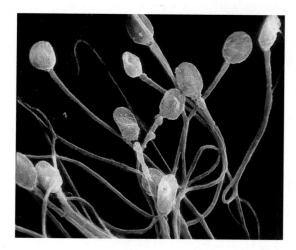

Figure 9.1 *Human sperm*

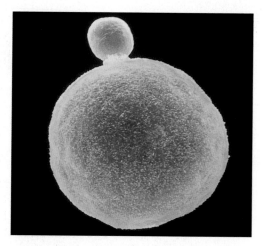

Figure 9.2 *A human egg at the end of its first meiotic division, just prior to ovulation*

The nucleus holds all the secrets of genetics. It contains all of the chemicals which are used to transfer genetic information from one individual to its offspring.

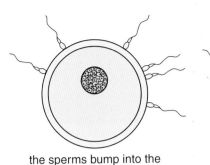

the sperms bump into the jelly coat around the egg

one of them penetrates the jelly

its head passes into the egg and the nuclei combine

Figure 9.3 *Fertilisation*

A closer look at the nucleus

Coursework Activity

To investigate the genetic material in a root tip

The best material to use is the growing region of a root tip of garlic. This plant is available throughout the year and is easy to grow. Simply place the garlic bulb on the top of a test tube containing water. In a few days, roots will appear.

You will be given root tips which have been stained with Feulgen's stain. This stain reacts with chemicals in the nucleus to produce a pink colour.

1 Carefully cut 2 mm off the end of the root tip using a sharp scalpel.

2 Place the tip on a microscope slide in a drop of 10% acetic acid. Use two mounted needles to pull the root tip apart. Try to break the tissue into very small parts.

3 Place a cover slip on the material. There should be just enough acetic acid to fill out the cover slip.

4 With the slide resting on some filter paper, put a few more layers of filter paper on top of it. Press your thumb straight down on the region of the cover slip, avoiding any sideways pressure. This should flatten the cells and separate the genetical material, the **chromosomes**.

(a)   (b)   (c)

(d)   (e)

Figure 9.4 *Cells from a bluebell displaying the various stages of mitosis – (a) interphase, (b) prophase, (c) metaphase, (d) anaphase, (e) telophase*

5 After about 5 seconds, peel off the filter paper. The acetic acid should fill the space under the cover slip.

6 Examine the slide under the microscope. Use the high power objective after focusing first under low power. Draw the cells.

You should be able to make out the chromosomes. Chromosomes contain **genes** – the carriers of genetic information.

7 Try to find the earliest stage at which the chromosomes are visible as double structures.

8 Look at several cells and compare them to the series of photographs (Figure 9.4).

As a result of your observations you should be aware of the following:

● the nucleus is the most likely site of the genetic material
● the nucleus can contain chromosomes
● chromosomes are only visible in cells which are actively dividing.

Cell division

The cell division seen in the above example is called **mitosis**. Apart from gamete formation, which is the exception to the rule, most cell divisions include mitotic division of chromosomes.

Figure 9.5 shows cells from a root tip. Different cells at different stages of mitosis can clearly be seen.

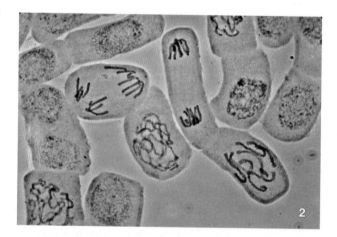

Figure 9.5 *Cells from a root tip at different stages of mitosis*

Cells alive – mitosis
http://www.cellsalive.com

The nucleus divides in four main stages:

● Prior to mitosis, each chromosome makes a copy of itself.
● At the start of mitosis, the original and the copy separate and migrate to opposite poles along a spindle.
● Two daughter nuclei are formed by this process.
● Division of the cytoplasm and the formation of a new cell wall then occurs.

Mitosis enables each new cell (the daughter cell) to have an identical set of chromosomes to the original cell. It is the means by which all the cells of an organism are derived from a zygote. It is also the way in which organisms reproduce asexually. As a result, all offspring produced asexually have the same genetic information as their parent.

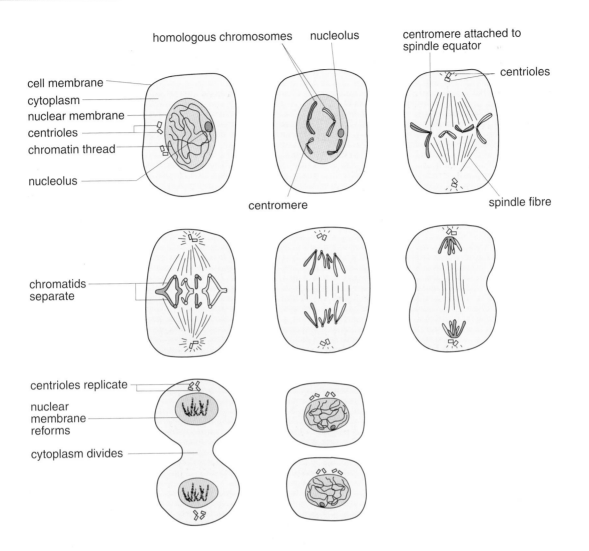

cell membrane
cytoplasm
nuclear membrane
centrioles
chromatin thread
nucleolus

homologous chromosomes
nucleolus

centromere attached to
spindle equator
centrioles

centromere

spindle fibre

chromatids
separate

centrioles replicate
nuclear
membrane
reforms
cytoplasm divides

Figure 9.6 *Mitosis*

Sexually produced offspring arise from the fusion of male and female cells. The production of these cells takes place by a special form of cell division called **meiosis**.

Sex cells and fertilisation

The largest known cells are eggs (see Figure 9.2). They contain little but cytoplasm – their bulk is mostly water and stored food. The important part of the egg is the nucleus. Sperm cells are hundreds or even thousands of times smaller than eggs – they are little more than a nucleus attached to a vigorous 'tail'. When a sperm finds its 'goal', its nucleus joins with that of the egg to form the nucleus of a new and separate cell.

The nuclei of both kinds of sex cells generally have fewer chromosomes than other cells in the body of the same organism. The reason for this becomes clear when we see what would happen if they did not. Cells in the human body have 46 chromosomes. If each matured sex cell, or gamete, also had 46, then a baby would have 92, and its children would have 184. Human cells normally contain 23 pairs of chromosomes, with one set coming from the mother's egg and the other set coming from the father's sperm. Mitosis ensures that each new cell gets a full set of chromosome pairs.

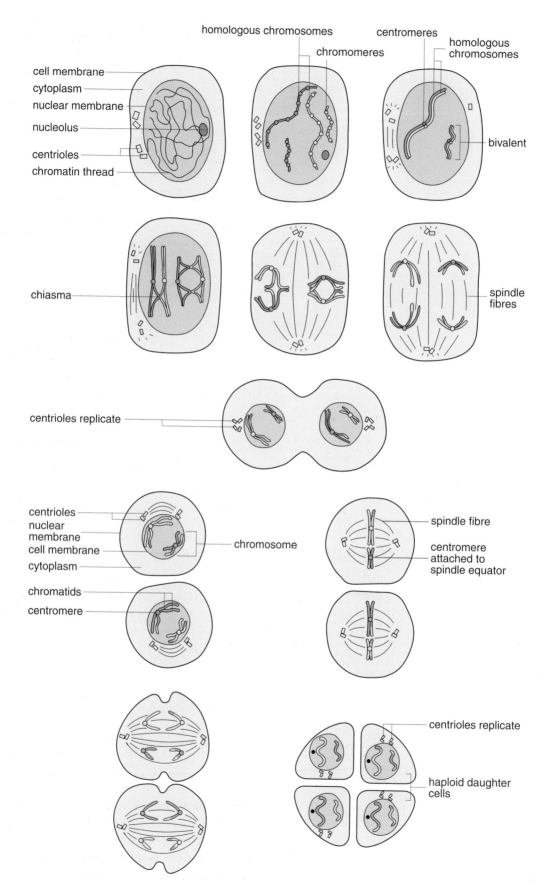

Figure 9.7 *Meiosis*

Microscopic studies of developing human sperms and eggs show that they have only 23 chromosomes, one from each pair. How does an organism produce cells with half the number of chromosome pairs? Of all the countless millions of cells in our body, only egg- and sperm-producing cells divide in such a way that the chromosome pairs are split. Logically enough, the process is called reduction-division or meiosis. To see how it works we can follow **meiosis** as it occurs in an animal that has only two pairs of chromosomes.

The first step in meiosis is similar in some ways to mitosis. Each chromosome pairs off with its opposite number across the middle of the nucleus, and each chromosome duplicates itself. There is a double chromosome for each original, the halves of which are **chromatids**. Now, just as in mitosis, the nuclear membrane disappears, but unlike mitosis, each double member of a pair goes to the new cells. At this point we have two cells, each containing two double chromosomes – one from each original pair.

A brief resting period follows, before a new wave of nuclear events begins, during which the double chromosomes break apart and each chromatid becomes a separate chromosome. The cells then divide again, so we now have four cells, each with two chromosomes, one of each pair of chromosomes in the original. The process of meiosis is illustrated diagrammatically in Figure 9.7. Both sperm and egg cells undergo meiosis. When the sperm unites with the egg, each provides half the chromosomes for the new individual.

A cell with the full set of chromosomes is called **diploid**.

A cell with half the normal number of chromosomes is called **haploid**.

As a result of the random separation of chromosomes in meiosis, each fertilised egg cell contains a different set of chromosomes and can be considered to be unique. This is the main advantage of sexual reproduction, each new life is just a little different from either of its parents. This variation among offspring means that sexually-reproducing organisms are better able to adapt to changing conditions in the environment.

Once the egg has been fertilised, all further cell divisions produce cells with the full number of chromosomes. Eventually the new organism will reach maturity, and its time will come to reproduce. Its reproductive organs will then produce sperms or eggs and the cycle of life will have come full circle.

Coursework activity

To make a model showing a stage of meiosis

You will need:

- four pipe-cleaners of one colour and four pipe-cleaners of a different colour to represent chromosomes
- two dustbin liner wire ties
- some self-adhesive tape and four small self-adhesive labels
- a piece of plain A4 paper.

1 Draw a horizontal line through the middle of the A4 paper. This represents the equator of the spindle (see Figure 9.6). Mark with a cross, 6 cm above the line, the position of a pole of the spindle. Do the same below the line to show the opposite pole.

2 Use the pipe-cleaners to make a model which shows the structure of a pair of chromosomes as they would appear on the equator of the spindle. Use a pipe-cleaner of one colour to show the chromosome from the mother and a pipe-cleaner of the other colour to show the chromosome from

the father. Use the dustbin liner ties to represent the points of contact between the chromosomes.

3 Assume that the chromosome carries the gene A and your model represents a heterozygote for this gene. Add the appropriate labels to your model to show the position of the gene. (Use the adhesive labels for this.)

4 Use adhesive tape to attach your model to the piece of paper to show the correct positions.

5 Indicate, by drawing arrows on the paper, the direction of movement of the chromosomes at the next stage of meiosis.

Chromosomes and genes and DNA

An organism's characteristics are passed down from generation to generation by genes. But what are genes, where can they be found and what do they actually do?

Life is a series of chemical reactions. It is not surprising, therefore, that quite early in the history of genetics, scientists understood that genes must be chemicals. Since proteins are the most essential chemicals found in living cells, the early geneticists guessed that genes probably existed as protein contained within the chromosomes in the nuclei of cells.

By 1950, it became clear that it was not the protein in chromosomes that passed on the code of life from generation to generation, it was another component of cells – **nucleic acids**. These are some of the largest and by far the most fascinating of all life's molecules. Two forms are known: **deoxyribonucleic acid (DNA)** which is found in all chromosomes, and **ribonucleic acid (RNA)** which is found in the cytoplasm and nuclei of cells.

A Dynamic Duo

In 1953, two scientists made one of the most famous discoveries of all time. The British researcher, Francis Harry Compton Crick, collaborated with the young American, James Dewey Watson, in a partnership which proved to be perhaps the most rewarding example of Anglo-American co-operation in the history of science. Watson is quoted as saying, 'He taught me physics, I taught him biology. It worked out rather well'.

Crick had spent the years during the Second World War designing mines for the Royal Navy and had then changed the direction of his interest to become fascinated by molecular biology. In America, he used techniques to find the structure of large protein molecules, but then moved to Cambridge where he met Watson who had a research fellowship in biology. A brilliant, unpredictable young man, Watson studied at a college in America at the age of 15. This dynamic duo of physicist and biologist set about building models of DNA until they made one which fitted with all the known facts about DNA. They carefully constructed exact scale models with precise lengths and angles to match the lengths and angles of the chemical bonds in the molecule.

Amazingly, the whole model of DNA was worked out within six weeks. It is said that during the work, Watson continued his habits of having a leisurely cafe breakfast each morning and a game of tennis each afternoon.

The term, *double helix*, is used to describe the shape of DNA (see Figure 9.9). The work was published in 1953 in one of the most famous research papers ever to have appeared in the scientific journal *Nature*. There was immediate worldwide appreciation of the sheer elegance and simplicity of Crick and Watson's work. Each shared the Nobel Prize for medicine and physiology, which they received in 1962. Crick built a symbolic copper helix outside his house in the centre of Cambridge. Legend has it that he stated, 'People keep asking me when I'm going to gild it'.

DNA is made up two chains of nucleotides twisted around each other like a rope ladder. This is what Watson and Crick called the **double helix**. Each nucleotide is made up of three components: a sugar group, a phosphate group and a **base**. The bases act as rungs of a ladder, joining the two chains together. Figure 9.8 shows a model of a strand of DNA.

Figure 9.8 *James Watson and Francis Crick who discovered the structure of DNA in 1953*

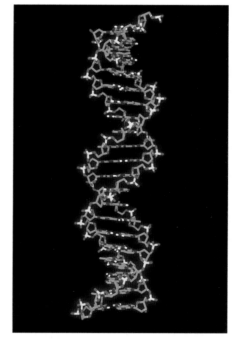

Figure 9.9 *The structure of DNA*

Watson and Crick discovered that the rungs of the ladder are made of four different types of bases: **guanine**, **cytosine**, **thymine** and **adenine**. The bases fit together as shown in Figure 9.10. Guanine only pairs with cytosine, and thymine only pairs with adenine. The differences between one DNA molecule and another – or one gene and another – depend on the pattern of these base pairs. This is how genes produce certain effects in organisms. For example, the order of base pairs which produces blue eyes is different from the order of base pairs which produces brown eyes.

There is an almost unlimited number of possible arrangements of base pairs if you consider that a strand of DNA can be over 10 000 base units long. There is, therefore, an almost unlimited number of possible genes in plants and animals. The DNA contains the genetic code which tells an organism how to develop.

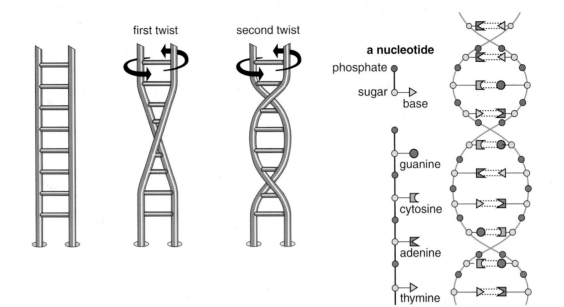

Figure 9.10 *The structure of DNA*

www

School Science – The human genome
http://www.schoolscience.co.uk

Genetic Science Learning Center
**http://gslc.genetics.utah.edu/
basic/index.html**

How do genes work?

How do genes control the development of an organism? How can such microscopic particles have such a staggering effect on life?

Genes consist of DNA. DNA expresses a code that determines which chemical reactions take place in a cell and at what speed. It does this by determining which proteins are made, or synthesised, in the cell. The growth and development of a cell is determined by the type and speed of the chemical reactions taking place within it. Hence, by controlling protein synthesis, DNA controls the life of the cell, and hence the development of the organism.

How does DNA control protein synthesis?

Proteins are made of building blocks called amino acids (see p. 39). The amino acids are linked together in chains. The different ways in which amino acids are linked together determines the type of protein synthesised. DNA is able to regulate how the amino acids are arranged – the types and arrangement of the bases in the DNA molecule act as a code that determines which amino acids are linked together. Thus, by determining the form and arrangement of these basic building blocks, DNA controls protein synthesis. The following is a very simplified account of how DNA is used for making proteins:

1 The long molecule of DNA (remember it is like a twisted ladder) unwinds and splits along its length as the bonds between the bases break.

2 One half of the molecule now acts as a pattern for the formation of a messenger molecule. This molecule consists of a particular type of RNA, known as **messenger RNA** or **mRNA**, which is made by new bases found as a mixture in the nucleus. These strings of mRNA line up opposite their partners on the original half of the DNA. In this way, they form a single strand. The result is that the code originally present in the DNA is now also found on the messenger molecule (see Figure 9.11).

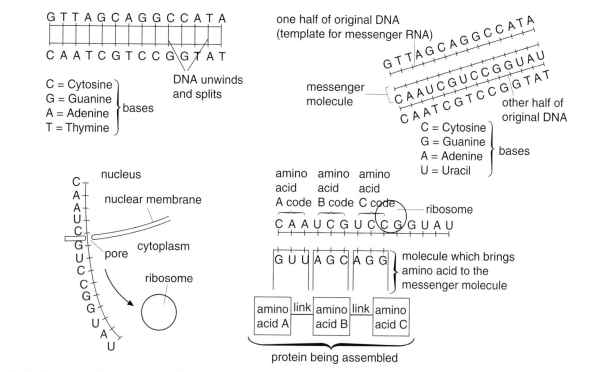

Figure 9.11 *Protein synthesis*

3 As shown in Figure 9.11, the messenger molecule, mRNA, then passes through the nuclear membrane to structures in the cytoplasm of the cell called **ribosomes**.

4 The code on the messenger molecule then determines which amino acids from the cytoplasm of the cell become linked together, thereby determining the type of protein synthesised. The amino acids are brought to the template mRNA strand by a second type of RNA molecule known as **transfer RNA** or **tRNA**. The ribosomes then 'read' the code of bases on the mRNA and a protein is assembled from the amino acid residues.

The discovery that DNA carries the code of life was an enormous step forward in molecular biology. The next major step was the discovery of how the molecule replicates itself.

DNA replication

Remember that before a cell divides, the chromosomes duplicate themselves. How do they achieve this? The two long strands of DNA separate and the free

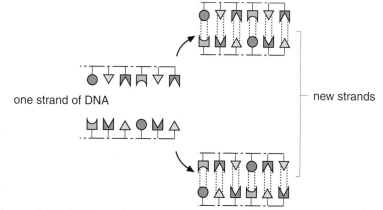

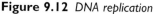

Figure 9.12 *DNA replication*

bases present in the cell nucleus align themselves with the separated strands (guanine with cytosine, thymine with adenine). This results in the creation of two new double helices.

Sex chromosomes

The discovery of the special chromosomes which determine the sex of an organism took place in 1910. An American geneticist, Thomas H Morgan (Figure 9.13), was studying the genetics of the fruit fly, *Drosophila melanogaster*.

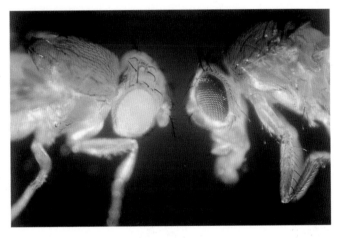

Figure 9.14 *The fruit fly,* Drosophila melanogaster *– on the right is a normal fly and on the left is a white-eyed mutant*

Figure 9.13 *Thomas H Morgan*

You may have seen this small fly hovering around over-ripe fruit (especially bananas), sometimes in vast numbers. In the same way that Gregor Mendel's significant discoveries were made using very common, but perhaps unlikely, organisms (see p. 156), Morgan's discoveries from his investigations with the fruit fly played a major role in expanding scientific knowledge. Among thousands of red-eyed flies raised under laboratory conditions, Morgan found one mutant fly with white eyes. This fly was a male and was mated with a normal red-eyed female. The F1, the first generation of offspring, consisted entirely of red-eyed flies. Using Mendel's logic, this meant that the gene for white eyes was recessive to the gene for red eyes. Next, members of the F1 were mated to produce the F2, or second, generation. The results agreed with Mendel's observations on peas – i.e. the F2 comprised a 3:1 ratio of red-eyed flies to white-eyed flies. Morgan noticed, however, that all of the white-eyed flies were males! He concluded that the gene for eye colour was in some way linked to the sex of the animal. White eye colour is controlled by a sex-linked gene.

A clue to the solution of this puzzle was seen in the chromosomes. It was already known that there is a difference between the chromosomes of male and female *Drosophila*. Of the four pairs of chromosomes in each cell, three pairs are identical in males and females, the other pair is different. The straight, rod-shaped chromosomes of this pair are called **X chromosomes**. The hook-shaped member of this pair (found in the male only) is called the **Y chromosome** (see Figure 9.15).

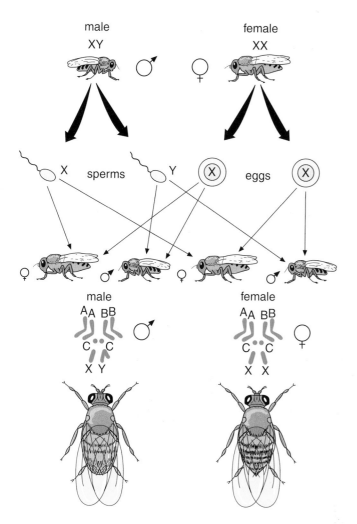

Figure 9.15 *X and Y chromosomes in fruit flies*

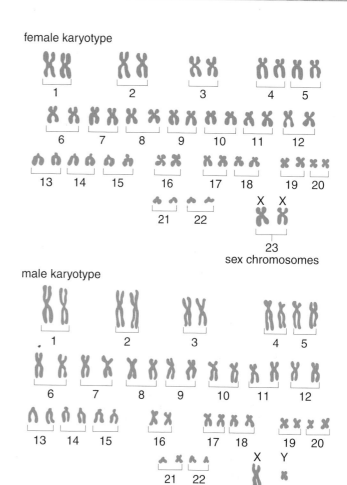

Figure 9.16 *The human karyotype (the complete set of chromosomes)*

When combined with a knowledge of meiosis, these observations led to an important conclusion: males produce two different kinds of sperms as far as these chromosomes are concerned. Half the sperms carry an X chromosome and the other half carry the Y chromosome. Females, on the other hand, produce only one kind of egg – with one X chromosome. Both eggs and sperms, of course, carry one chromosome of each of the other pairs.

Because of their connection with the sex of the flies, the X and Y chromosomes are called **sex chromosomes**. All other chromosomes are called **autosomes**. The discovery of two kinds of sex chromosomes suggested that they could provide an explanation for the determination of sex. Flies with two X chromosomes are always females, while those with an X and a Y chromosome are always males. The sex of a fly is then dependent on whether the egg (with an X chromosome) is fertilised by a sperm with an X chromosome or one with a Y chromosome. Thus it is the male fly's sex cell that determines the sex of the offspring.

Since the time of Morgan, experimental and research techniques have been improved. It is now possible to show that this difference between sex chromosomes is found in all animals. (In contrast, most plants do not have separate sexes, but those with separate male and female individuals have sex chromosomes.) The human pattern of sex chromosomes is similar to that of the fruit fly.

Humans have 23 pairs of chromosomes (Figure 9.16). Twenty-two pairs of these are autosomes (non-sex chromosomes) and one pair consists of the sex chromosomes. In men, the Y chromosome is very small compared to the X chromosome. We can explain sex determination in humans in the same way as we can in fruit flies. (*Note*: not all animals have sex-determining *sperms*. Birds and butterflies have males with XX chromosomes and females with XY chromosomes.)

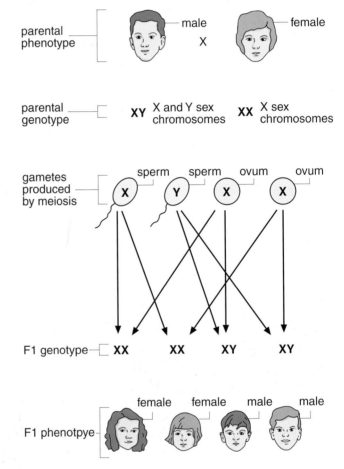

Figure 9.17 *Human sex chromosomes*

What is inheritance?

We have seen that the bridge that connects one generation to the next is microscopic, consisting of an egg cell and a sperm cell. Within these tiny bits of living matter are the plans for the next generation. When the sperm fertilises the egg, one of the most remarkable series of changes known to science begins.

The instructions within the human cell determine that the embryo will develop into a human rather than into an elephant or a mouse. This is the same for every organism that reproduces sexually. These instructions are in the form of chemical messages. The way in which these messages are passed from one generation to the next is **inheritance**. The study of inheritance has become a branch of science called **genetics**. Today most people have heard of the term 'genetics'. Genetic engineering, genetic counselling and genetically-inherited diseases are terms which are commonly used in newspapers, radio and TV. We tend to be much more interested in the medical aspects of genetics than anything else. This is not surprising because we hear of so many disorders that can be passed from parents to their children through genetic inheritance.

If you were a farmer or a gardener you would certainly be interested in knowing about the methods of passing useful characters from one generation to the next so you could make use of it through **selective breeding**.

Selective breeding

For thousands of years the selected pedigree animal has been prized. Such animals have a recorded ancestry which goes back many generations.

The dairy farmer wants selected pedigree cattle from which to breed his milking cows (Figure 9.18). The hunter wants a pedigree dog. A farmer wants pure lines of cultivated plants.

Figure 9.18 *A pedigree dairy herd*

Figure 9.19 *The wheat in this field was chosen because of its desirable qualities*

Characters such as grain yield (Figure 9.19), fruit yield and disease resistance are desirable qualities that can be maintained through selective breeding. Although humans have learned a great deal about selective breeding, we do not pretend to know all the solutions to our problems. Some attempts have had little or no success. We know that selective breeding sometimes gives the results we want, but often does not. We have long understood that inheritance was involved in selective breeding, but the actual mechanism of operation remained a mystery until the nineteenth century.

It might seem strange to you now, but the whole science of genetics began with an Austrian monk experimenting with pea seeds in 1865. Using this unlikely material and a great deal of patience, this Augustinian monk, Gregor Mendel, set out the first principles of inheritance. For his unique contribution to science, he is often called the 'father of genetics'.

Mendel – his life

Gregor Mendel was born in 1822 and christened Johann Mendel. His family was of peasant ancestry and lived in Moravia, now a province of the Czech Republic. After simple early instruction by an uncle, Mendel attracted the attention of the clergy and, at the age of 21, became a monk in the monastery of Brunn. At his ordination, he took the name of Gregor, by which he has been known ever since.

Mendel attended the University of Vienna from 1851 to 1853, where he studied mathematics and physics, and then became a teacher of science at the local secondary school. He continued to teach until 1968, when he was made abbot of the monastery, a position of such responsibility that he did no further teaching and gave up his research as well. It is interesting to speculate on what might have happened had the scientific world responded to Mendel's two publications which led ultimately to the foundation of the science of genetics. Mendel was discouraged by the almost complete indifference of the scientific community to his work. It must, indeed, have been a prime factor in his failure to continue his experiments.

For a period of about eight years, from 1865 to 1866, Mendel conducted his famous breeding experiments with the common garden pea for his long and meticulous studies. His first paper was published in the *Transactions of the Natural History Society of Brunn*, the obscurity of which may account for the indifference with which the paper was received. Thirty-four years later, in 1900, three scientists from different countries independently discovered Mendel's work and realised its significance. They were, H. De Vries from Holland, C. Correns from Germany and E. Tschermak from Austria. They completely confirmed Mendel's findings which were to become such a dynamic science in the 21st century. Mendel died in 1884 before his work was recognised for what it was. Today, we call him 'the founder of heredity' or even 'the founder of molecular genetics' and the first mathematical biologist.

Figure 9.20 *Gregor Mendel, the father of genetics*

The work of Mendel

Although it is likely that Mendel performed very few experiments that had not been done before, he succeeded where others had failed. His success may have been due to the unusual combination of skills he brought to the task. He was trained in mathematics as well as in biology, and with this background, he planned experiments that at the time were novel in three respects:

1 Instead of studying a small number of offspring from one mating, Mendel used many identical matings. As a result he had enormous numbers of offspring to study.

2 Because he had large numbers to study, he was able to apply statistical methods to analyse the results.

3 He limited each cross to a single difference – a single pair of contrasted characters at a time. People who had carried out genetic crosses with plants and animals before Mendel did not concentrate on one character at a time. Pure-breeding stock was not always used (pure-breeding individuals receive similar genes from both parents), so characters were often masked by each other. Mendel selected garden peas for his experiments because he knew that they possess many varieties. In addition, the plants are easy to cultivate and cross, and the generation time is reasonably short. Finally, and of great importance, the plants are self-pollinating. The significance of this requires an explanation.

Let us consider the structure of the pea flower (Figure 9.21) and see how fertilisation usually takes place: pollen from the anthers falls onto the stigma of the same flower before the flower opens fully; pollen tubes develop from the pollen grains to carry the male gamete to the female gamete in the ovule. If you want to pollinate one pea flower with pollen from another plant, you must remove the anthers from the flower before its own pollen is mature. Later, when the stigma is ready to receive pollen, you can dust it with pollen taken from another flower of your choice. In this way the parents of the next generation can be controlled.

Mendel made sure that the plants he started with were all pure-bred for each character he was studying. He did this by letting the plants fertilise themselves for a number of generations. The offspring of each generation were studied to make sure they were like one another and like the parent plant. Mendel then made hundreds of crosses by dusting the pollen from one kind of plant onto the stigma of plants of another kind. For example, he pollinated plants from a type whose seeds were always round, with pollen from a type whose seeds were always wrinkled.

In every case he found that the offspring all resembled one of the parents and showed no sign of the character of the other parent. Thus the crosses between plants with round seeds and plants with wrinkled seeds all produced offspring with round seeds. One character seemed to 'dominate' the other. Mendel therefore called this character the **dominant character**.

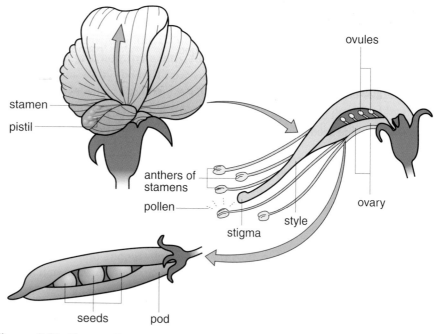

Figure 9.21 *The pea flower*

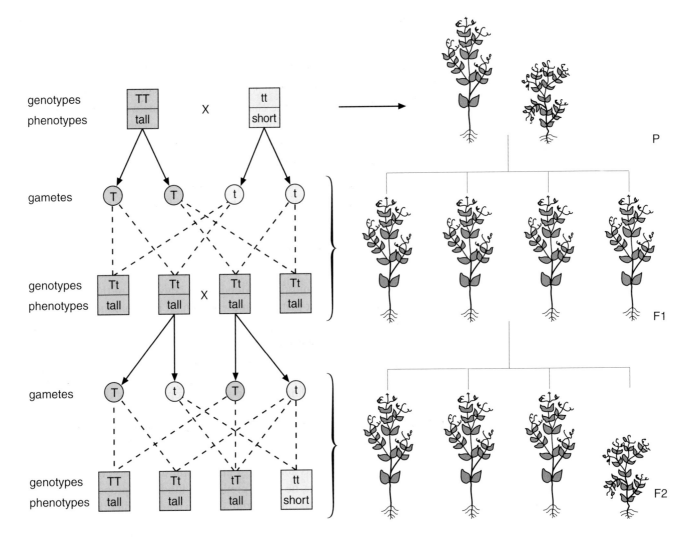

Figure 9.22 *Mendel's results*

Mendel thus arrived at a general rule – the **law of segregation**.

"The two members of each pair of genes must separate when gametes are formed, and only one of each pair can go to a gamete."

If a parent is **TT**, its gametes will all inherit one or other of its **T** genes, but not both. If the parent is **tt**, its gametes will all inherit one of its **t** genes. If the parent is **Tt**, half the gametes will inherit its **T** gene, and the other will inherit its **t** gene.

www

Mendel Web
http://www.netspace.org/MendelWeb/home.html

Summary

1 Organisms grow by a type of cell division called mitosis.

2 Each daughter cell produced in mitosis has the diploid chromosome number and the chromosomes of the daughter cells are identical to those of the parent cell.

3 All body cells of members of the same species contain the same kind and number of chromosomes.

4 Sperms and eggs are produced by meiosis and are haploid.

5 When sperms and eggs join at fertilisation, the diploid number is restored.

6 The synthesis of proteins is one of the most important processes in living cells.

7 DNA controls protein synthesis through a code of bases. By transcription, this code is passed on to messenger RNA.

8 Messenger RNA carries the code into the cytoplasm where it acts as a template for the building of proteins.

9 Units of another type of RNA (transfer RNA) bring amino acids to the template where a ribosome reads the code and a protein is assembled from the amino acids.

10 More than a century has passed since Gregor Mendel's experiments with garden peas led to the formulation of the basic laws of genetics.

Homework Questions

1 What does 'genetics' mean?

2 What were the advantages of Mendel using peas for his experiments?

3 State Mendel's principle of dominance.

4 What do you understand by the term genotype?

In-Depth Questions

1 Gregor Mendel's first law of genetics states 'Of a pair of contrasted characters, only one can be represented in a gamete by its germinal unit.'

(a) Give the modern name for 'germinal unit'.

(b) State where these germinal units are found in the gametes.

(c) A red-haired woman marries a brown-haired man, and all the children are brown haired. Explain this genetically.

2 In humans, the gene for tongue rolling, R, is dominant to the gene for the inability to roll the tongue, r.

(a) Using these symbols, give the genotypes of the children that could be born from a marriage between a heterozygous father and a non tongue-rolling mother.

(b) State whether the children would be tongue-rollers or not.

3 Figure 9.23 is part of a family tree showing the distribution of brown eyes and blue eyes.

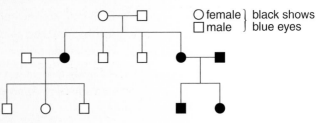

Figure 9.23

(a) Which number represents a man who is homozygous for blue eyes?

(b) Which number represents a woman who must be heterozygous?

(c) Which of the eye colours is controlled by a dominant gene?

(d) Which part of the family tree enables you to answer part (c)?

4 A boy was interested to see how eye colour was inherited in his family, so he wrote down the colour of the eyes of all the members of his family. The information and his deductions are given in Figure 9.24. Unfortunately, he could not finish it.

Fill in the gaps after copying the table.

(a) Write the correct words for the numbers 1–17.

(b) From the results, state the dominant eye colour.

(c) Also from the results, state what recessive means.

(d) How many factors for eye colour do the gametes shown contain?

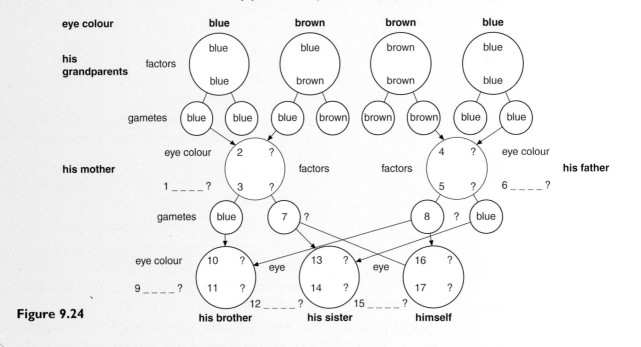

Figure 9.24

10 Variations – Their Causes and Significance

Learning objectives

By the end of this chapter you should be able to understand:

- the difference between continuous and discontinuous variation;
- that variation leads to evolution through natural selection;
- that fossils are used as evidence of evolution;
- that the major causes of variation can be genetic and environmental;
- that mutation is a source of genetic variation;
- the effects of radiation in terms of mutation;
- the effects of radiation on human health.

Variation

One of the most fascinating things about living organisms is their enormous variety. They differ in appearance, behaviour and habitat (where they live). A garden snail, a cockle, a lion, a horse and a zebra are all animals. They all differ from each other. However, the garden snail and the cockle can be grouped together, and the lion, horse and zebra can be grouped together. The zebra and the horse resemble each other more than either resembles a lion and so they can be divided into a separate group. Living organisms can, therefore, be divided into groups based on the presence of similar features. Inside each large group, smaller groups can be made.

Linnaeus and classification

Carl von Linné (1707–1778) was born in Rashult, a small town in southern Sweden. His father wanted him to become a priest, but thought shoemaking a better career. As a boy, von Linné used to go into the country collecting specimens and was fascinated by the variety of plants and animals he found. A local doctor noticed his interest in natural history and encouraged him to go to university.

Von Linné was probably inspired by the work of John Ray (1627–1705), the 'father of English natural history'. Ray was the son of a blacksmith and became an internationally honoured naturalist and author of numerous books in which he attempted to classify the specimens he collected. He had the idea of a natural system clearly in his mind but was unable to produce it himself. Indeed it was an impossibility at the time because of lack of sufficient information.

Lack of money forced von Linné to end his studies in Sweden and eventually he went to Holland to complete his university course. While there, he wrote his famous work *Systema Naturae*, consisting of only 12 printed folio pages. This work was his passport to the scientific world.

Figure 10.1 *Carl Linnaeus*

Figure 10.2 *John Ray*

Scientists of repute acknowledged it and this enabled him to travel to England and France to meet some of the most respected scientists of that time. Eventually, he became Professor of Natural History at Uppsala University in Sweden.

His great contribution to science was to name and classify plants and animals in a simple logical way using a binomial method, where organisms were given two Latin names. For example, to animals strongly resembling one another, like the lion, tiger and leopard, he gave the overall name, or genus name, *Felis*. Each would then be given a second or species name. So the lion is *Felis leo*, the tiger *Felis tigris*, and the leopard, *Felis pardus*. His love of Latin influenced von Linné to change his own name to Carolus Linnaeus in his published works.

He is often criticised as being narrow minded and arrogant. This view was probably reinforced by his own proud motto '*Deus creavit, Linnaeus disposuit*' – 'God created, Linnaeus arranged.' Although he did not look beyond the external anatomy of a plant or animal when he classified them, he directed zoological and botanical thoughts towards a logical systemic plan upon which our present science of taxonomy is based. In this way, he encouraged scientists to look at the origin of these species, a question which was to be of prime importance in the last half of the 19th century.

Variation in humans

Let us consider ourselves and see how we are different from most other organisms but how we are also similar to some (Figure 10.3). Right at the end of this branched, tree-like system of classification we find humans as a distinct **species** of animal. A species is defined as a group of individuals which can interbreed to produce fertile offspring. In other words, their offspring must be able to breed between themselves.

There may be a great deal of variation within species, for example in humans, Asians, Africans, Scandinavians and American Indians are very different in appearance, but they all belong to the same species and can interbreed successfully to produce fertile offspring.

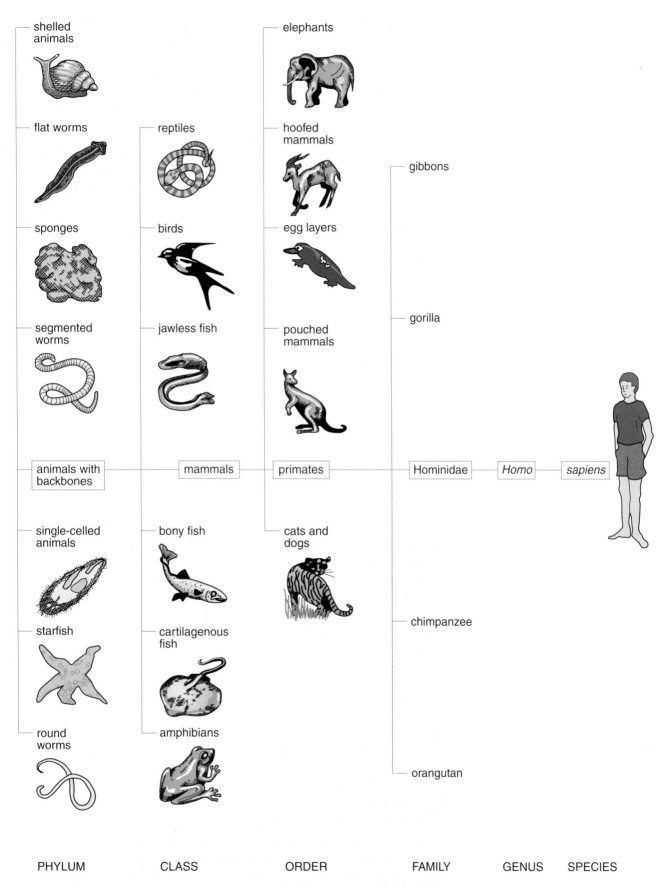

Figure 10.3 *The positions of humans in the animal kingdom*

PHYLUM	CLASS	ORDER	FAMILY	GENUS	SPECIES

In humans there are hundreds of features which illustrate variation. Some can be measured and show a continuous trend from one extreme to another, for example the **continuous variation** in height in a population. Another type of variation shows two extremes without any intermediate types, for example, tongue rolling (see Figure 10.5).

This is **discontinuous variation**. You can either roll your tongue completely or you can't. There is no such thing as a 'half tongue roller'. Tongue rolling does not change with age or with learning.

Figure 10.4 *These photos show the variety between some of the different races of humans*

Figure 10.5 *This boy is able to roll his tongue*

Coursework Activities

A great deal of variation can be observed by examining certain characters in students from your school or college. A character is a single feature of an organism which is under observation, for example hair colour or eye colour. Variation means the distribution of these characters throughout the group. This can only be seen by collecting all the results for the whole group.

Ability to taste phenylthiocarbamide (PTC)

PTC is a chemical which tastes bitter to some people – it tastes just like the rind of a grapefruit. You won't know what this tastes like if you are a 'non-taster'! You can either taste it or can't, there is no in-between.

1 Take one PTC paper strip.

2 Touch your tongue with the paper strip and record whether you can taste anything.

3 Calculate from the class results the percentage of 'tasters' and 'non-tasters'.

Is this a clear cut test? Are there any people who cannot say definitely whether they are tasters or non-tasters? Perhaps your class is not typical. Suggest a reason for this. Below are data for the frequency of non-tasters in various populations:

Race	Number tested	Non-tasters %
Hindus	489	33.7
Danish	251	32.7
English	441	31.5
Spanish	203	25.6
Portuguese	454	24.0
Malays	237	16.0
Japanese	295	7.1
Lapps	140	6.4
West Africans	74	2.7
Chinese	50	2.0
S. American Indians	163	1.2

Tongue rolling

1 Try to roll your tongue from side to side as shown in the photograph (Figure 10.5).

2 Find the percentage of tongue-rollers and non-tongue-rollers in your class.

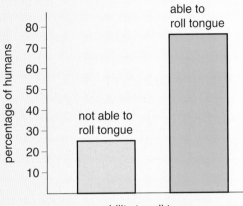

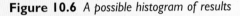

Figure 10.6 *A possible histogram of results*

This example is similar to the PTC example. A histogram may be plotted which should resemble the one shown in Figure 10.6.

This illustrates discontinuous variation.

Eye colour

1 Work in pairs. Each member of a pair should look at his/her partners' eyes in good light.

2 Record blue/brown if they are definitely one of these colours. If not, describe the colour as precisely as you can.

3 Collect the data for blue and brown eyes for the class.

You must now decide on a description of the other colours. When you have done this you must decide whether certain colours may be grouped together or whether there is a continuous gradation which does not allow grouping. Is there anyone in the class with two eyes of different colour? What could be the explanation for this?

Hair

Texture: classify your partner's hair as being straight or curly and find the percentages of each for the class. Is this a distinct grouping or is there a gradation?

Colour: hair colour is not at all easy to define. Hair can be black, dark brown, medium brown, light brown, blond, red. Look at your class' hair colour and modify your colour code if necessary. Record the numbers in each group. Are the differences within groups as great as those between groups? If so, what does this tell you about the variation of hair colour compared with the variation in tongue-rolling ability?

Variation in behaviour – reflexes

1 One partner holds a 30 cm rule vertically while the other places a thumb and forefinger at each side at the bottom end without touching it.

2 The first partner lets the rule drop without warning, and the second catches it as quickly as possible by closing the thumb and forefinger.

3 Record to the nearest cm how many cms the ruler fell by measuring the distance from the end of the ruler to the middle of the catcher's thumb and forefinger.

4 Do this test three times without practice and calculate the average length for each member of the class. The more rapid the reflex action, the shorter will be the distance through which the ruler is allowed to fall.

5 Display the class results as shown below and construct a histogram by plotting numbers of individuals against classes of distances fallen.

Distance fallen/cms	1	2	3	4	5	6	7	8	9	10
Number of individuals										

Height

Record the height of each member of the class, complete a table similar to the one shown below and construct a histogram as you did for reflex times.

Heights/cm	150–5	156–60	161–5 etc.
Number in each class			

Continuous and discontinuous variation

We can use discontinuous variations to sort individuals into distinct groups with no overlapping. In continuous variation there are no distinct groups and individuals are evenly spread over a range of measurements. By plotting histograms in the way suggested in the investigations we obtain an idea of the limits within which most individuals fall. We can also see how the more extreme cases are spread on each side. Before making measurements we should follow these rules:

1 Make sure that the character you are measuring does not depend on another factor. For example, if you are measuring height in a population of humans or the length of leaves, the sample must all be of the same age group. The age of an individual will certainly affect these measurements.

2 When measurements involve judgements of degrees of a character, such as hair colour, everyone involved in measuring must agree with the judgement and use the same descriptions.

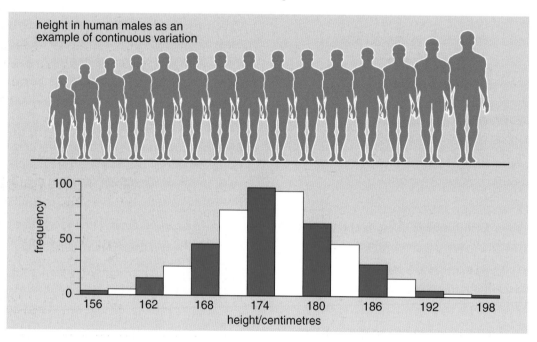

Figure 10.7 *Continuous variation in height*

Use the Variation program to calculate the frequency of your characteristics such as hair colour, eye colour and ear lobes. Find out how these characteristics are inherited. (Program available from 'Games for Life', The Wellcome Trust, 210 Euston Road, London NW1 2BE.)

Causes of variation

The outward appearance of an organism is dependent on a combination of inherited characters and those due to the effects of the environment. The name given to the outward appearance of an organism is **phenotype**. We can say

Phenotype = Effects of genes + Effects of the environment

The following example can illustrate this. Imagine a litter of Alsatian puppies. They all have genes (units of inheritance) from the same parents. If we compare the growth of these puppies, we might see that one out of the litter becomes weaker and smaller than the rest. The reason could be that it has not been given the correct diet and exercise. In other words, the effects of the environment have influenced its phenotype. By altering the environment we can alter the phenotype.

In contrast, a litter of Corgis will grow up to be small dogs no matter how well fed they are. The genes determine the phenotype if the environment is kept the same. We cannot alter the genes by changing the environment.

Environmental factors

The environment of an organism means the type of place where it lives. However, in biological terms, environment means every factor which influences the organism from the outside. It includes food (and any other materials taken into the organism), temperature, degree of acidity, light and any physical forces acting on the organism from the outside. Some examples will serve to show how important these factors are in shaping the phenotype.

Nutrients

The types of food eaten by animals and the types of mineral salts used by plants influence their growth. Figure 10.8 shows the effects of improved diet on the growth of some Japanese children.

The children were brought up in different environments. Some were born and raised in the USA. Others were raised in Japan with and without an improved diet. From the graphs you can see that the American-born children are the tallest at all ages. The improved diet and standard of living in Japan between 1900 and 1952 has also resulted in an increase in height. The same has happened in Britain. Children are now taller and heavier, age for age, than they were 60 years ago.

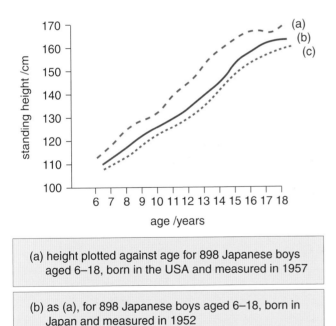

(a) height plotted against age for 898 Japanese boys aged 6–18, born in the USA and measured in 1957

(b) as (a), for 898 Japanese boys aged 6–18, born in Japan and measured in 1952

(c) as (a), for 898 Japanese boys, aged 6–18, born in Japan and measured in 1900

Figure 10.8 *The effect of improved diet on growth in Japanese children*

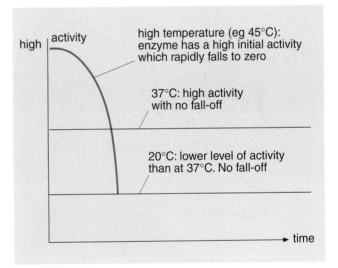

Figure 10.9 *The effect of temperature on enzyme activity*

An abnormal phenotype can also be shown in humans as a result of a deficiency of iodine. Lack of iodine in drinking water may be the cause of **goitre** formation. These swellings are the result of an enlarged thyroid gland. This gland makes a hormone which contains iodine. Vitamin deficiency can also result in abnormal phenotypes. For example, lack of vitamin D causes rickets (see p. 34) in which the bones become soft and are distorted under the weight of the body.

Chemicals

Some chemicals which enter the body from the environment cannot be called 'food'. They are not needed for growth or energy release and may affect the phenotype. One such chemical which had a disastrous effect was **thalidomide**. This drug was given to pregnant women to prevent sickness. Many of these women gave birth to deformed children without limbs. In these cases the fetus had developed in an environment consisting of amniotic fluid and the mothers' blood. Thalidomide exerted its effects by entering the mothers' blood and crossing the placenta.

Temperature

Temperature changes act mainly by affecting the rates of enzyme-controlled reactions in the cells. These effects are shown in Figure 10.9.

The higher the temperature, the faster the enzymes work up to a maximum rate. This explains why animals and plants generally grow more slowly at lower temperatures and why most organisms cannot survive at temperatures higher than 45°C.

Light

The browning of human skin when exposed to light is an obvious change of phenotype due to an environmental factor.

Physical forces

Training by using muscles more than they are normally used can alter the phenotype. Muscle enlargement is obvious (see Figure 10.11).

Another effect of training is that the blood vessels to the muscles enlarge in order to supply them with more nutrients and oxygen.

Figure 10.10 *A sun tan is an obvious environmental change*

Figure 10.11 *This body builder has trained to increase the size of his muscles, and thus his phenotype*

The Great British Naturalist – Charles Darwin (1809–1882)

The theory of evolution is always associated with Charles Darwin, whose genius in the late 1850s gave the world the new idea of natural selection (see p. 175). Darwin was born in Shrewsbury, the son of a wealthy doctor. At a local public school, he received the usual course of Latin and Greek verses, with classical history and geography. It is interesting to note that this curriculum did not contain any natural history. He performed chemical experiments in the garden shed and wandered the countryside, fishing, shooting and collecting minerals, rocks and insects. His father thought his pursuits were disgraceful.

This supposedly idle boy was eventually sent to Edinburgh to study medicine. The sight of two operations performed with no anaesthetic revolted the 17 year old Darwin and after two years, when it was apparent that he was totally unsuited to medical studies, he returned to Shrewsbury. His family now decided that he should study for the clergy and in 1828 he was a student of theology at Cambridge. He proved to be far from studious and continued to annoy his father who disapproved of the company he was keeping and his way of life.

On graduating with a pass in 1821, he prepared to take Holy Orders when fate intervened. On the advice of his professor, John Henslow, Darwin joined HMS *Beagle* on a voyage around the world, as an unpaid naturalist. This was the turning point in Darwin's life because it set an apparently unambitious man, with little distinction, on the way to show the world his spark of genius and depth of reasoning. The observations and conclusions that he made on this voyage became the foundations of one of the most famous books ever written in any language. In 1859, Darwin published '*Origin of species by means of natural selection, or the preservation of favoured races in the struggle for life*,' more commonly known as '*The Origin of Species*'.

Figure 10.12 *Charles Darwin*

Darwin's voyage on the *Beagle*

At 22 years old, Darwin applied to the equally young Captain Fitzroy for the post of naturalist on board HMS *Beagle* for its epic voyage, which took place between 1831 and 1836. Darwin was accepted on board, having been funded by his uncle, Josiah Wedgwood, of pottery fame and wealth.

After being driven back to harbour twice by heavy seas, HMS *Beagle* finally weighed anchor on 27th December 1831, and set out towards South America on a journey which was to be the spark for a flame that would set the scientific world alight. It was then that Darwin's worst fears materialised. The voyage soon changed to a nauseous routine of tough shipboard life and endless seasickness. He sometimes spent whole days below deck, but fortunately, Fitzroy treated Darwin's lack of sea legs with sympathy, allowing him to share his table for meals.

Although Darwin was convinced that variations within species could be passed on to future generations, he had no understanding of hereditary genetics until the importance of Mendel's work was recognised, almost 50 years later.

It might have been a misunderstanding, after not having read and understood Darwin's work, but it was unfortunate that one of Darwin's friends, Herbert Spencer, coined the phrase, 'survival of the fittest,' to sum up Darwin's conclusions. The media of the time sensationalised the idea to mean survival of the strongest but actually Darwin meant the survival of the fittest to breed. Thus, some drab, insignificant-looking animals are more efficient breeders than some of the more spectacular looking types and therefore have greater 'fitness'.

Did you know?

The word 'biology' was invented by Jean-Baptiste Lamarck. He suggested a logical theory of evolution of animals without backbones (invertebrates). His ideas were, however, fundamentally flawed because he believed that characteristics which developed during the lifetime of a species could be inherited by the offspring. For example, according to Lamarck's theory of evolution, the children of well-developed weight lifters would inherit their parents' strength and large muscles.

An alternative view

Before Charles Darwin's time, there were two main schools of thought: one believed that all species were created as they appear today and have not changed, the other maintained that one species could change gradually into another by evolution. A conflicting idea to the theory of natural selection was proposed a long time before Darwin commenced his studies by Jean-Baptiste Lamarck (1744–1829). In the year of Darwin's birth, 1809, Lamarck published his ideas on evolution in *Zoological Philosophy*.

Hard evidence for evolution

Both Lamarck and Darwin built up large collections of fossils to provide evidence that species change over time. They found that the more primitive animals and plants occurred as fossils in the oldest rocks. The word 'fossil' comes from the Latin *fossilis*, meaning something dug up from the ground. Today the term is applied to any organism preserved in the Earth's crust or traces of such organisms. In past ages, when a plant or animal died, it was occasionally caught in some liquid that cut off air and so prevented the dead body's decay by bacteria. In such cases, the organism often remained virtually intact. Some examples are the ancient insects found preserved in amber, which itself is a fossilised resin once produced by trees.

Figure 10.16 *This insect has been preserved in amber*

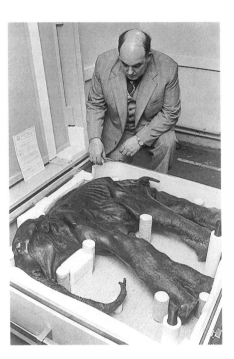

Figure 10.17 *A baby mammoth which has been preserved in ice*

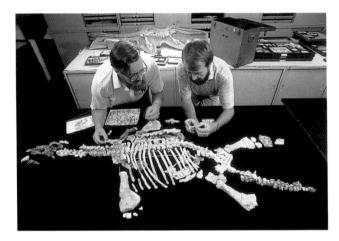

Figure 10.18 *The fossilised remains of a dinosaur being studied by palaeontologists*

In some instances, the liquid destroys the flesh, leaving the bones intact, as in the animal skeletons found in the tar pits of California. But fossils of whole bodies or skeletons are extremely rare. Most animals and plants are eaten or decay when they die. The chance of being fossilised depends on when and where you die. The chances of the fossil actually being found are also very remote. The finds are usually just fragments – a few teeth or bones. In some cases the fossil may just be a shell, the tunnel of a worm in sand, a foot print or an impression of an animal or plant in mud. Coal is probably the best known fossil of all.

Many parts of the Earth's crust have proved rich with fossil specimens. Ice has preserved organisms and their parts, often in a near complete condition. Mammoths are examples of such well-preserved remains.

The best sources of fossils are the floors of seas past or present. Unless they are eaten first, dead organisms sink to the bottom. Their shells or bony parts are converted to hard limestone by chemical action. Sand settles over millions of years and, though the soft parts decay, the hard parts remain. These fossils may not be found until long after the sand has become solid rock and the waters of the sea itself have receded.

How the damage is done

Radiation may damage a cell by directly harming molecules, for example molecules of DNA may be damaged by the passage through them of an electron or other atomic particle. From a biological point of view, the most important damaging radiations are alpha particles, beta particles, X-rays and gamma rays.

Alpha particles spread their energy very quickly, forming an enormous number of pieces of ions. There is little danger from alpha particles unless they get inside the body. The skin easily stops the particles entering from outside sources. If, however, an organism takes in food exposed to alpha radiation, hence contaminating the body cells, the alpha particles become a serious hazard. The most active tissues in the body are the blood-producing bone marrow, the liver, testes and ovaries. Once alpha particles get into these tissues, they will do two kinds of harm:

1 the marrow and liver cells will suffer damage – this will shorten the life of the person.

2 the damage done to the sex organs will be inherited via DNA and passed on to future generations.

Products from nuclear reactors are one source of alpha particles and pose a serious problem. For example, plutonium-239 is a long-lasting element which can easily enter food chains. Once in the body, it accumulates in the bone and is thought to cause anaemia and leukaemia. Leukaemia is a particularly distressing form of cancer which affects the blood cells in the bone marrow. It occurs when mechanisms which control blood cell manufacture break down. An imbalance in the correct proportions of red cells, white cells and platelets then occurs (Figure 10.20).

Nuclear waste leaked from the Sellafield reprocessing plant in Cumbria has been detected in the Irish Sea.

Fish are also tested for radiation contamination (Figure 10.22).

Grass samples near power stations are analysed to check that the radiation levels are not too high.

Figure 10.22 *The level of radiation in these fish is being sampled*

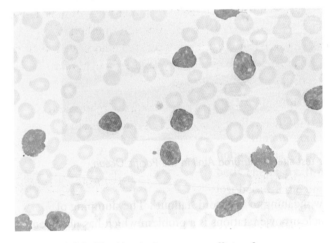

Figure 10.20 *The blood of a person suffering from leukaemia showing numerous white blood cells stained purple*

Figure 10.21 *This sample of water is being tested to measure the levels of radiation*

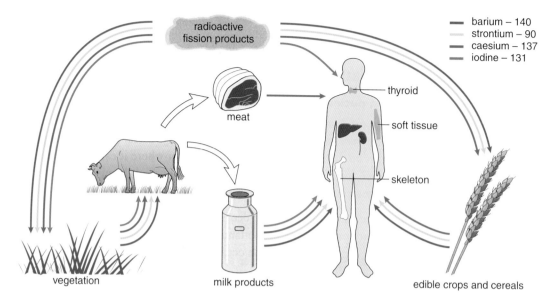

barium – 140
strontium – 90
caesium – 137
iodine – 131

thyroid
soft tissue
skeleton

radioactive
fission products

meat

vegetation

milk products

edible crops and cereals

Figure 10.23 *How radioactive materials affect the human body*

Beta particles are high speed electrons which can penetrate the skin. Like alpha particles, they are also a hazard internally. Radioactive fallout contains beta particles as well as alpha particles. Strontium-90 and caesium-137 have attracted considerable attention because they readily accumulate in living organisms. Fish caught in the North Sea have been found with caesium-137 in their flesh. Strontium-90 is similar to calcium and becomes localised in bones. Emissions can damage the red bone marrow and cause anaemia and leukaemia. Caesium-137 is absorbed by all cells.

X-rays and gamma rays have great penetrating power. They are a massive hazard when their source is outside the body. Great care must be taken to minimise exposure when X-rays are used. Again, the most active tissues – developing embryos for instance – are the most sensitive. X-raying pregnant women is risky for the embryo and is rarely, if ever, carried out.

Nuclear energy, radioactivity and the environment

One of the main environmental concerns today is the disposal of nuclear waste from power stations. The problem of the extremely long 'half-lives' of radioactive waste chemicals is the main consideration when deciding on a method of disposal. The **half-life period** is the time that it takes for the radioactive levels in the chemical to be reduced by half. The radioactivity can be thought of as something which decays away over a period of time.

Table 10.1 below lists the half-lives of some important radioactive elements. Some of these may enter our environment as a result of human activities.

Table 10.1

Chemical	Half-life	Chemical	Half-life
Carbon-14	5760 years	Strontium-90	28 years
Phosphorus-32	14.3 days	Iodine-131	8.04 days
Sulphur-35	87.2 days	Caesium-137	30 years
Calcium-45	165 days	Plutonium-239	24 400 years

Life saving genetics

Until recently, certain hormones were only obtained from dead animals, but it was difficult to produce enough to satisfy demand in this way. Genetic engineers have solved the problem of mass production by using bacteria. The method is summarised in Figure 11.2. The main advantage of this technique is the mass production of many otherwise scarce and expensive proteins which help save lives. Bacteria can be used as living factories to produce these proteins on demand. Theoretically, any protein can be mass produced using the same principle.

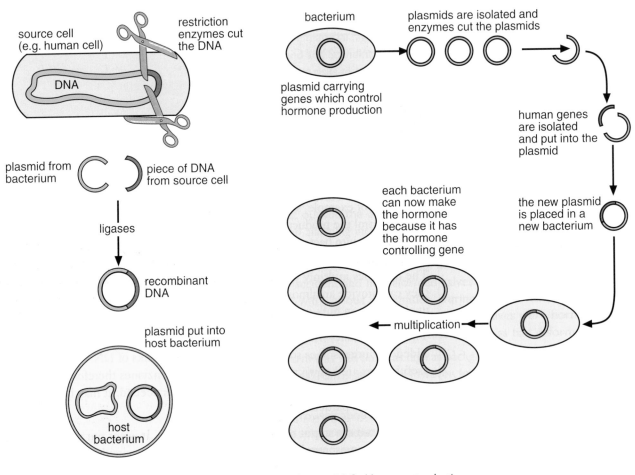

Figure 11.1 *Recombinant DNA technology*

Figure 11.2 *Hormone production*

Genetic fingerprinting

The fact that the order of bases in our DNA (see p. 150) is as individual as our fingerprints is the basis of a method of identification which can be used to help solve crimes. The technique is called **genetic profiling** and was first used in the late 1980s as evidence to establish the guilt of a murderer. The term **genetic fingerprinting** was soon used to describe its role in criminology, although it has nothing to do with the patterns on the skin of fingers! The process is dependent on the police or forensic scientists being able to find DNA in cells left at the scene of the crime. Only very small amounts of blood, skin, hair or other tissue

are needed. The DNA is extracted from the cells in a complex way and analysed to determine the order of bases in the DNA molecule. At the end of the process, the scientist will have a type of photograph on which the order of bases is seen as a pattern which looks very much like a bar code on a shop-bought product.

There is now a computerised database holding the DNA profiles of all convicted criminals and this promises to be the greatest breakthrough in criminal justice since the discovery that fingerprints are unique to individuals.

Figure 11.3 *Genetic profiles*

Did you know?

The first test case using genetic fingerprinting proved that a suspect who had confessed to a rape and murder was, in fact, innocent. Two girls had been raped and murdered in the same part of the country, but the crimes were committed three years apart. Investigators suspected a connection between the two and a suspect was soon cross-examined. He admitted to one of the crimes but denied being involved with the other. Scientists used the technique of DNA profiling which clearly showed that both crimes were committed by the same person and that the suspect was not that person. All men from the area were tested and genetic profiles were made of 5000 samples. Finally, one sample matched those from both crime scenes and the person was arrested and convicted.

Other uses of genetic profiling include investigations into the parenthood of children when there is a legal dispute over who is the father of a child, and the identification of bodies after mass disasters by comparing the profiles with those of known close relatives.

Did you know?

In the 1990s, the remains of Czar Nicholas II of Russia and his family were identified using DNA extracted from their skeletons which had been buried since 1917. The DNA profiles were compared to a sample from Prince Philip, Duke of Edinburgh, who was found to share the same line of ancestry as Alexandra, the wife of the Czar. In 1991, a 5000-year-old mummified body, 'Otzi the iceman', was found in a glacier on the Austrian–Italian border in the Alps. Some scientists believed that the body was brought there from South America as a hoax, but analysis of its DNA showed that the iceman was found to be related closely to inhabitants of Northern Europe. Although the analysis of DNA after such a long time is possible, the hope of ever extracting DNA from extinct dinosaurs and creating a 'Jurassic Park' will have to remain a dream. DNA would be decayed and useless after the millions of years between the age of dinosaurs and the present.

www

Human genome project
http://www.schoolscience.co.uk

Human Genome Mapping Project
http://www.hgmp.mrc.ac.uk

The Human Genome Project

Since the 1980s, advances in the fields of both genetics and medicine have led to developments in medical genetics which have allowed medical practice to evolve at a rapid pace. The Human Genome Project is an international research effort that has succeeded in analysing the structure of human DNA. Scientists have mapped the location of an estimated 100 000 genes. It is anticipated that the end product of this research will be the standard reference for biomedical science in the 21st century and will help us to understand, and eventually treat, many of the 4000 plus recognised human genetic afflictions.

The aims of the Human Genome Project are:

- to map and sequence the human genome (all human genes)
- to map and sequence the genomes of certain other organisms
- to support the collection and distribution of data between research groups
- to promote research training
- to encourage the sharing of ideas in gene technology across international boundaries.

Initial estimates suggested that all this would take up to 15 years. In fact the completion of the initial map took place in 2000, which was before the predicted time schedule. The purpose of the enormous research programme was to sequence the four bases which make up human DNA, i.e. adenine, cytosine, guanine and thymine. (See DNA structure on p. 150.) The bases are represented no less than 3000 million times in our genome. If typed in order, using their initial letters, A, C, G and T, our sequence of bases would fill the equivalent of 134 complete sets of *Encyclopaedia Britannica*. The size of an individual gene within the whole length of human DNA is similar in comparison to the size of an ant on Mount Everest! This mind-boggling project will provide an invaluable reference for medical science in the study of human genetical disorders throughout the 21st century.

Genetically-altered plants

What if plants could be made to make their own pesticides? This question was first asked in the 1980s and was answered soon afterwards. Potatoes were the first crop plants to be genetically engineered to make their own insecticide. Scientists isolated the appropriate gene from a bacterium which naturally produces a poisonous protein which kills beetles, caterpillars and most other insect pests but not useful insects. They succeeded in putting the gene into the cells of the potatoes and thereby improved the yield of the crop. The methods of inserting the genes into the potato cells include shooting them into the plants using a microscopical gun, or using viruses to carry them in when they invade cells.

Once these techniques were perfected, the scope for introducing genes into plants became almost limitless. Today, soya beans, cereals and many other crops have been made resistant to insects, fungi and herbicides.

In the latter case, herbicides can be sprayed on the crop to kill weeds without harming the crop. The genes which are inserted into plants occur naturally in various types of bacteria.

www

Greenpeace – genetic engineering
http://www.greenpeace.org

World Health Organisation
http://www.who.int

The Why Files
http://whyfiles.org/o62ag_gene_
eng/index.html
http://whyfiles.org/shorties/
crop.weed.html

Did you know?

The life-threatening liver disease, hepatitis B, could soon be treated using genetically-engineered bananas! Scientists have produced bananas which are able to make a protein which is the antigen to hepatitis B virus. When people eat the bananas, they produce antibodies which make them immune to hepatitis B. It could provide a very cheap method of protecting the populations of developing countries and could possibly be extended to the prevention of other viral diseases such as measles, yellow fever and polio.

Food technology is an important science today in our world where giant supermarkets have to store food in bulk. This is another area that is benefiting from genetic engineering. The genetically modified Flavr Savr tomato was one of the first fruits to demonstrate the wonders of genetic engineering to the public. The tomato has had a gene inserted which prevents the manufacture of an enzyme which normally causes tomatoes to soften when they ripen.

The modified tomatoes are less likely to be damaged when they are harvested and can remain longer on the plant to ripen naturally. They should therefore have a much better flavour besides having a longer shelf life.

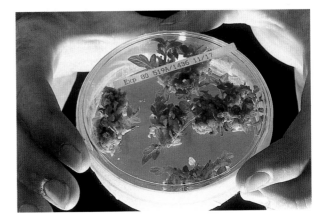

Figure 11.4 *The petri dish contains cultures of genetically-modified Flavr Savr tomato plants*

Did you know?

The world's first caffeine-free coffee plants were grown in Hawaii in 1998. Coffee from the plants does not need to be decaffeinated by expensive chemical means. The natural flavour is kept and the coffee can be used by the growing number of people who prefer it to be decaffeinated. A gene is inserted into the coffee plant to switch off the gene that normally controls the production of caffeine.

Figure 11.5 *Root nodules on the roots of field bean, a legume*

Plants of the future?

Very few organisms can use the nitrogen which is abundant in the atmosphere and convert it into essential proteins. If plants could use it, we would not have to add nitrates to the soil in the form of fertilisers. Genetic engineering could, in the future, take the place of fertilisers, so avoiding the high costs and environmental problems (see p. 217) associated with their use. As a rule, plants are adapted to keep microbes out of their tissues. **Legumes** are plants that produce pods like peas, beans and clover. They are exceptions to this rule (see Nitrogen cycle p. 248) because they welcome the invasion of their roots by a type of bacterium that can convert nitrogen from the atmosphere into a form which can be used by the plants to make protein. The bacteria are called **nitrogen-fixing** and can live in swellings called **nodules** in the roots of legumes.

What if genetic engineers could alter cereal crops like rice, wheat or maize so that they would accept these nitrogen-fixing bacteria? If they could insert a gene into cereal crops to produce the chemical which attracts the bacteria into cells, it would be one of the greatest breakthroughs in the history of agriculture. Feeding the world without nitrate fertilisers would be possible.

Genetically-altered animals

In 1996, Rosie, a cow with a difference, was born. Her birth ensured the survival of thousands of premature babies born each year. Scientists genetically engineered Rosie to produce a human protein in her milk. This particular protein is essential for the survival of new born babies.

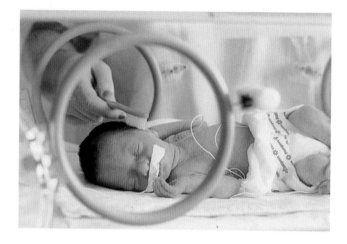

Figure 11.6 *This baby in an incubator could have its life saved through genetic engineering*

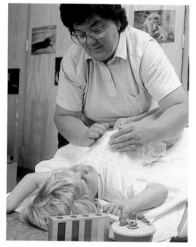

Figure 11.7 *A patient receiving therapy for cystic fibrosis*

In 1993, sheep were genetically modified to produce a valuable protein in their milk that contained a blood clotting factor. This factor is essential for people suffering from haemophilia (see p. 192). A protein needed to treat cystic fibrosis is also produced in the milk of genetically-altered sheep.

In all of these cases, the human genes which normally control the production of these proteins have been inserted into the cow or sheep cells and these cells now produce the useful proteins.

Did you know?

As a result of genetic engineering, 'super-salmon' are now farmed which have a very high growth rate. In doing this, however, the genes for the salmon's normal homing behaviour have been prevented from working. If these salmon escape into the natural wild population and breed, they could introduce mutated genes into the wild population and thus prevent them from finding their way home to lay eggs.

Figure 11.8 *Wild salmon could be affected by genes from farmed salmon*

IT Use the Internet to look up further examples of genetic engineering, genetic disease and genetic fingerprinting.

When things go wrong

Inheritance of abnormal genes can be seen in various forms of disorders in humans. Perhaps the best known example of a genetically-controlled blood defect is haemophilia. This is a condition in which the blood fails to clot, or clots very slowly. People with extreme cases of haemophilia can bleed to death from relatively minor injuries.

The chemistry of blood clotting is very complicated and involves over a dozen different enzyme-controlled reactions. If one or more of the enzymes is not made by the body, blood clotting is hindered or perhaps (in rare cases) prevented altogether.

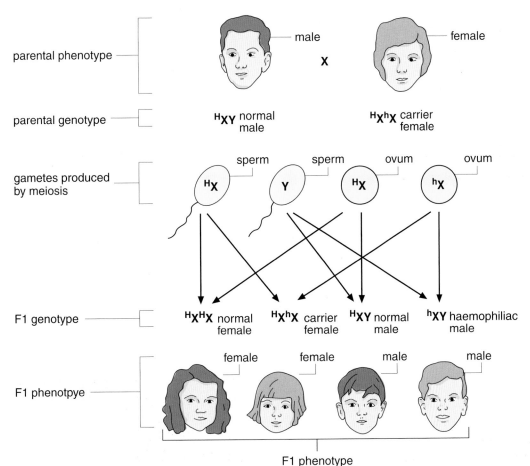

Figure 11.10 *Inheritance of haemophilia*

Men only

Haemophilia only appears in males (except in very rare circumstances), although the condition is inherited from the mother. This form of inheritance is called 'sex-linked' recessive, which means that the gene is carried on the X chromosome. Males have only one X, whereas a female has two X chromosomes. Thus in females, the condition is masked by the normal gene on the other X. Males also have one Y chromosome. Thus, if an affected male becomes a father, then all his daughters will be carriers and all his sons normal (they receive their X from the normal mother).

Did you know?

Haemophilia is a genetic defect with a royal history. The gene for the problem became so widely distributed in European royalty during the nineteenth and twentieth centuries that the course of history was affected – particularly in Spain and Russia. The gene for the condition probably first appeared as a mutation in Queen Victoria, since there is no record of haemophilia in her ancestry. Because of marriages among the royalty of Europe, the gene became distributed in a number of royal families.

Figure 11.9 shows the pedigree of the distribution of haemophilia in Queen Victoria's descendants. Note that the present royal family of the United Kingdom is free of the gene.

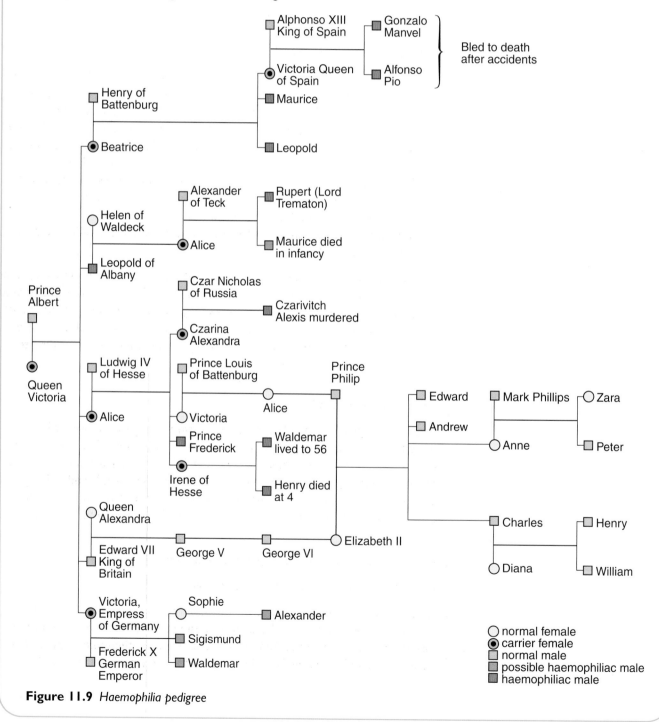

Figure 11.9 *Haemophilia pedigree*

Let h = gene for haemophilia and H = normal. Since the condition can only be carried on the X chromosome, an affected male must be X^hY.

Parents $\qquad\qquad X^hY = X^HX^H$

$$\downarrow$$

Children $\qquad\qquad X^hX^H\ X^hX^H\ X^HY\ X^HY$

X^hX^H is a carrier female, X^HY is a normal male.

If a carrier female becomes a mother, the chances are that half of her sons will be unaffected and half her daughters will be carriers:

$$X^hX^H \times X^HY$$

$$\downarrow$$

Children $\qquad\qquad X^hX^H\ X^hY\ X^HX^H\ X^HY$

The problem is that, in this situation, there is no perfect method of telling the carrier daughter from the normal daughter. Obviously, it is extremely difficult to give guidance on family planning to such women. The councillor can only say with confidence that daughters of an affected man will be carriers. The daughter of a haemophiliac female carrier cannot be identified as a carrier herself until she has given birth to a haemophiliac son. In approximately one-third of all patients, no history of the condition can be detected in the family ancestry. This may be due to the transmission through several generations of female carriers without an affected male being born. Furthermore, all record of a previously affected male could be lost to the memory of that family. Alternatively, the condition may have arisen by a gene mutation.

It is not possible to provide accurate statistics for all countries, but in Europe and in North America the incidence of haemophilia is approximately one per 8000 to 10 000 of the population. There have been major improvements in treatment of the condition and the chances of survival have undoubtedly improved in recent years. In addition, the number of recognised patients is increasing, leading to more meaningful counselling.

The common errors

Possibly the most common human genetic disorder is **cystic fibrosis**. It is an inherited condition which affects the pancreas and the bronchioles of the lungs. It results in several serious problems, including failure of the pancreas to function properly, intestinal obstruction and the inability of sweat glands and salivary glands to work properly. Cystic fibrosis is still one of the most common serious disorders of childhood, and is inherited as a recessive gene in the following way:

Let N = the gene for a normal pancreas and bronchioles.

Let n = the recessive gene for cystic fibrosis.

A person suffers from the disease only if he or she has two genes for cystic fibrosis, i.e. the genotype cc. A person with the genotype Cc is a carrier of the disorder but does not suffer from the disease. There is, therefore, a one in four chance of a child suffering from the complaint if two carriers have a child.

	Carrier man		Carrier woman	
Genotype	Nn	×	Nn	
Gametes	N + n		N + n	
Children	NN	Nn	Nn	nn

The condition occurs once in about 2000 births and it accounts for between 1 and 2% of admissions to children's hospitals. Many children die as a result of pneumonia, though some survive to adulthood.

A dominant problem

In 1872, an American doctor, Fraser Roberts, wrote the following observation in his note book: "The boy George Huntington, driving through a wooded lane in Long Island while accompanying his father on professional rounds suddenly saw two women, mother and daughter, both tall and very thin, both bowing, twisting and grimacing". Fifty years later, George Huntington made a major contribution to science by describing and studying the inherited disease, now known as **Huntington's disease**. This is an inherited disease characterised by involuntary muscular movement and mental deterioration. The age of onset is about 35 years. The majority of those affected can therefore produce a family before being aware of their own condition. It is transmitted by a dominant gene and both sexes can be affected equally. An estimate of its frequency is roughly five in 100 000 and affected people are heterozygous:

H = gene for Huntington's disease

h = normal gene

	Mother			Father
Genotype	Hh	×		hh
Gametes	H + h			h + h
Children	Hh	Hh	hh	hh

Theoretically, two parents could be affected and a homozygous child could be produced. The effect of this would probably be lethal. The gene is so rare that it is most unlikely to occur in the homozygous condition.

A gene disorder – sickle-cell anaemia

This is an often fatal condition which is quite common in West Africans. If there is a low level of oxygen in the blood, the red blood cells of a person suffering from this disorder collapse into a sickle shape and may form blockages in blood vessels. The disease is inherited as a single mutant recessive gene. If a child inherits the gene from both parents it only has a 20% chance of surviving into adulthood. The gene that controls the formation of haemoglobin is not formed properly, therefore the haemoglobin in the sickle-shaped cells is not very efficient at carrying oxygen.

As the condition is so severe, you might think that, over thousands of years, the mutant gene would have disappeared from human chromosomes because carriers would die before having children. Under certain circumstances, however, it is actually an *advantage* to have some sickle-shaped red blood cells. The reason being that the malarial parasite is less likely to attack people who are heterozygous for the mutant gene.

Did you know?

It is estimated that the mutant gene that causes cystic fibrosis has survived for more than 2500 generations in the human race. Does this suggest that in the heterozygous condition, it may be an advantage to some people?

www

Sickle cell anaemia
http://schoolscience.co.uk

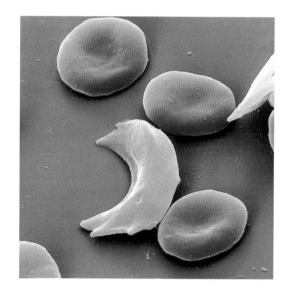

Figure 11.11 *A blood smear from a person with sickle-cell anaemia. Note the sickled shape of a red blood cell*

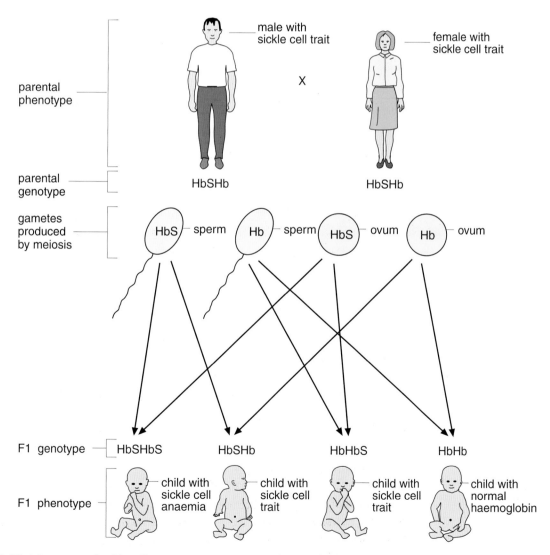

parental phenotype

male with sickle cell trait

female with sickle cell trait

X

parental genotype

HbSHb

HbSHb

gametes produced by meiosis

HbS — sperm   Hb — sperm   HbS — ovum   Hb — ovum

F1 genotype — HbSHbS   HbSHb   HbHbS   HbHb

F1 phenotype

child with sickle cell anaemia

child with sickle cell trait

child with sickle cell trait

child with normal haemoglobin

Figure 11.12 *Inheritance of sickle cell anaemia*

For example, let us assume that the gene for haemoglobin is Hb and that the gene for sickle-cell haemoglobin is HbS. A normal person will have the haemoglobin genotype HbHb. A person with the sickle-cell disorder will have the genotype HbSHbS and usually dies. A person with the genotype HbSHb, however, can survive and will be resistant to malaria. If two people, each with the genotype HbSHb have a child, then the predicted genotype of the child can be shown as follows:

Parents	HbSHb		×		HbSHb	
Gametes	HbS + Hb				HbS + Hb	
Children	HbSHbS	HbSHb		HbHbS	HbHb	

It can be seen that there is a one in four chance of the child dying with the sickle-cell disorder (HbSHbS), a one in two chance of the child being a carrier of the sickle-cell gene but probably surviving (HbSHb) and a one in four chance of the child being perfectly normal for the haemoglobin gene (HbHb).

An extra chromosome

Down's Syndrome is caused by the presence of an extra chromosome 21 in all body cells.

The extra chromosome results from failure of the chromosomes (pair 21) to separate properly at meiosis, probably during egg formation. The disorder results in mental retardation and some abnormal physical features such as an unusual heart structure, enlarged tongue and weak muscles. About one in 600 babies are born with Down's Syndrome, but this will vary according to the age of the mother. With mothers under 35, less than one baby in 1000 has the syndrome, but at 45 and over, the odds are one in 60.

www

Down's Syndrome Association
http://www.dsa-uk.com

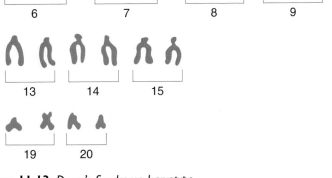

Figure 11.13 *Down's Syndrome karyotype*

Summary

1 Genetic engineering is revolutionising the ways in which scientists can mass produce proteins such as hormones which can save lives. Useful genes, responsible for the production of proteins, can be taken from one organism and put into another.

2 These organisms are usually bacteria because such microbes can multiply rapidly and produce vast quantities of useful proteins.

3 Gene technology is now an important science which is used in genetic fingerprinting and to alter plants and animals so that food production may be increased.

4 Occasionally, mutations lead to inheritable abnormalities in humans.

5 Such genetic disorders may be caused by altered genes or altered chromosomes.

6 Common errors in chromosomes can show as symptoms which often require medical treatment.

Homework Questions

1 Give an account of how genetic engineering can be of use in (a) medical technology and (b) agriculture.

2 Write an account of genetically-inherited disorders in humans.

3 Explain why it is so difficult to prevent the gene for Huntington's disease from being inherited.

4 Explain the chromosome abnormality responsible for Down's Syndrome.

5 The diagrams show stages in the evolution of the modern horse.

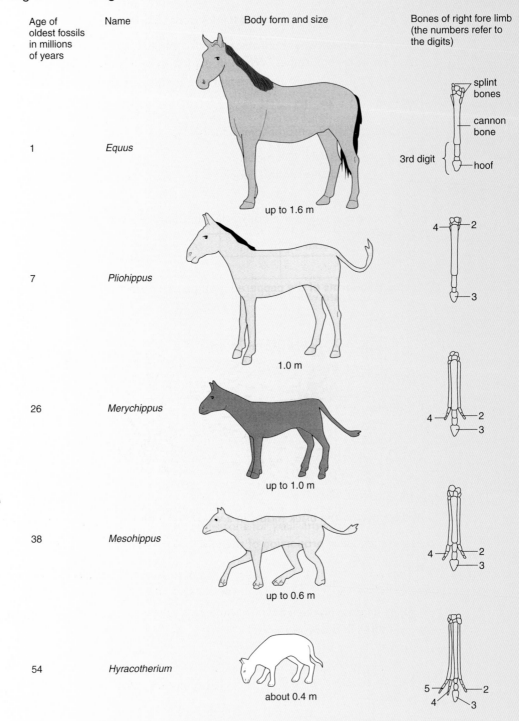

Age of oldest fossils in millions of years	Name	Body form and size
1	*Equus*	up to 1.6 m
7	*Pliohippus*	1.0 m
26	*Merychippus*	up to 1.0 m
38	*Mesohippus*	up to 0.6 m
54	*Hyracotherium*	about 0.4 m

Bones of right fore limb (the numbers refer to the digits)

splint bones
cannon bone
3rd digit
hoof

The body outlines are shown, together with some bones of the right forelimb. All examples shown are extinct, apart from the modern horse (*Equus*). *Hyracotherium* is the earliest example. It is thought to have lived near streams where it fed on leafy vegetation growing in the soft ground. Later forms of the horse became adapted to living in drier, firmer and more open grassland. They still fed on vegetation.

(a) The body size of the modern horse (*Equus*) is different from the size of its early ancestors. Explain how this change may be an advantage to the modern horse.

(2 marks)

(b) (i) Describe the changes that have taken place in the bones of the forelimb during the evolution of the modern horse.

(2 marks)

(ii) Suggest one advantage to *Hyracotherium* of having several digits touching the ground.

(1 mark)

(c) The process of evolution is believed to involve natural selection. Describe the process of natural selection.

(5 marks)

EDEXCEL

6 (a) The diagram below shows a stage in the replication of a short section of DNA:

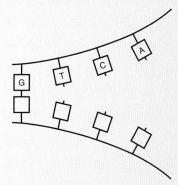

(i) Copy the diagram and complete the boxes by filling in the correct letters (A, G, C or T) for the four unlabelled bases.

(2 marks)

(ii) During which cell process does DNA replicate?

(1 mark)

(b) The DNA triplet codes for some amino acids are shown below.

TTT = lysine   CCC = glycine   GCC = alanine
TAC = methionine CAT = valine   CCG = proline
GTA = histidine   AAA = phenylalanine ATG = tyrosine

Part of a strand of DNA, with the 12 bases shown below, codes for a short sequence of amino acids.

T A C C C C C G A T G

(i) Using the triplet codes, start from the left hand end and write the sequence of amino acids which would be produced. The first one has been done for you.

T A C   C C C   C C G   A T G
 ↓   ↓   ↓   ↓
methionine

(1 mark)

(ii) Using the triplet codes, start from the right hand end and write the sequence of amino acids which would be produced. The first one has been done for you.

T A C   C C C   C C G   A T G
 ↓   ↓   ↓   ↓
histidine

(1 mark)

(iii) Sometimes children are born with a genetic defect in which a short sequence of bases on a DNA molecule has been reversed. As a result, the body cannot make a certain protein. Use the information in the diagrams to explain why this protein cannot be made as a result of this defect

(3 marks)

EDEXCEL

7 Insulin is a hormone which is used to control diabetes. Insulin can be extracted from the pancreas of pigs and cattle but genetic engineering allows bacteria to produce human insulin. The diagram outlines the first stages in the preparation of insulin from bacteria.

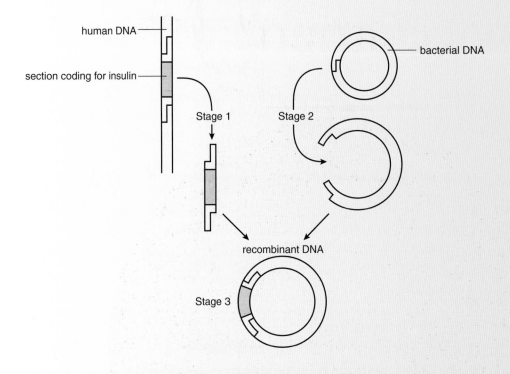

(a) Describe in detail what is happening between stage 1 and stage 3.   *(3 marks)*

(b) Describe briefly how these modified bacteria could be used to produce large amounts of insulin.
                                                                               (2 marks)

(c) Suggest one reason why insulin produced by genetic engineering is preferable to insulin from pigs and cattle.   *(1 mark)*

(d) State the function of insulin in the body.   *(1 mark)*

(e) Explain why insulin-dependent diabetics should be aware of the amount of carbohydrate in their diets.
                                                                               (2 marks)

                                                                               WJEC

Organisms and their environment

This brown ant is infected with a parasitic fluke. The parasite causes cramp in the mouthparts of the ant, clamping it to the blade of grass for several hours. During this time the ant may be eaten by a grazing sheep or cow, inside which the parasite can continue the next stage of its life cycle.

12 Relationships

Learning objectives

By the end of this chapter you should be able to understand:

- why photosynthesis is important to all animals;

- the significance of food chains, food webs and food pyramids;

- that pyramids of energy are more useful in understanding energy flow than pyramids of numbers or pyramids of biomass;

- the extent of human impact on the environment including the effects of population growth and pollution of air, water and land;

- how food production can be managed to improve the efficiency of energy transfer;

- that the production of food crops may be kept at a high level by using fertilisers, controlling pests and diseases and using selective breeding;

- that management of the production of cheap, high quality food imposes a duty of care to damage natural ecosystems as little as possible and to treat domesticated animals humanely.

Relationship between organisms and with the environment

The branch of biology which concentrates on the relationships between organisms and their environment is **ecology**. This can be studied at different levels: at one end of the scale, the ecologist can study the interactions of a single organism and its environment; at the other extreme, the largest unit is the **biosphere**. This is the total of all living things on Earth and their environment. The environment of an organism includes not only its physical surroundings, but also other living organisms in its surroundings. Units smaller than the biosphere are:

- **Population**. A geographically localised group of individuals of the same species – for example, a penguin colony. See Figure 12.1.
- **Community**. A localised group of several populations of different species – a rocky shore, sandy shore or mud flat. See Figure 12.2.
- **Ecosystem**. A localised group of communities and their physical environment – a pond or river. See Figure 12.3.
- **Biome**. A collection of similar ecosystems in a particular region – a desert, prairie or tundra. See Figure 12.4.

Adaptations of organisms to their environment

We can divide the factors which affect the environment into **physical** and **biotic** (the influence that one organism has on the environment of another). Both groups of factors have resulted in the survival of those best suited to cope with them.

Figure 12.1 *A colony of penguins*

Figure 12.2 *A rocky shore*

Figure 12.3 *A pond*

Figure 12.4 *The tundra*

All organisms living today have become adapted in many specialised ways. Each particular biome has its own special animals and plants.

The arctic fox is closely related to the desert fox but they both show adaptations to aid their survival.

The large external ears of the desert fox help to radiate heat away, thus cooling the animal, while the very small ears of the arctic fox help it to retain as much heat as possible.

Figure 12.5 *A desert fox*

Figure 12.6 *An arctic fox*

Figure 12.7 *An arctic hare*

Figure 12.8 *A European hare*

The arctic hare has a white coat in winter whereas the European hare has a greyish brown coat. These colourings are designed to enable the hares to be camouflaged in their respective habitats.

The thickness of both body fat and insulating fur coat of arctic mammals are much greater than those of desert living types.

Plants too will show many adaptations to their environment. Survival in dry conditions depends on how efficient a plant is at retaining water and preventing water loss. Reduction of leaves to spines, succulent stems, thick cuticles and a lack of stomata are all methods used to conserve water. These adaptations are all visible in a cactus.

Physical and chemical factors

The physical and chemical factors which affect survival are given below.

Figure 12.9 *This cactus has adapted to be able to survive in desert conditions*

- *Light intensity*. Light is essential for photosynthesis and as a result, green plants can only grow where there is light.
- *Oxygen and carbon dioxide*. These are important because of their functions in respiration and photosynthesis. Only anaerobic organisms can survive without oxygen (see p. 21).
- *Temperature*. The enzymes which control living processes will only work in a narrow temperature range.
- *Minerals*. An adequate balanced supply is essential for all living things.
- *Water*. This is essential for all life because chemical reactions in cells take place in solution.

---

www

Explore these different ecosystems
http://www.pbs.org/edens/
http://arctic.fws.gov/habitat.html

Ecology
http://www.homeworkhelp.com

Biotic factors

All living organisms have some influence upon the environment of their neighbours. This influence may be small, consisting only of a limited competition for water and light, or it may be very great. For example, many animals play an important part in the environment of plants: animals may pollinate flowers, help to disperse fruits and seeds, carry disease or trample vegetation. Of all the animals, humans have had the greatest influence on the environment of other organisms. To illustrate this, consider what happens when a family moves into a house which has been unoccupied for a few years. Usually the garden is overgrown and neglected. Many grasses, herbs and young trees may be found on what was, perhaps, a vegetable patch. These plants support several animal species, among them insects, small mammals and birds. As the new occupants of the house clear all this 'rubbish' away, they destroy the environment of these organisms, which will gradually disappear from the garden. In doing this, the gardener becomes the biotic factor in the environment. If you scale this up to billions of people on a world-wide scale destroying millions of hectares of natural ecosystems, it becomes obvious that humans have perfected the art of destroying the environment.

Figure 12.10 *Humans are responsible for destroying vast areas of rainforest*

Life in communities

Life within a community can be summarised by one word – relationships. Three types of relationships are recognised:

1 **Competition** – this describes the relationship that many organisms have with one another. It may be between many members of the same species, or between members of different species.

2 **Dependence** – this type of relationship links many living organisms together, for example a parasitic tapeworm living inside the gut of a mammal (see Figure 2.16).

3 **Interdependence** – the cycling of materials through animals and plants illustrates this form of relationship. It is best illustrated by the study of feeding inter-relationships.

Figure 12.11 *These red deer stags are displaying competition within a species*

Figure 12.12 *Competition between different species*

Competition

A struggle is seen when too many mouths reach for too little food – for example when one plant slowly dies because its neighbour is taller and shades it from sunlight. The competition between organisms is of two types:

1 Between members of the same species

This arises because far more offspring are produced in each generation than can possibly survive. If a species can produce large numbers of offspring which vary slightly, there is a good chance that it will be able to adapt to natural changes in the environment. Secondly, if a species produces large numbers of offspring which are dispersed over a wide area, the chances of the next generation becoming successfully established are greatly improved. While it leads to competition, the formation of large numbers of offspring is, therefore, an advantage to the species. Some insects lay hundreds of eggs (see Figure 12.13).

The number of seeds produced by many plants is far greater than most of us would care to count.

Figure 12.13 *Some insects lay hundreds of eggs*

Figure 12.14 *A dandelion 'clock' dispersing its seeds*

Figure 12.15 *This chimpanzee is caring for its young*

Figure 12.16 *This leaf insect matches its background perfectly*

Wherever you look, you can find examples of this general rule of organisms producing very large numbers of offspring. The exception to the rule occurs in mammals (particularly humans) and birds. Here, more parental care is given and there is less competition between individuals compared with other groups (see Figure 12.15).

2 Between members of different species

There are many ways in which the members of one species can compete with those of another. There is some competition between an animal and its prey, for example between an owl and a field mouse or a thrush and an earthworm, as all are competing for survival. Animals are able to protect themselves in many ways against the threat of attack from another animal. Some fight back, some live in large groups, and others conceal themselves because their colouring matches the background (Figure 12.16).

Figure 12.17 *The trees and plants in this wood are competing for light, minerals and water*

A different sort of competition exists when several different species rely on the same source of food. This can be demonstrated by throwing a handful of bread crumbs outside on a frosty morning. Birds such as blue tits, sparrows, starlings, blackbirds and perhaps a robin, all jostle for position. The larger birds drive off the smaller ones who, through cunning and cheek, never seem to leave with less than their share.

Competition for a limited supply of food is also found in plants. It can be illustrated by the fate of an acorn when it falls to the ground and starts to grow. As it grows it has to compete with, and dominate, a succession of different plants at various stages of development. The forest floor may be closely covered by a variety of woodland grasses and herbs. The oak seedling must compete successfully with all these in turn as it grows through them. Having done this it may have to face competition from other young saplings, or from other plants such as bramble. When a full grown tree falls in the forest and opens up a gap in the canopy of leaves, it is a common sight to see 50 to 100 young saplings all reaching towards the light. Oak, ash, beech, sycamore and other species are commonly found competing with one another until one dominates the rest to replace the fallen tree. The competition, with many individuals pushing roots down towards the same source of water and minerals or stretching up towards the same patch of light, is severe. The plant that can outgrow its neighbour will have a valuable advantage.

Dependence

Some organisms appear to have found an easy way of life, letting larger organisms protect them and prepare their food. These are the uninvited guests called **parasites**. Their specialised behaviour does, however, bring them different problems. They have very complicated life cycles and thus an enormous number must be born if a few are to survive and carry on the species.

It appears that the parasitic way of life developed at a very early stage in the evolution of life on Earth. This relationship involves one living organism obtaining food and shelter on or inside another living organism called the **host**. All major groups of organisms have representatives that are parasites. Some are of world-wide importance because they cause many diseases. The malarial parasite, for example, is a single-celled animal which feeds on human blood and liver cells and kills over two million people a year.

Similar relationships have evolved in which both partners benefit from a relationship between two organisms of a different species. This is **symbiosis** and it is very well illustrated by a **lichen** – a permanent association between an alga and a fungus. The alga photosynthesises and gives some of the products to the fungus which in turn produces enzymes and digests the substrate on which it lives. The products of digestion are shared by the partners.

Interdependence

Animals depend on plants either directly or indirectly for food, as plants are able to make their own food by converting the energy from sunlight to chemical energy. Photosynthesis is a process in which carbon dioxide and water, in the presence of light and chlorophyll, are converted to the basic building blocks of energy-containing foods (see p.24). The energy from sunlight is changed to chemical energy in food. Photosynthesis occurs only in cells which contain the green pigment, chlorophyll. We can call these cells 'self-fuelling'. Only the self-fuelling cells, through photosynthesis, can make glucose. With very few

Ecological Interactions
http://www.hcs.ohio-state.edu/hcs300/ecology.htm

Food chains and webs
http://www.marietta.edu/~biol/102/ecosystem.html#

exceptions, all other organisms depend on these cells for energy. The dependence may be *direct*, as it is in herbivores or strict vegetarians (vegans), or it may be *indirect* when a person eats beef or drinks milk from a cow. In the end, all human life depends on photosynthesis.

To understand this dependence more fully, imagine that photosynthesis suddenly stopped. Suppose, for example, that the Earth were somehow cut off from sunlight. No glucose could be formed and green plants would soon die. Other organisms might survive for a time – carnivores could eat herbivores, fungi and bacteria could eat dead organisms – but eventually, food would run out and almost all life would end. What if the sun kept on shining, but all the green plants were somehow removed? The result would be the same. The remaining organisms would have light energy all around them but they could not use it. Eventually all would die.

In the living world, matter is recycled constantly. Simple molecules are organised into complex ones, and the complex substances are broken down to simple ones. This process has been repeated over millions of years, but it requires energy as its source. This energy comes from sunlight.

Food chains

Plants are always the first link in a food chain because they can change energy in sunlight into stored chemical energy. When plants are eaten by herbivores, some of the energy is passed to this next link in the food chain. When the herbivore is eaten by a carnivore, the process of energy transfer is repeated. In this way, energy passes from carnivores to scavengers and decomposers which feed on dead organisms. Not all the energy stored by a herbivore is stored by the carnivore that feeds on it. Much is used to fuel life processes such as movement, growth and reproduction. Some is also lost as heat during respiration. Only the left-over energy becomes stored.

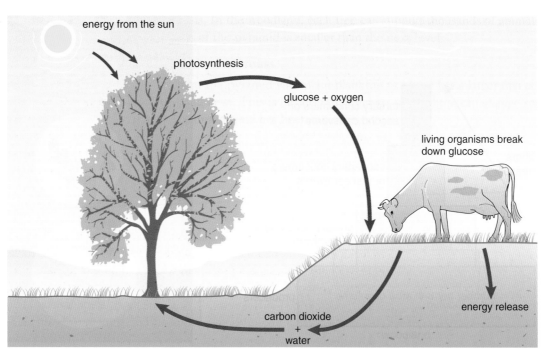

Figure 12.18 *Energy and living things*

Did you know?

The four warmest years world-wide have all been it the 1990s, with nine of the ten warmest occurring since 1980.

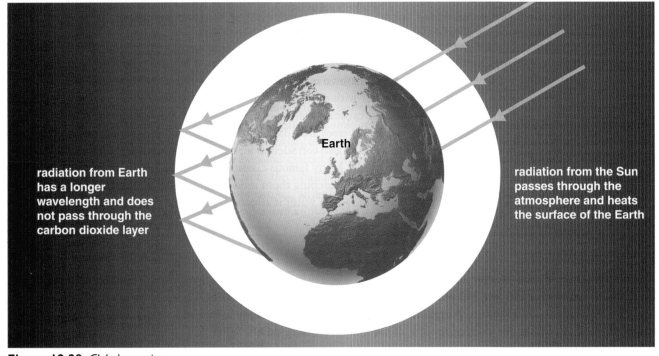

radiation from Earth has a longer wavelength and does not pass through the carbon dioxide layer

Earth

radiation from the Sun passes through the atmosphere and heats the surface of the Earth

Figure 12.28 *Global warming*

Important air pollutants which are not products of combustion are the **chlorofluorocarbons (CFCs)**. These are responsible for breaking down the **ozone layer** which surrounds the Earth. Ozone works by preventing cancer-inducing **ultraviolet rays** from the Sun from reaching harmful levels. CFCs were until recently used in refrigerators and aerosols. They are now substituted by harmless alternatives.

Did you know?

In 1985, the world produced a million tonnes of ozone-destroying CFCs. By 1995, despite the fact that the use of CFCs was banned by industrialised countries, world production was still 360 000 tonnes. This was because developing countries are allowed to continue producing them until 2010.

In 1997, the world's highest-flying spy plane, the Russian M-55, was used to monitor the destruction of the ozone layer.

It is impossible to entirely eliminate air pollution from industrial nations but it can be reduced to below danger point. Alternative sources of energy can help but no-one pretends that wind, solar or tidal power will be enough to satisfy the ever-growing energy needs of society. An increase in the use of nuclear energy would eliminate the problem of most of the polluting gases, however, the issue of nuclear waste disposal has not yet been solved (see p. 183). Pollution from traffic can be reduced by the use of **catalytic converters** which greatly decrease emissions of sulphur dioxide and oxides of nitrogen. Lead-free petrol can be used to help reduce lead pollution.

Coursework Activity

To investigate acid rain

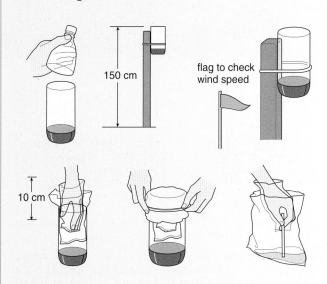

150 cm

flag to check wind speed

10 cm

Figure 12.29 *Procedure for collecting and testing acid rain*

1 Cut open a 2 litre plastic bottle as shown in the diagram above.

2 Fix the bottle to a post (at least 1.5 m long and 5 cm in diameter) with a strong elastic band.

3 Use polythene bags (18 × 30 cm) to collect rain and to act as 'gloves'.

4 Choose a site in the open, away from over-hanging trees or buildings. (Why?) Make sure the site is hidden from vandals.

5 At the same time every day (say 9 am) put a polythene bag into your collecting bottle. Use the polythene bag as a glove to stop you from touching the inside of the bag (Why is this important?). Fix the collecting bag to the bottle with an elastic band.

6 Check on the wind direction by using a flag and a compass.

7 At the end of school, test the pH with indicator paper as shown. Record the pH, wind direction, the volume of rain and the time you took the readings.

8 Repeat the readings over about 20 days.

When you evaluate the data, bear in mind the following:

● Are there any local features which may affect the acidity of rain (power stations, busy roads, industrial burning)?
● Do your results indicate long distance pollution from a known industrial area?
● Lichens may be used as indicators of pollution. Most do not live well in the presence of sulphur dioxide. Are there many types of lichens growing in your area?

Coursework Activities

What is the pH of the rain that falls on your school or your house?

Which direction does the acid rain come from? Are there any sources of acid rain in your area?

Water pollution

Many of our lakes and rivers are polluted. We have even managed to pollute the oceans. When the fore-runners of our cities were first set up, they were small settlements, often built near large rivers. One reason for this choice of location was waste disposal. Inhabitants poured untreated sewage and other refuse into the water which carried it to the sea.

It was not a serious problem at first, when settlements were small and far apart, as the pollutants were decomposed by natural processes.

Figure 12.30 *This outlet pipe is discharging sewage, polluting the water*

Today, the story is completely different. Natural decomposition cannot possibly deal with the volume of waste produced by inhabitants of modern towns and cities. Strict laws are now enforced concerning the use of waterways for sewage and other waste disposal. Although untreated sewage is often poured into the sea, there are now sewage works (see p. 265) to deal with the waste before it becomes the effluent suitable to be poured into rivers.

When allowed into waterways, sewage will encourage bacteria to thrive. The bacteria use all of the oxygen in the water, causing aerobic life to die. It may also contaminate water with pathogens and help to spread diseases such as typhoid and cholera (see p. 268). It is therefore dangerous to eat animals that come from polluted waters. Cases of typhoid, hepatitis and other infectious diseases are often traced back to mussels or other sea-life that filter water and capture the harmful bacteria.

The problem of oxygen depletion also occurs with over-use of fertilisers on crops. Fertilisers containing nitrate and phosphate will encourage the growth of aquatic plants when washed into waterways by the rain. The plants reproduce to such an extent that they pile up and prevent light getting to those at the bottom layers. These plants die and decompose, encouraging the growth of bacteria. These bacteria flourish with the excess of food available, depleting the amount of oxygen in the water, thus reducing the oxygen available to aquatic life.

Did you know?

In some waterways in Australia, blue-green algae multiply in the high summer temperatures and produce a poison which affects the livers of the livestock which drink the water.

Australian scientists have discovered a bacterium that feeds on the poisonous algae which could be used to control them without adding harmful chemicals to the environment.

The millions of gallons of detergents reaching drains daily are adding to water pollution problems. Many contain phosphates and so act as fertilisers, leading to similar problems as those caused by over-fertilising crops. Agriculture is also responsible for other forms of water pollution including those caused by pesticides. As before, these are washed into water by the rain and, though not usually in sufficient concentrations to harm humans, they become highly toxic as

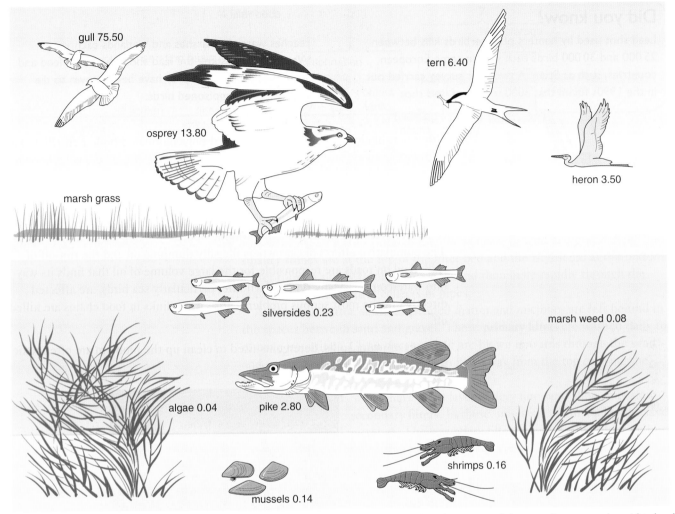

gull 75.50

osprey 13.80

tern 6.40

heron 3.50

marsh grass

silversides 0.23

marsh weed 0.08

algae 0.04   pike 2.80

shrimps 0.16

mussels 0.14

Figure 12.31 *The concentration of DDT in a food chain. The DDT becomes stored in the tissues of the organisms at each trophic level of the food chain, and can build up to very high levels in the top carnivores. The figures indicate parts per million of DDT*

they build up through food chains. Those animals at the top of the food chain will receive such a high concentration that they are poisoned.

Perhaps the most important long-term form of water pollution is that due to industrial wastes such as heavy metals like mercury, lead, zinc and cadmium. These are often bi-products of manufacturing processes in paper mills, steel works, refineries and car factories. The concentration of heavy metals increases through food chains until those feeders at the top are poisoned. The heavy metals interfere with the action of many vital enzymes in animals causing death.

IT Use the Internet to look up further examples of the ideas in this section. For example, look up keywords such as acid rain, air pollution, global warming and CFCs. Alternatively, visit the web sites of the environmental pressure groups and Government environmental agencies.

water). This chemical kills any remaining harmful microbes. Fluoride may also be added at this point to protect against dental decay.

6 The water is tested regularly throughout the day for impurities.

7 The water is pumped to high level storage reservoirs for distribution.

Did you know?

Recycled sewage water will be the most important source of extra water in many developed countries in the next decade. Re-used water may provide a fifth of total water supplies and one-third of the demand for irrigation.

Refuse and land pollution

Wherever humans go, they leave a trail of wastes. In fact, archaeology is dependent on the discovery of materials left behind by previous civilisations. There is litter in the streets, on beaches and along roadsides. Abandoned cars, refrigerators and other useless rubbish are left as eye sores in areas used as scrap yards. Litter is a costly and serious aspect of a waste problem that we have made for ourselves. We live in a society in which more and more disposable materials are made because we depend on a constant turnover of manufactured products to create jobs and wealth. We produce billions of tonnes of rubbish each year. It is estimated that over two kilograms of rubbish are produced per person per day in Britain. People often take rubbish disposal for granted until something happens to prevent it from being collected each week. Food scraps, newspapers, wood, lawn mowings, glass, cans, old appliances, tyres, furniture and many other items make up the contents of rubbish collection trucks. There are several ways in which these solid wastes are disposed of. Some are dumped at sea, several miles out in the ocean, some are burned in incinerators, most are used as land fill.

Any method is certain to pollute the environment to some extent, but land fill is probably the safest. Problems arise, however, when organic material decomposes, resulting in an accumulation of methane. On the occasions when this has reached the surface and ignited, there have been disastrous consequences – houses have been known to explode. Good use is made of much of the methane produced in this way by collecting it and using it as a fuel (see p. 266).

Figure 12.35 *A land fill site*

Did you know?

Bacteria which feed on sulphur are helping to reduce the mountains of used car tyres in the USA. Two-hundred million used tyres must be disposed of each year. The bacteria alter the rubber so that it can be recycled.

Figure 12.36 *Bacteria enable us to recycle these car tyres*

Recycling
http://www.alcan.co.uk

One solution to the problem of rubbish is to use it over again in the process of **recycling**. This reduces the production of waste materials that are a source of pollution and helps save our irreplaceable resources, such as minerals, and our replaceable resources, such as trees. It is possible to recycle paper, glass and certain metals. In the past, cost and the abundance of natural resources limited the development of recycling technology. In addition, an efficient method of separating reusable wastes from the remaining wastes was lacking. Today, with the reduction of natural resources, we are forced to consider recycling. However, recycling is still far from being totally accepted. Lack of public interest, recycling centres, funding for research, recycleable goods and government incentive have slowed the process. Attitudes are beginning to change.

Environmental groups have been active in setting up collection points. The public are becoming increasingly aware of the need to take bottles, cans and paper to be recycled. It is now up to industry to start recycling on a large scale and up to governments to propose legislation to help solve the problem.

Figure 12.37 *A recycling collection centre*

Intensive farming of animals

Domesticated animals can be improved in similar ways to the methods used for the increase of crop yields. Farmers select individuals which have desirable characteristics, for example, high meat and milk production in cattle, good egg production in chickens or good wool and meat production in sheep. When they cross two animals which show perhaps one of these desirable characters, they often see a combination of useful characters in the offspring. The enormous number of varieties of domesticated animals, bred for particular characteristics, have been produced by this type of selective breeding for thousands of years.

Today there are new technologies which speed up the process of selective breeding. They include:

- **Artificial insemination (AI)**. Sperm from male animals which show desirable characteristics is artificially introduced into the female's reproductive system to fertilise an egg. Many females can be inseminated in this way using the sperm of the same male.
- **In-vitro fertilisation (IVF)**. Eggs are extracted from a female and fertilised in a Petri dish using sperm obtained from a male. The fertilised eggs are then placed inside the uterus of the female.
- **Genetic engineering**. New DNA is introduced into young embryos produced by IVF. In this way sheep have been given human DNA to enable them to produce a clotting factor in their milk that helps haemophiliacs (see p. 191). Animals have also been given genes to produce more growth hormone so that milk production is increased.
- **Cloning**. This is an artificial way of producing twins. Young embryos have their cells separated and each cell then grows into an individual. Many genetically-identical clones can then be produced once they have been transferred into females.

Cloning – Dolly the Sheep
http://www.nmsi.ac.uk/science_museum_fr.htm

New Scientist magazine report on cloning
http://www.newscientist.com/nsplus/insight/clone/clone.html

Why Files
http://whyfiles.org/034clone/index.html

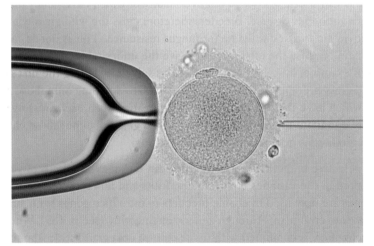

Figure 12.39 *A needle about to inject the DNA of a sperm into a human egg during the process of IVF*

Figure 12.40 *Chickens are often reared intensively in battery farms*

A duty of care for animal welfare

The figures for sales of animal products suggest that consumers want cheap, high quality meat, eggs and milk. Most people want animals to be kept well but many are unwilling to accept that good welfare costs money and that this extra cost will increase the price of the product. Farmers are under pressure to produce animal products cheaply and many people are questioning whether animal welfare is being put at risk. For example, hens in battery cages cannot dust bath or scratch the ground as they do when they are in farmyards. Are they suffering? Similarly, pigs confined to stalls with solid floors cannot root about in soil as they would in the wild. It has been suggested that when animals gnaw the confining bars, it is a sign of frustration or distress. However, proving in a court of law that animals suffer by being confined can be difficult.

Use the Internet to look up further examples of the ideas in this section. For example, look up key words such as genetic manipulation, animal welfare, water pollution, oil pollution and recycling. Alternatively, visit the web sites of the environmental pressure groups and Government environmental agencies.

You could also look at a CD-ROM encyclopaedia or 'Biosphere' about the environmental effects of human activities. (Available from AVP Software, School Hill Centre, Chepstow, Gwent, NP6 5PH.)

Did you know?

In Austria, scientists have developed an animal feed which could be used in place of antibiotics on factory-farmed livestock. Animals kept in confined conditions easily catch diseases caused by bacteria. Antibiotics are often given to control these diseases in pigs and chickens kept in batteries. This practice has been criticised because the bacteria could become resistant to the antibiotics and the resistant bacteria might be transferred to humans.

The Austrian scientists have developed a milk-based feed which has been successful in keeping factory-farmed livestock free from bacterial disease. The feed works by controlling the growth of disease-causing organisms in the digestive tract. It contains a culture of bacteria which occur naturally in the digestive tract of calves. The bacteria help digestion and control the reproduction of harmful bacteria. The cultures are grown in ordinary cows' milk and dried at a temperature which does not destroy the bacteria. The powder can then be fed to the animals.

Battery-farmed animals are reared in a carefully controlled environment so that balanced diets can be given, temperature is regulated, pests, predators and disease will be eliminated and the minimum legally agreed space to individuals is given. In this way, the yield of hens' eggs or pork will be kept at a high enough level to meet the demands of the public. The Farm Animal Welfare Council states that good animal management systems should provide Five Freedoms:

● from hunger and thirst – fresh water and a balanced diet;
● from discomfort – shelter and a resting area;
● from pain, injury or disease – prevention or rapid diagnosis of disease;
● to express normal behaviour – providing sufficient space and company of others of the same species;
● from fear and distress – treatment which avoids any suffering.

The Animal Health Act of 1981 safeguards the welfare of animals in markets and while being transported within Britain. The Slaughterhouse Act of 1974 specifies humane methods of slaughter.

Conservation

The public image

The word 'conservation' brings to mind different images to different people. Conservationists usually aim to protect species or whole ecosystems. Conservation has in the past been placed rather low on government's lists of official concerns. However, with the massive development of tourism throughout the world, it is now to the advantage of many countries to conserve their wildlife and habitats in order to attract wealthy tourists.

With the launch of the World Conservation Strategy (WCS) in 1980, it was hoped to improve the image of conservation. The strategy recognises the need for development, without which a large proportion of the world's population will remain poor. It argues that, for development to be long lasting, it must rely on established conservation principles.

Conservation and development are in fact dependent on each other. This is illustrated in underdeveloped countries where the dependence of communities on nature is direct and immediate. For the 500 million people who are malnourished, or the 1500 million whose only fuel is animal dung or crop waste, conservation is the only thing between them and misery or even death.

Unhappily, people on the margins of survival are compelled by their poverty to destroy the few resources available to them. They cut down trees for fuel, leaving the soil exposed to erosion by wind and rain. The 400 million tonnes of animal dung and crop waste that rural people burn each year are badly needed to fertilise and maintain soil structure. If the dung and crop waste was ploughed back into the soil, it would bind the soil together and help protect it from erosion.

The WCS defines conservation as, *the management of human use of the living systems of the planet so that it may yield the greatest lasting benefit to present generations, while maintaining its potential to meet the needs of future generations.* Thus conservation, like development, is for the people.

Development aims to achieve improvements through the use of the natural resources of the planet. Conservation aims to achieve these improvements by ensuring that such use can continue. The aim of the WCS is the blending of conservation and development to ensure that changes to our planet secure the survival and well being of all people.

Conserving species

We sometimes forget that however varied nature is, it is not inexhaustible, and some species cannot cope with the changes we make to their environments. The conservation of as many species as possible, together with their habitats, is a matter that should concern us all. It is crucial if the diversity of animals and plants (biodiversity) on the planet is to be maintained. Furthermore, the losses suffered over the last 200–300 years have been so great that just preserving the present situation is not enough. For many countries, that would simply mean isolating a few small remains of natural landscape from the process of industrialisation. There would be no room for the more sensitive species; the specialists of the living world such as the giant panda and the koala bear.

Figure 12.41 *Giant pandas live in bamboo forest, which is under threat*

Preserving habitats

Nature conservation means preserving nature in its original form so that all species have a suitable habitat in which to live. Once a species has become extinct through the destruction of its habitat, nothing can bring it back. Even gene technology has its limitations. DNA is biodegradable therefore the dream of bringing extinct dinosaurs back to life from fossilised DNA in *Jurassic Park*, will have to remain a dream. However, careful breeding programmes have saved some species which were on the brink of extinction. This has happened to the wild horse, a few specimens of which can still be seen – but only in zoos. Much as we might wish to see these and similar rare species in their natural surroundings, this is impossible, because their natural habitat has been destroyed.

There are many animals and birds which have only relatively recently come under pressure and have managed to survive to the present day in remote areas, away from human beings. Lynx, bear and wolf disappeared from most of Europe within historical times. They were exterminated because they were regarded as competitors. However, these animals still live in very remote areas of Europe and also in countries such as North America.

There are species that we have tried repeatedly to eliminate. For example, the malaria-carrying mosquito, the housefly and the locust. It is interesting to note that, with all of our advanced technology, we have not been able to *purposely* eradicate any species, apart from the smallpox virus.

Figure 12.42 *Grizzly Bears still live in remote parts of North America*

However, as a result of over hunting and habitat destruction, we have unwittingly speeded up the extinction of many species of animals and plants. The dodo, passenger pigeon, the Tasmanian wolf and Steller's sea cow, are some of the larger vertebrates that have been hunted to extinction. Many other lesser-known invertebrates and plant species are probably becoming extinct before they even become known to science.

We have an obligation to repair the damage already caused by our ancestors. For some species on the brink of extinction it may be possible to restore their natural habitats and re-introduce them after breeding in captivity. This has been attempted for some of the great apes, like the gorilla and orang-utan, and also for some birds like the Hawaiian Goose.

Trading in endangered species

Each month, special agents of the United States Fish and Wildlife Service seize tens of thousands of furs which are illegally smuggled into the USA. In Europe, the situation is similar. There are many horror stories of wild animals, such as chimpanzees, reptiles and parrots, found dead after being smuggled into Europe.

Figure 12.43 *Illegally imported animal products*

Rhinoceros horn, tiger skins, snake skins, ivory and other products from rare species are also smuggled across borders. In an attempt to reduce this shameful traffic, airports have display cases showing the types of things that are illegal to bring into the country. Governments are now taking action. Long prison sentences are given to those who are caught. The law enforcement relies on the Convention on International Trade In Endangered Species (CITIES). The convention became law as long ago as 1975 and now has 100 member countries, including most of the important exporters and importers of wild animals and plants. The aim of the convention is to establish worldwide controls over trade in endangered species and their products. It recognises that this sort of trade is one of the major threats to the survival of species. Almost 30 years after its introduction, there are some signs that governments are treating it with the seriousness that it deserves.

Safeguarding natural habitats

Most countries in Europe now have nature conservation laws and protected areas. There are a number of different categories of protected area, which differ greatly in the amount of human use which continues within them and the legislation in place to preserve them. The Greenland National Park is almost uninhabited and its environment is totally free of human influences, whereas the Camargue reserve in France is subject to many external influences. The International Union for Conservation of Nature (UCN) has produced a report reviewing the various types of habitat protection that exists throughout the world. These are:

Scientific reserves (Sites of Special Scientific Interest, SSSI)

These are free from any human interference or artificial influences. They are areas set aside exclusively for scientific research and often protect species or habitats which are important for their biological value. Their size is determined by the area which can be preserved intact. For example, the whole of Surtsey Island (which is the island formed after a volcanic eruption off the coast of Iceland in the 1960s) or much smaller areas of wetland in Britain.

National or state parks

These parks serve some of the same purposes as reserves, that is, conservation of the environment and its species. For example, the marine reserves around West Wales. Their regulations do not exclude the public or the provision of access routes. The parks are generally zones to meet the aims of strict conservation, recreation and education. Most national parks in the United States prohibit human activities, though this is not the case in European parks. For example, managed herds of reindeer are grazed in the protected parks of Sweden.

Beauty spots or sites of national interest

These sites, which are often spectacular, include gorges, canyons, waterfalls and caves. They are protected in the same way as historic monuments but are accessible to the public.

Managed nature reserves and sanctuaries

These reserves are designed to protect a species or a community. They include forestry, game and fishing reserves. In such cases, the species must be managed to ensure they are preserved. An example is the grassland ecosystem of Mont Ventoux in France. This area has particularly interesting plants which are maintained by sheep grazing; without the sheep, the environment would rapidly change.

Man-made landscapes and protected landscapes

Man-made environments can also provide valuable havens for wildlife, for example hedgerows around agricultural fields. However landscapes which have been shaped by agricultural activities are destined to disappear once their economic value ends. Protecting such environments involves maintaining or reviving human activity. The regional national parks of Europe are good examples of this.

Summary

1 Almost all forms of life depend on photosynthesis which only occurs in green plants.

2 Through photosynthesis, carbon dioxide and water are organised into organic compounds such as glucose, the basic fuel for all cells.

3 Light energy is necessary for photosynthesis. It is converted to chemical energy which is stored in glucose.

4 Food chains begin with plants and represent the energy flow from one feeding level to the next.

5 Feeding relationships can be shown in the form of pyramids which demonstrate the rule that biomass decreases from the base of the pyramid to the apex because of the energy loss between feeding levels.

6 A stable population density depends on a balance between birth rate and death rate. Present trends in human populations suggest that future generations will have difficulty in providing enough food for themselves.

7 The large numbers of people living in limited space, with the consequences of industrial demands, cause pollution problems.

8 Air is polluted with many harmful gases, mainly from industrial combustion and traffic.

9 Water is polluted by chemicals including fertilisers, detergents, oil and those produced as by-products of industry.

10 Land is being used and polluted by the disposal of both biodegradable and non-biodegradable wastes.

11 We are now making a conscious effort to conserve wildlife and their habitats.

Homework Questions

1 Explain why photosynthesis is essential to almost all forms of life.

2 Define photosynthesis using a word equation and chemical formulae.

3 Starting with the food producers, name and define the various types of organisms in a food chain with five links, ending with humans.

4 Explain what you would need to know to convert a food chain into a pyramid of biomass.

5 List four types of water pollution and suggest the steps that would be necessary to solve the problem.

6 Explain how the decomposition of sewage in water kills aquatic life.

7 List four toxic gases associated with air pollution.

8 Explain how recycling can help solve the problem of waste disposal.

In-Depth Questions

❶ Give an account of the conditions that affect photosynthesis.

❷ Make a diagram of a food web that exists in your local area.

❸ Discuss the statement 'Air pollution is a necessary evil'.

❹ Explain how overproduction leads to mineral depletion.

❺ What will be the possible consequences to a wide variety of other organisms of increased industrialisation.

13 Healthy Living

Learning objectives

By the end of this chapter you should be able to understand:

- the importance of exercise and fitness to the individual;
- the need for diet and weight control;
- the use and abuse of drugs including antibiotics;
- personal and social implications of drug addiction.

Good health

Health is not only the absence of illness. It is a positive and enjoyable feeling of well-being as a result of an effort to maintain an all-round state of mental and physical fitness. Although there is no need to be as fit as an Olympic athlete, you should be fit enough to be able to live the lifestyle that you want. Our lifestyles are probably less strenuous than they were 100 years ago, but we all have to exert ourselves from time to time, whether it is running for a bus or dancing all night. If we can do these things without collapsing, it is obviously to our advantage. Taking regular exercise has several benefits:

- your fitness will increase
- it reduces the chances of obesity
- it is fun as long as you exercise in ways that suit your life and that give you pleasure
- it will help you feel better and more self-confident.

Biologically speaking, fitness helps your body to function. For example, sustained regular exercise improves blood circulation to your muscles, increases the stroke volume of your heart, reduces your rate of heart beat and makes your breathing system more efficient. Combined with a healthy balanced diet and a non-smoking life-style, exercise is certain to be beneficial to you.

Healthy eating

We need to eat a varied and balanced diet to maintain health and avoid malnutrition or starvation. The difference between these terms is that malnutrition means the lack of a balanced diet while starvation means not having enough food to provide the energy that the body requires. You can be overweight and still suffer from malnutrition.

Everybody requires slightly different amounts of each type of nutrient. Guidelines have been set up by Government medical and nutritional experts relating to the amounts of different nutrients which most of us require. These are now called **Dietary Reference Values** and are similar to Recommended Daily Amounts (RDAs) which are part of the labelling of many foods and drinks. The easiest way to eat a healthy diet is to ensure that we eat a variety of foods each day.

For example, a balanced diet could be made up of foods shown in Table 14.1.

Table 14.1

Food group	Typical food
Starchy (carbohydrate)	bread, pasta, rice, cereals, potatoes, yams, millet
Dairy products (mainly fat, protein, vitamins and minerals)	milk, cheese, yoghurt
Meat and meat alternatives (mainly protein)	meat and meat products, poultry, eggs, beans, lentils, nuts, soya, mycoprotein
Fruit and vegetables (vitamins and minerals)	leafy, root and salad vegetables, pears, bananas, oranges, apples

Other foods like cakes, sweets, biscuits, butter and margarine can be eaten as part of a well balanced diet, but should not form the main part of your diet. Starchy foods will make you fat if you eat more than you need, but not as easily as fatty foods. Starchy foods contain only half the energy of fatty foods and are much more bulky. **Obesity** occurs when we take in more **calories** (energy) than we use up. Any diet which is high in fat and sugar but low in dietary fibre may cause such conditions as bowel cancer, heart disease and strokes. For example, too much **cholesterol**, a fatty substance found in meat, can lead to a heart attack. When there is too much in the blood, it becomes deposited on the walls of arteries, making the central space narrower.

The coronary arteries have an enormous blood supply, so deposits often occur here. A deposit may break off and pass down the artery until it jams in a smaller artery, blocking it completely. The heart muscle is then deprived of oxygen, its cells die and the heart stops beating.

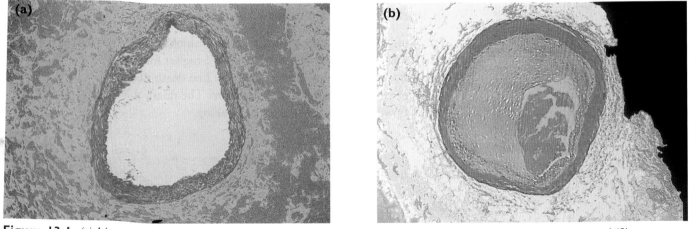

Figure 13.1 *(a) A healthy coronary artery. (b) A coronary artery which has become blocked by a diet high in cholesterol (fibrous blockage is coloured orange)*

Self-inflicted problems: tobacco, alcohol and other drugs

A **drug** is any substance which alters your physical or physiological state. The problems resulting from the use of them are not new. They have always caused social and health problems and can all prove harmful when improperly used. The facts about some common drugs are given here and will form a basis for decisions concerning their use.

Alcohol in the body

Alcoholic drinks contain **ethanol** which is a poison. It is made by the action of yeast on sugars and it can be absorbed into your blood system directly through the stomach lining without being altered by digestive enzymes. Within two minutes of reaching your stomach, it starts to enter your bloodstream. It is carried to your tissues and is rapidly absorbed by the cells. In the cells, most of the ethanol is oxidised very quickly, releasing a lot of heat which raises your blood temperature. The temperature-regulation centre of the brain is consequently stimulated and responds by increasing the circulation to the skin. Excess heat is radiated away by the increased circulation which gives a superficial rosy glow to your appearance. The rush of blood to the skin is at the expense of the blood supply to the internal organs, which themselves are deprived of an adequate supply of blood and heat.

Effects of ethanol on body organs

Only part of the consumed ethanol is oxidised. Some is released into the lungs as vapour causing the alcoholic breath odour, some goes to the skin and leaves in sweat and some goes to the kidneys and leaves in urine. All body organs absorb ethanol and, consequently, are affected by its presence to some extent. The oxidation of ethanol in cells produces water and this is excreted by the skin to control the body temperature. Tissues become dehydrated and urea is concentrated in the kidneys to such an extent that it can lead to permanent kidney damage. Excessive drinking of ethanol can also affect the stomach. It causes an increase in stomach secretions which can lead to **gastritis**, a painful swelling of the stomach lining.

The effects of ethanol on nerves

Ethanol is a **depressant** because it has an anaesthetic or numbing effect on the nervous system. Some people, however, mistake it for a stimulant because the numbing effect on the nerves makes some people less inhibited and less concerned about their behaviour.

The cortex of the brain shows the first effects of ethanol. Loss of judgement, will-power and self-control are the first signs of drunkenness. When ethanol reaches the vision and speech areas of the brain, blurred vision and slurred speech result. Muscle co-ordination is affected when ethanol reaches the cerebellum (see p. 100) and this becomes apparent as dizziness and the inability to walk properly. The final stage of drunkenness is unconsciousness which can become life-threatening because of the possibility of choking on vomit or even dying because of a severely depressed heart rate.

Alcoholism – the disease

People who suffer from **alcoholism** depend on ethanol continually. It may start with occasional social drinking but may lead to a form of escapism with people drinking to avoid stressful situations experienced because of a multitude of reasons. About one in 10 alcoholics reaches a stage of **alcohol psychosis**. This is a form of mental illness requiring professional treatment and hospitalisation. Symptoms include confusion to the extent that even members of the patient's family are not recognised. Terrifying hallucinations occur involving delirium tremens, or DTs, in which uncontrollable trembling takes place.

The physiological causes may include shortage of the vitamin B complex. Indeed, vitamin deficiency diseases are common among alcoholics because they often eat very little during periods of heavy drinking. As a result, the liver releases its food stores and swells as the carbohydrates are replaced by fats. Over a long period, a serious liver disorder called **cirrhosis** can result. Here, the fatty liver shrinks and hardens as the fats are used.

Drinking and driving – the facts

Recent controlled experiments have thoroughly tested the relationship between drinking and driving. A sample of experienced motorists were given a driving test similar to the one needed to gain a driving licence. All passed the test. The same motorists were given measured amounts of ethanol, but not enough for them to show any signs of drunkenness. All but one passed a breathaliser test. They were then given the same driving test again. All the drivers made a number of errors that could lead to accidents. Most had slower braking reaction times and were inaccurate in performance, but *all* the drivers thought they were doing well. Their judgement was found to be impaired after only one or two drinks and this was proved graphically by psychological tests.

It is, therefore, not surprising that ethanol is a factor in a large proportion of all fatal traffic accidents. In one-vehicle accidents, 70% of the drivers killed had been drinking. Fifty per cent of multi-vehicle accidents are drink-related.

The facts are that alcohol

- increases reaction time
- impairs vision and distance judgement
- decreases the time span of attention
- makes it harder to associate danger-signals with danger
- gives a false sense of security
- leads to aggressive driving.

Drugs and the body

The main reason why people become involved with drugs is that they make them feel good. Eventually, however, drugs can lead to brain, liver, kidney and lung damage. This problem is made worse by the fact that drugs can be addictive, so the user cannot stop taking them easily.

Dangers of some useful drugs – antibiotics

An **antibiotic** is a chemical made by a microbe that can kill bacteria. No antibiotic should be used unless prescribed by a doctor for two reasons:

1 They may produce harmful side-effects which may give rise to allergic reactions. In some cases the reaction is strong enough to be fatal. Certain antibiotics destroy helpful bacteria living in the intestine. Other bacteria may then grow in the intestine and cause diarrhoea or other disorders.

2 Like all organisms, bacteria show variation (see p. 164). Some have varieties that allow them to resist the effects of an antibiotic and these will survive repeated use of an antibiotic. They reproduce rapidly so that a new strain may evolve in which all members are resistant to the antibiotic.

Drugs – the facts

Table 14.2

Examples	Legal status	Damaging effects
Alcohol	May be bought from 18+ years, drunk at home from 5+ years. A licence is needed to sell it	Addictive. Slows down nervous actions (sedative effect). Can cause liver, brain and kidney damage. Can cause cardio-vascular problems
Barbiturates (downers, barbs)	Available on prescription only	Drowsiness (sedative effect). Psychological dependence
Tranquillisers (tranx, sleeping pills)	Available on prescription only	Drowsiness (sedative effect). Psychological dependence
Solvents, glue, lighter fuel	Illegal as a drug of abuse	Dizziness, loss of co-ordination, blurred vision, nausea. Permanent damage to the brain, liver, kidneys
Cannabis (pot, dope, ganga, hash, marijuana)	Illegal	Impaired judgement, lung disease through smoking. Psychological dependence. Hallucinations
Amphetamines (uppers, speed, whizz)	Available on prescription only. Illegal to sell	Impairment of judgement and vision. Hallucinations (stimulant effect)
Tobacco	Legal from 16+ years	Addiction. Lung cancer. Cardio-vascular diseases. Bronchitis, emphysema
Cocaine (coke, snow)	Illegal	Addiction (stimulant effect). Nervous anxiety
Cocaine freebase (crack)	Illegal	Aggression. Feelings of fear
Caffeine (coffee, tea, chocolate, soft drinks)	Legal	Stimulant
LSD (acid)	Illegal	Hallucinations. Increased blood pressure. Trembling. Nausea. Brain damage because of damage to nerve cells.
Hallucinogenic amphetamines (ecstasy, E)	Illegal	Hallucinations. Damage to nervous system
Heroin (derivative of opium)	Available on prescription only. Illegal to sell	Addiction. Permanent damage to nervous system

IT Use the Internet to look up keywords such as health education, drugs, alcohol and smoking. Alternatively, visit the web sites of the health education agencies. You might also look at a CD-ROM encyclopaedia or a CD-ROM about health or drugs.

Summary

1 Attention to a well-balanced diet and regular exercise prevent obesity and the health problems related to it.

2 Tobacco poses serious health problems by contributing to many diseases.

3 Ethanol (alcohol) is a depressant and, used excessively, leads to the health and social problems of addiction and alcoholism.

4 Misuse of drugs is harmful and may cause death to the user.

5 Drug addiction can be psychological, physical or both.

6 Many drugs are illegal to use or sell.

7 Under some circumstances, the use of antibiotics can be dangerous.

Homework Questions

1 Describe the possible dangers of excess cholesterol in the diet.

2 State some of the findings concerning the death rate among smokers.

3 What are some short-term disadvantages of smoking?

4 Explain the progressive effects of ethanol on the nervous system.

5 Give examples of addictive drugs which are illegal to take and sell.

In-Depth Questions

1 Why is inhaling smoke from a cigarette injurious to your health?

2 Why is drinking alcoholic drinks on an empty stomach more dangerous than drinking after eating?

3 Why does the presence of ethanol in a person's body give the feeling of warmth?

4 Explain the possible relationship between drug addiction and juvenile delinquency.

14 Microbes and Biotechnology

Learning objectives

By the end of this chapter you should be able to understand:

- that certain bacteria are essential to life as we know it, for example those involved in the carbon and nitrogen cycles;

- that many microbes are used in biotechnology, including food and drink manufacture, industrial production of detergents, waste disposal and mining, sewage treatment, biogas production and antibiotic production;

- the industrial use of enzymes taken from microbes;

- that disease can be caused by some microbes through droplet infection, contaminated food and water and by carriers;

- how the body defends itself against disease, including immunity.

Microbes – the essential, the useful and the harmful

It is unfortunate that when most people hear of microbes and bacteria they immediately associate them with 'germs' and disease. In fact, the vast majority of bacteria have nothing whatsoever to do with disease. Most are completely harmless, indeed many are so helpful to us that life as we know it would be impossible without them. Only a relatively small number, called **pathogens**, cause disease. In fact, we are constantly being colonised by millions of bacteria no matter how hygienically we live.

Essential bacteria

Certain bacteria are essential for recycling materials in our environment. One group is responsible for decomposing dead things, breaking them down to chemicals which can be used by a second group to start the building up process all over again. Without these bacteria we would be suffocated by millions and millions of years' accumulation of dead organisms. This can be illustrated by two cycles which are essential to our lives.

The first of these is the **carbon–oxygen cycle**.

Two basic life processes are involved in the carbon–oxygen cycle – respiration and photosynthesis. Both animals and plants take in oxygen for respiration (see p. 19). During respiration, glucose containing carbon is oxidised, releasing carbon dioxide into the environment. If this process continued unchecked, we would eventually run out of oxygen and the atmosphere would continually build up carbon dioxide. Nature has, however, developed a neat recycling trick to keep the oxygen and carbon dioxide levels in the atmosphere relatively constant.

When plants photosynthesise they take in the carbon dioxide that would otherwise build up in the atmosphere and they give out oxygen as a waste

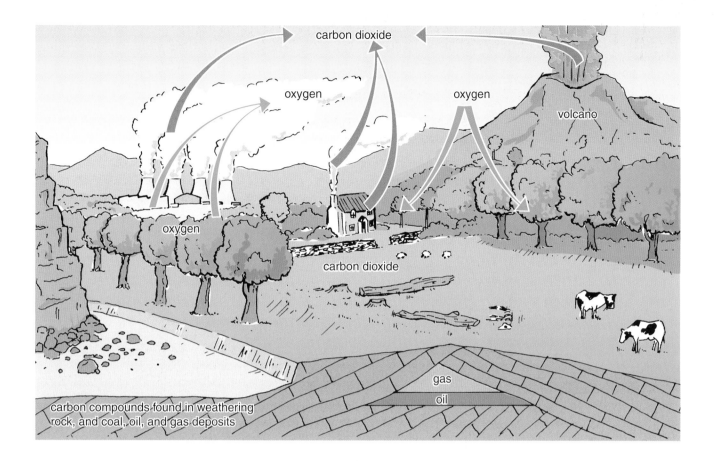

Figure 14.1 *The carbon cycle*

product. They do, however, make more than enough food for themselves. Plant-eating animals can take advantage of this and use the foods made in photosynthesis to make their own protoplasm. These herbivores are, in turn, eaten by carnivores. When an organism dies, the organic materials in it are broken down by essential putrefying bacteria. The carbon leaves the dead bodies during decay as carbon dioxide. The burning of fossil fuels also releases carbon dioxide into the atmosphere. The consequences of the interference by humans of this fine balance are discussed on pages 217–220.

A second cycle – the **nitrogen cycle** – also illustrates the point that bacteria are vital for our survival.

The nitrogen cycle involves plants, animals and several kinds of bacteria. The plants' roots absorb **nitrates** from the soil and use them in the manufacture of proteins. Why isn't all the nitrate in the world used up by plants? The following account should answer this question:

Herbivores obtain proteins by eating plants. Carnivores can obtain proteins by eating herbivores. Not all the protein ingested by these animals is used to build up their protoplasm. All the protein is digested to amino acids (see p. 39), but there are more of these building blocks than the animal needs for building its own body. The excess amino acids are converted into urea which is excreted in urine.

Putrefying bacteria break this waste material down, together with the dead remains of animals and plants. **Ammonia** is produced but because this is so reactive, it combines with chemicals in the soil to form ammonium compounds.

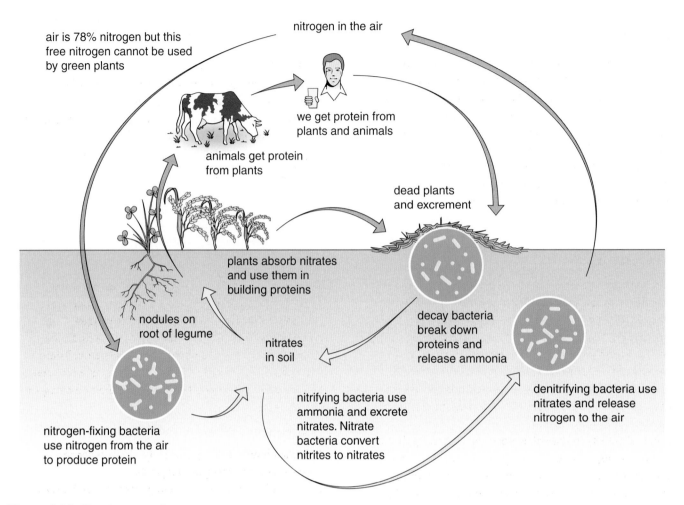

nitrogen in the air

air is 78% nitrogen but this free nitrogen cannot be used by green plants

we get protein from plants and animals

animals get protein from plants

dead plants and excrement

plants absorb nitrates and use them in building proteins

nodules on root of legume

decay bacteria break down proteins and release ammonia

nitrates in soil

nitrogen-fixing bacteria use nitrogen from the air to produce protein

nitrifying bacteria use ammonia and excrete nitrates. Nitrate bacteria convert nitrites to nitrates

denitrifying bacteria use nitrates and release nitrogen to the air

Figure 14.2 *The nitrogen cycle*

Nitrifying bacteria oxidise these compounds to form **nitrites** and then nitrates. The nitrates are absorbed by plants and the process begins all over again.

About 78% of the atmosphere is nitrogen but this cannot be used directly by plants. A type of bacteria which lives in the roots of **legumes** can, however, use atmospheric nitrogen and convert it into compounds which can be used by plants. Legumes are pod-bearing plants like peas, beans, clover and lupins. The bacteria get carbohydrates from the legumes and in return, supply them with a form of nitrogen that they can absorb. The process is called **nitrogen fixation**.

A fourth group of bacteria called **denitrifying bacteria** release nitrogen from nitrates in the soil. They carry out the process in anaerobic conditions (see p. 19) and are most abundant in tightly-packed water-logged soil. If the soil is well drained, loss of nitrate in this way is minimal.

IT

Look up the nitrogen cycle and carbon cycle in a CD-ROM encyclopaedia or in the 'Biosphere' (available from AVP Software).

Did you know?

German scientists have perfected a technique to rid drinking water of nitrates with the use of bacteria. Agriculture has led to rising levels of nitrates in ground water, and scientists believe that there may be a link between nitrates in drinking water and stomach cancer. High levels of nitrates can also cause anaemia in newborn infants. Scientists have now shown that a species of bacteria can successfully eliminate nitrates from water, converting them to harmless nitrogen.

Questions

1 Explain why agriculture has been responsible for an increase in nitrates in ground water.
2 Which of the following types of bacteria is responsible for the action described above:
(a) putrefying, (b) nitrifying, (c) denitrifying, (d) nitrogen-fixing?

Did you know?

A cocktail of microbes may soon provide an economic alternative to the burning of straw which often leads to air pollution. For hundreds of years, farmers have used fire to clear land and kill off crop diseases before the next sowing of seeds. The only real alternatives to burning are either to leave the straw to rot where it is, or to plough it into the soil. Both methods can lead to an increase in crop diseases. They also cause difficulties for seed drilling machines.

Bacterial activity in the soil is normally limited by the lack of a ready source of energy. Straw contains large quantities of cellulose which can be broken down by microbes to simple sugars. These can then be used by nitrogen-fixing bacteria and scientists have selected several types of microbes for this purpose. For example, there is a fungus which lives on other fungi that cause disease in root crops. This fungus can also break down cellulose.

There is a nitrogen-fixing bacterium which does the same. Another bacterium produces large amounts of gum to bind soil particles together. The oxygen consumption of this bacterium also helps provide the right conditions for the nitrogen-fixing bacteria. These microbes are all mixed together in a cocktail which can be sprayed on to straw. The straw can then be ploughed into the soil.

Questions

1 Explain how the spray acts as (a) a decomposer, (b) a fertiliser and (c) a fungicide.
2 Suggest how the spray would protect the soil against erosion.
3 What is meant by 'the right conditions for the nitrogen-fixing bacteria'?

Coursework Activities

RISK ASSESSMENT ESSENTIAL

To demonstrate how bacterial enzymes can cause decay

Some microbes produce an enzyme, urease, which breaks down urea in the soil to form ammonia and carbon dioxide. Ammonia is alkaline and can be detected using universal indicator paper.

1 Pour 20 cm^3 of urea (1 mole dm^3) into a specimen tube.

2 Stick half a paper clip in a cork to form a hook with which to suspend a strip of moist universal indicator paper.

3 Add 5 cm^3 1% urease to the urea in the specimen tube and place the cork with the suspended indicator paper in the tube as shown in Figure 14.3.

4 Set up a control tube with contents identical to those above but with 5 cm^3 boiled, cooled urease instead of the unboiled urease.

5 Leave both tubes for half an hour at room temperature.

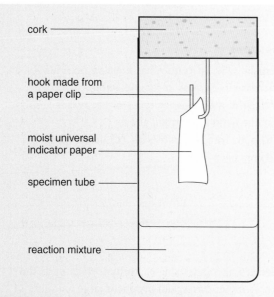

cork

hook made from
a paper clip

moist universal
indicator paper

specimen tube

reaction mixture

Figure 14.3 *Apparatus to demonstrate how urease breaks down urea*

6 Note any colour change in the indicator paper and compare these with the pH colour chart which accompanies the indicator paper.

Streaking plates

Materials needed are: a source of bacteria e.g. natural yoghurt, a sterile nutrient agar plate supplied by your teacher, a wire loop and a Bunsen burner.

This is really a dilution technique where a large population is separated into colonies.

1 Using a flame-sterilised loop, spread a loopful of culture onto the medium in zone A only.

2 Draw the loop across zone A and spread the bacteria over zones B and D as shown.

3 Rotate the Petri dish.

4 Flame the loop, dip it into the centre of the agar to cool then move the loop over the surface of the medium again (zone B) overlapping the end of zone A.

5 Repeat the procedure to produce zones C and D. Thus, beginning with a loopful containing millions of microbes, the streak D will consist of well spaced out organisms which will develop into isolated colonies.

6 Sellotape the lid on the Petri dish.

7 Turn the dish upside-down and incubate at 25°C for two days.

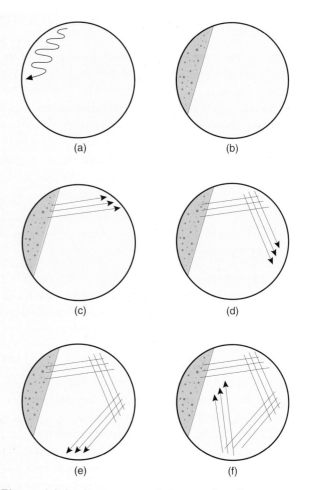

(a) (b) (c) (d) (e) (f)

Figure 14.4a *Apparatus needed to streak a plate*

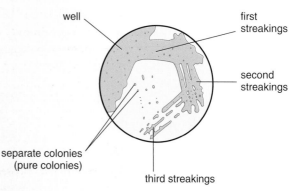

well

first streakings

second streakings

separate colonies
(pure colonies)

third streakings

Figure 14.4b *Appearance of a streaked plate after incubation*

To observe and culture nitrogen-fixing bacteria

1 Using a pea or bean plant, carefully wash the roots with nodules on them.

2 Dip them into Domestos disinfectant for 5 minutes.

3 Obtain two sterilised slides from your teacher.

4 Squash a nodule in a drop of water between the slides.

5 Make a very thin, stained smear of a loopful of the squash and crystal violet (0.5 g in 100 cm³ water).

6 Streak out a loopful of the remaining squash onto a glucose yeast extract agar and incubate at 25°C.

A raised, yellow, sticky colony of nitrogen-fixing bacteria (*Rhizobium*) will grow in 1–2 days.

Recipe for glucose yeast extract agar:

Peptone	10.0 g	Glucose	5.0 g
Marmite	10.0 g	Agar	15.0 g
K_2HPO_4 pH7 buffer	5.0 g	Distilled water	1.0 cm³

Coursework Activities

RISK ASSESSMENT ESSENTIAL

1 How do soil environmental factors affect decomposition?

2 Compare the microbial activity of different soil types (naturally-occurring or from a garden centre).

3 What are the best conditions for nodules to grow on the roots of peas or beans?

Consider the procedures in the activities suggested previously. You should be able to apply one or more of them to investigations where limiting factors such as temperature and pH will be important.

Consult your teacher about available materials and apparatus.

Refer to the Introduction to Coursework (see p. 1).

Exploited microbes

Microbes have been exploited by Mankind for thousands of years to make useful substances – a process that we now call **biotechnology**. Eight thousand years ago, the Babylonians fermented barley to make beer. Six thousand years ago yeast was used by the Egyptians to raise bread. Vinegar, yoghurt and cheese were also made by ancient civilisations. People knew that the processes worked, but did not know how. It wasn't until the early part of the 20th Century that the individual enzymes from microbes involved in fermentation were isolated and the various chemical products were identified in detail. The majority of enzymes used in biotechnology on a large scale come from microbes which include bacteria, fungi, and, sometimes, algae.

Microbial enzymes are used by biotechnologists in many processes today. The examples below will serve to illustrate how useful some microbes are.

- Biological washing powders
- Baking industry   – the breakdown of starch in flour by enzymes found in yeast
- Food technology   – the partial digestion of proteins in baby foods
                           – the changing of one form of sugar into a sweeter tasting form
                           – the partial digestion of milk sugar in pet foods e.g. 'cat milk'
                           – the production of soft-centred chocolates.
- Brewing industry   – the breakdown of starch and proteins to produce sugars and amino acids to improve alcohol production
- Textiles   – the coating of fibres to make them heavier and maintain twist

- Drug production — the production of the antiviral compound, interferon
- Mining — the recovery of valuable metals.

So why use microbes to produce enzymes?

1 There is a relatively high level of enzyme activity in microbes.

2 Other supplies of enzymes can be unreliable but microbes can be grown at any time of the year, almost anywhere and in any quantity.

3 A wide variety of microbes are available as a source of enzymes. There are over 1500 types of bacteria and 100 000 types of fungi that can be exploited.

4 Genetic engineering (see p. 185) allows even greater scope for efficient enzyme production through selective breeding and modification of existing types.

Useful bacteria in yoghurt production

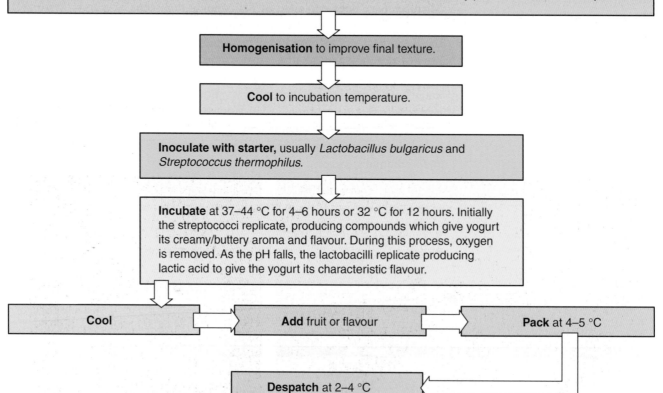

Figure 14.5 *Yoghurt production*

In the production of yoghurt, a starter culture of bacteria is added to milk at 30°C. The bacteria ferment the milk sugar (lactose), producing lactic acid which causes the protein in the milk to form a semi-solid product. The bacteria used are *Lactobacillus bulgaricus* and *Streptococcus thermophilis*. The stages are shown in the diagram on the previous page.

Milk is pasteurised (see p. 271) and homogenised (thoroughly mixed). A 2.5% starter culture of bacteria is added at 45°C and fermentation is allowed to continue for 4 hours at this temperature. During this time, lactose is changed to glucose, which is further changed to lactic acid. After cooling, the yoghurt will keep for up to 3 weeks. If fruit is added, however, the shelf-life is reduced.

Did you know?

Waste chicken bones are used to help make cheese. Scientists at a poultry processing firm needed to dispose of the unwanted bones cheaply, so they formed them into a substance which can hold the bacteria and enzymes needed to make certain foods.

The substance is called Biobone and was developed by the Canadian company, Bioprotein. In cheese-making, rennin is the enzyme needed to start the process that turns milk into cheese. It is poured into a vat of milk but is expensive and can only be used once. Because natural rennin is in short supply, most cheese is now made with rennilase, an enzyme made by microbes, which can give cheese an unpleasant flavour. If Biobone is placed in rennin, the rennin is held within the porous bone.

Milk is pumped through the Biobone to start the cheese-making process, leaving the rennin free to be used again. It is an example of how immobilised enzymes can be used in a continuous manufacturing process (see p. 259).

Questions

1 Suppose you own a cheese-processing factory and you want to use Biobone. What would you have to find out before using it as described?
2 Suggest why the demand of natural rennin exceeds supply.
3 Explain why chicken bones are better than mammal bones for Biobone manufacture.

Useful fungi – ethanol production

Yeast is a single-celled fungus. There are many different varieties of yeasts in nature. They grow wherever there is suitable food. For example, some types live on grapes and other fruits where they form a thin 'bloom' which you can rub off with your fingers.

Figure 14.6 *These grapes are showing a bloom*

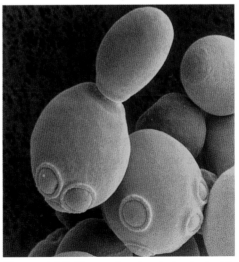

Figure 14.7 *Yeast cells reproducing by budding*

Coursework Activities

To demonstrate the fermentation of sugar by yeast

The apparatus should be set up as shown and the following steps taken to ensure the best conditions for fermentation:

1 10 g yeast and 10 g sugar are placed in the flask with 500 cm³ boiled, cooled water.

2 A further flask is set up to which boiled yeast should be added.

3 Both flasks should be kept at 30°C and the bubbles passing into the boiling tube should be counted per minute.

Commercially available laboratory fermenters are available which can monitor changes in oxygen, pH and temperature. They may also connect to a computer to display and examine changes in these factors.

Questions

1 Why was the sugar added?

2 Why were the flasks kept at 30°C?

3 What happened to the indicator in the boiling tube?

4 How did you show that yeast was respiring anaerobically?

To make bread rise

You are provided with three different mixtures of dough labelled A, B and C. These have been prepared as follows

A	B	C
100 g plain flour	100 g plain flour	100 g plain flour
5 g sugar	–	5 g sugar
7 g yeast	7 g yeast	–
120 cm³ water	120 cm³ water	120 cm³ water

1 Carefully pour each dough to a standard depth into measuring cylinders. Label these A, B and C. Make sure that you can read the graduation on each measuring cylinder.

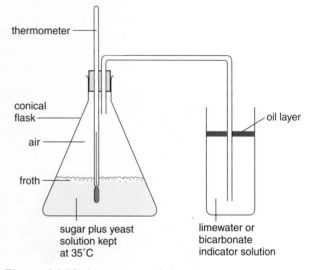

thermometer

conical flask

air

froth

oil layer

sugar plus yeast solution kept at 35°C

limewater or bicarbonate indicator solution

Figure 14.10 *Apparatus needed to demonstrate fermentation*

2 Record the exact amount of dough and take readings every five minutes. Use longer or shorter intervals if you think they are more suitable.

3 Plot a graph of increase in volume against time.

Questions

1 In what ways do doughs B and C differ from dough A?

2 What was the purpose of dough A?

3 What differences did you observe from your results?

4 What causes the dough to rise?

5 Why can't you taste ethanol in bread?

To make bread rise – an alternative procedure using a computer

1 Mix the ingredients as described above.

2 Add water to make the dough and place the mixture in a large syringe.

3 Connect a position sensor to a data logging system and set up a system as shown in the diagram.

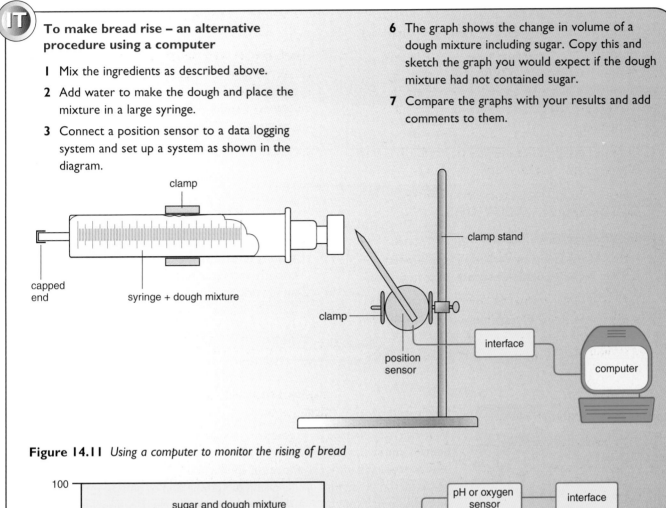

Figure 14.11 *Using a computer to monitor the rising of bread*

6 The graph shows the change in volume of a dough mixture including sugar. Copy this and sketch the graph you would expect if the dough mixture had not contained sugar.

7 Compare the graphs with your results and add comments to them.

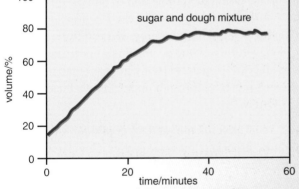

Figure 14.12 *Graph to show change in dough volume over time*

Notice that the barrel of the syringe needs to push the arm of the position sensor and this allows you to monitor the change in dough volume over time.

4 Start recording and leave this to record as long as necessary.

5 Repeat the experiment, this time adding sugar to the dough mixture.

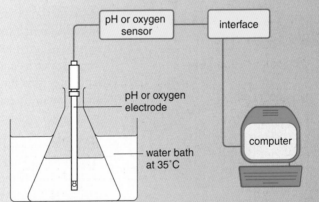

Figure 14.13 *Using a computer to monitor fermentation*

To monitor fermentation – an alternative procedure using a computer

Oxygen sensors can be used to monitor the uptake of oxygen during fermentation. Similarly, pH sensors can be used to monitor the change in acidity during yoghurt production.

1 To try either of these, place 200 cm³ of milk and 10 cm³ of yoghurt into a flask in a water bath at 35°C.

2 Connect the pH or oxygen electrode to its sensor and the sensor to the computer interface.

3 Start recording and continue to record for 10 hours.

4 Predict the shape of the graph that you would expect.

Does fermentation begin immediately after setting up the experiment? If not, suggest a reason why. Why won't fermentation continue indefinitely?

Coursework Activities

RISK ASSESSMENT ESSENTIAL

1 Which of the following carbohydrates is most suitable for fermentation: sucrose, lactose, glucose or starch?

2 Is fermentation using yeast more or less efficient in the presence of oxygen?

3 Investigate how good various types of flour can be at making bread rise. Apply the procedure described previously and refer to the Introduction to Coursework on page 1.

Figure 14.14 *This product is produced from mycoprotein*

Single-cell protein (SCP)

Microbes may be used as alternatives or supplements to the normal diet of humans and domesticated animals. These microbes are rich in protein and can be used to replace traditional sources of animal and plant protein. In 1964, research began on the possibility of increasing the production of protein by harnessing the metabolism of a fungus. *Fusarium graminearum* was the fungus and it proved to be capable of providing a food which is rich in both protein and fibre. When given wheat starch as a food, along with water and a suitable temperature in a fermenter, this fungus produces vast quantities of what has come to be known as **mycoprotein** (literally fungus-protein). It is sold under various brand names, the most popular of which is **Quorn**.

Mycoprotein is collected from the fermenter and, after pasteurisation, is processed into food products, especially pies and curries. Compared to lean steak it has the following composition:

| | Percentage weight without water | |
	Mycoprotein	Lean steak
Protein	44.3	68.2
Fat	13.8	30.2
Fibre	37.6	0.0

Although lean steak is higher in protein, it has the disadvantages of having a lot of fat and no fibre. Problems related to cholesterol intake and lack of fibre can be reduced by eating mycoprotein.

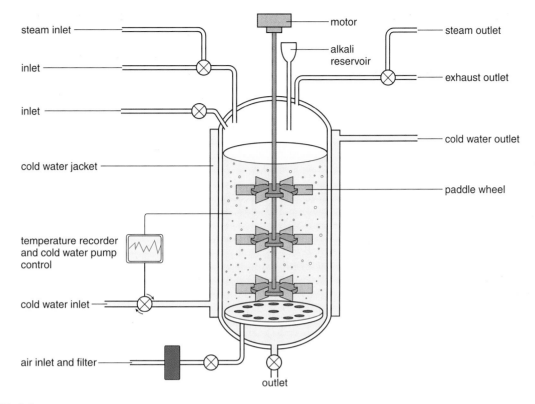

steam inlet

inlet

inlet

cold water jacket

temperature recorder
and cold water pump
control

cold water inlet

air inlet and filter

motor

alkali
reservoir

steam outlet

exhaust outlet

cold water outlet

paddle wheel

outlet

Figure 14.15 *A fermenter*

Enzymes and industry

The majority of enzymes used in industry have been taken from microbes. They can be used cheaply because they do not require high temperatures to work and so do not require the use of expensive fuels. The costs for industrial processes are, therefore, reduced considerably. The best known application of enzymes for domestic use is probably in biological washing powders and other detergents. Since the 1960s, the detergent industry has been the largest of all enzyme users. In the 1970s, consumers became painfully aware of allergies to some washing powders containing enzymes and so non-biological washing powders continue to have a market. The most widely-used enzymes in detergents are all made by bacteria or fungi. They are:

- alcalase   – works best at pH 7–10. Digests protein.
- esperase   – works best at pH 10–12. Digests protein.
- savinase   – works best at pH 10–12. Digests protein.
- termamyl   – works best at pH values up to 9.5 and at temperatures up to 90°C. Digests carbohydrates.
- lipases   – work best at pH 7–10. Digest fats.

Coursework Activity

To investigate the action of a biological washing powder

You will be given a piece of lamb's liver and four liquids at 40°C:

A Soap flakes

B Water

C Biological washing powder

D Trypsin (a protease) in an alkaline medium

1 Take four pieces of clean white cloth and stain them by rubbing with the liver. Wash hands thoroughly before continuing.

2 Using forceps, put one stained piece into the same volume of each of the four liquids.

3 Leave them to soak until one cloth has had its stain removed. Note which one this is.

Questions

1 Explain why biological washing powders are considered to be energy saving.

2 Why do biological washing powders not work at 100°C?

Coursework Activities

RISK ASSESSMENT ESSENTIAL

1 Use a fair test to compare how effective a biological washing powder is compared with a non-biological washing powder.

2 What is the best temperature for a biological washing powder to work?

3 Does the pH of the water affect the activity of biological washing powders? Apply the same method as previously described and refer to the Introduction to Coursework (see p. 1).

Waste disposal and mining with microbes

Biotechnology provides us with a way of disposing of waste products safely and can thus help solve the pollution problems that we create. Microbes have been used for many years to make sewage harmless (see p. 265). They can even help clear up the mess we make when oil is spilled over our beaches. If we provide them with nitrates and phosphates, they will multiply and will, in due course, break down and digest the oil. We can also use bacteria to break down metal-containing rocks called **ores**. The metal is dissolved in a liquid and then drained away by bioleaching. The metal can be extracted from the liquid and purified. Some bacteria and algae can concentrate metals inside themselves and in this way can remove poisonous heavy metals, such as zinc and cadmium, from contaminated soils.

Biotechnologists are now finding ways to recover and recycle valuable metals from places where this was once considered impossible. Deposits of high grade ores (those containing large amounts of metals) are decreasing at an alarming rate. Methods of mining low grade ores are often very expensive. Microbial mining may be the answer to this problem.

Did you know?

The bacterium *Thiobacillus ferro-oxidans* obtains all its nutrients from carbon dioxide from the air and mineral salts from the soil. It is now used on a large scale in copper mining because it oxidises insoluble copper ore to soluble copper sulphate. Sulphuric acid is a by-product, which helps maintain the acidic conditions which the bacteria like. *Thiobacillus* can be used on copper waste tips containing as little as 0.25% copper!

Low grade uranium ore (0.02% uranium) has been mined in this way in Canada, cutting costs by 75%. The rock face is hosed down to encourage the growth of microbes and the resulting solution is pumped out.

Research and development is taking place on other bacteria for the extraction of cobalt, nickel and vanadium.

Microbiologists think that there are dozens of species of bacteria capable of breaking down poisonous chemicals. Already they have found microbes to break down all the main classes of dangerous chemicals found in tips. Some of these bacteria need oxygen, so in 1974 a scientist designed a process to provide oxygen and salts of nitrogen and phosphorus to microbes in soil. This encourages them to break down oil-based pollutants, such as many solvents and pesticides.

Coursework Activity

To use enzymes from microbes to recover silver

Any exposed photographic film, for example X-ray film, has a layer of gelatine (a protein) containing silver grains stuck onto one side of a transparent cellulose base. Silver is expensive, so the photographic industry wants it back! We can recover some on a small scale using trypsin as the enzyme. What kind of molecule do you think it is capable of digesting? Eye protection should be worn during this investigation.

1. Using a syringe, add 2 cm³ of freshly made 1% enzyme solution to tubes A, B and C.

2. Using a clean syringe add 2 cm³ of boiled cooled enzyme solution to a tube labelled D. Wash hands thoroughly after contact with enzymes.

3. Using a clean syringe add 2 cm³ of distilled water to tubes A and D.

4. Using the same syringe add 2 cm³ of 0.1 M ethanoic acid to tube B.

5. Using a clean syringe add 2 cm³ of 0.1 M sodium hydroxide to tube C.

6. Place the tubes in a water bath at 30°C.

7. Place a strip of exposed film in each of the four tubes.

8. After 15 minutes remove one tube at a time and look carefully for silver salts falling off the strips.

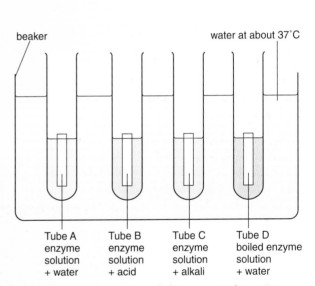

Figure 14.16 *Apparatus needed to recover silver using enzymes from microbes*

9. Record your observations in a table.

Look carefully at the sludge that might have collected in the bottom of one or more of the tubes. You may be able to see some grains of silver!

Questions

1. In which tubes did digestion take place?

2. What effect does boiling have on the enzyme?

3. Under what conditions did the enzyme work best?

4. Why were the tubes kept at 30°C?

Microbes and food technology

In the confectionery industry, sweet foods are produced from not-so-sweet foods with the use of enzymes extracted from microbes. Fructose sugar tastes much sweeter than either glucose or sucrose sugars. Consequently, less is needed in sweets and chocolates, so it makes good economical sense to use the sweeter type of sugar in smaller quantities. Enzymes are used to convert one form of sugar to another.

Coursework Activity

To make soft-centred chocolates

Have you ever wondered how it is possible to have chocolates with soft centres but hard outsides? How did they get the soft cream into the middle? This relies on the ability of an enzyme, **invertase** (extracted from yeast), to convert sucrose sugar into a mixture of glucose and fructose.

Enzyme

Sucrose   ⟶   Glucose + Fructose
(Glucose–Fructose)   (fructose can now be
(taste of fructose   tasted)
is masked)

You will need the following:

- A bowl of melted baking chocolate. (This may be supplied by your teacher or you might have to prepare it yourself by following the instructions on the packet. Eye protection should be worn when melting chocolate.)
- Six sugar cubes
- 1% invertase solution

1 Take three sugar cubes and treat them as shown in the diagram. Avoid direct contact with the invertase. Wash hands immediately if splashes touch skin.

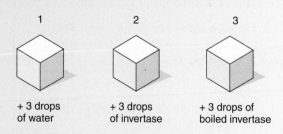

+ 3 drops   + 3 drops   + 3 drops of
of water   of invertase   boiled invertase

Figure 14.17 *How to prepare the sugar cubes*

2 Quickly dip each into the melted chocolate using forceps and place them on a clean Petri dish. (Make sure no holes are left in the chocolate covering where the forceps have been.)

3 Set up the apparatus shown below.

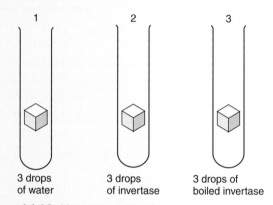

3 drops   3 drops   3 drops of
of water   of invertase   boiled invertase

Figure 14.18 *How to treat the three sugar cubes*

4 Leave the chocolates and the tubes for one week.

5 After one week, break open the chocolates and see what has happened. Describe what you see in the centre.

Questions

1 What has the enzyme done?

2 Since YOU MUST NEVER TASTE ANYTHING IN A LABORATORY, you cannot observe the sweetness in this way, but you can carry out a simple test to show what has happened. Carry out the Benedict's test (see p. 40) on the contents of tubes 2 and 3. Explain the results.

The large scale use of enzymes

Most enzymes used by industry have been taken from microbes. The enzymes work in batch systems, i.e. once the reaction is over, the products are extracted and the enzymes are disposed of safely. Such processes are wasteful, so to overcome this disposal problem, enzymes are now often recycled. The enzymes are immobilised in insoluble substances in such a way that the substrate (see p.16 for details of enzyme action) can still react with the enzyme. The enzyme can then be recovered at the end of the process. In industry these insoluble substances are fixed to permanent supports. The substrate is trickled over them and the products pass out at the other end. The enzyme stays in the system.

This is called a **continuous system** because there is no need to stop it to separate the enzyme and products. The advantages of the use of immobilised enzymes are:

- the enzyme can be re-used and so the cost of buying new enzymes is reduced
- the products do not have to be separated from the enzymes
- waste disposal of used enzymes is not necessary. Waste from factories does not, therefore, cause so much pollution
- they can be used in continuous systems. Normal soluble enzymes can only be used in batch systems
- industrial processes involving more than one enzyme can be set up and can run continuously.

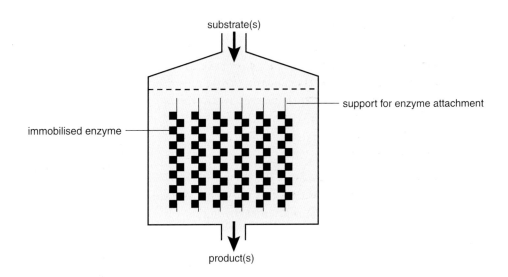

Figure 14.19 *The use of immobilised enzymes*

Did you know?

Some French champagne makers use immobilised enzymes in yeast. In the traditional way of making champagne, live yeast is added to bottled wine. Over a period of time, it ferments the sugar in the wine and releases bubbles of carbon dioxide. Each bottle is placed upside-down in special racks and must be turned by hand to ensure that all the yeast settles on the cork.

When this happens, the bottle's neck is frozen before it is turned upright again. Pressure from the gas expels the frozen plug of yeast and the bottle is re-corked. The new 'high tech.' process uses yeast in capsules of non-reactive gel. About 300 capsules are added to each bottle and are far easier to remove than free yeast cells. They quickly sink to the cork when the bottle is upside-down and allow the bottles to be stored in any position, thus saving space.

Antibiotics

As long ago as 1939, mass production of the antibiotic, **penicillin**, made by the fungus *Penicillium*, was attempted. Although it was Alexander Fleming who discovered the antibiotic in 1928, the pioneers in mass production were Howard Florey and Ernst Chain several years later.

In the production of penicillin, the starter culture of *Penicillium* is added to a liquid culture medium in a fermenter. During the first 24 hours, the cells multiply rapidly. When the sugar in the medium becomes less, the fungus produces penicillin. After seven days, the concentration of penicillin in the medium reaches its maximum. The medium is filtered and the penicillin is extracted from the filtrate.

Figure 14.20 *(a) Fleming, (b) Florey and (c) Chain*

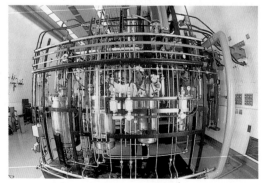

Figure 14.21 *A commercial fermentation unit used for mass production of such products as penicillin*

The problem that had to be solved in mass production was that the fungus uses up all its food and air as it grows, producing waste products that build up and harm it. Biotechnologists designed production units which bring new food and air to the fungus while removing its waste products. Giant fermenters with capacities of over 1000 gallons are used for this process today.

Microbes and waste disposal

About 400 litres of sewage are produced per person per day in the UK. Only about half a litre of this is the solid which could cause a health risk. The problem stems from the variety of bacteria which live in the solids. Many are harmless to humans but can still cause pollution (see p. 221). Because of this, untreated sewage can no longer be legally dumped into water sources in Britain. It must be treated at a sewage works so that the organic matter in the material leaving the works (effluent) is minimal.

Microbes are involved in three processes in sewage treatment:

- biological filtration
- activated sludge
- anaerobic digestion.

The helpful microbes responsible for the treatment are:

- bacteria which digest cellulose (fibre in sewage)
- fungi which break down industrial wastes in acid conditions and destroy nematode worms in the sewage
- algae to provide oxygen which helps to kill harmful bacteria which live without oxygen.

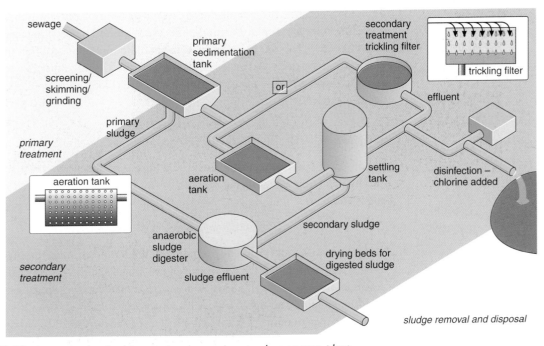

Figure 14.22 *The processes involved in treating sewage in a modern sewage plant*

Primary treatment

First the sewage is passed through wire screens. These collect the large objects which would otherwise damage the pumps. The sewage then flows through grit channels, where the relatively heavy grit and gravel settle to the bottom. The grit can be collected for use in industrial processes. Most of the remaining solids are organic and are pumped into large sedimentation tanks where they settle as sludge. Some coastal cities remove the sludge at this stage and pump the effluent into the sea. Chlorine is added to the effluent to kill harmful bacteria.

Secondary treatment

From the sedimentation tanks, the sewage passes into trickling tanks. These consist of beds of stones about 200 cm deep. On the stones is a slime of microbes. These are mainly bacteria which digest dead matter. The sewage trickles onto the stones from a pipe and the bacteria break down the organic matter. Any remaining solids settle out and are pumped to a humus tank where anaerobic digestion takes place by bacteria. The sludge is dried and used as fertiliser. The effluent is treated with chlorine and can now be discharged into streams.

The captivated sludge process

In the 1980s, a novel method of waste water treatment became popular. Older biotechnology made use of trickling filters or activated sludge methods (activated sludge is solid matter from sedimentation tanks mixed with bacteria and single-celled organisms). The mixture was aerated and passed to the trickling tanks. It was then able to kill anaerobic microbes. The newer captivated sludge process no longer needs settling tanks to separate the treated effluent from active sludge. Surplus activated sludge can be automatically taken out of the reactor as quickly as is necessary.

In older processes, the microbes are present as films of slime which can move freely in the waste water. Settling tanks are therefore needed to separate the films of microbes from the treated effluent. The microbes are then pumped back to the reactor vessel. In the more recent captivated sludge process, small foam pads are placed in the reactor vessel. These are colonised by microbes and never leave the reactor vessel.

Biogas – fuel from microbes

When bacteria are used in the anaerobic digestion of sewage, methane is produced. The name, **biogas**, is given to this because it is produced from rotting plant and animal material.

$$\text{Decaying organisms} \rightarrow \text{Methane} + \text{Energy}$$

In China and India, rotting vegetation and animal dung are fermented to produce biogas for use as a fuel for families. Indeed, many families in rural districts in the Far East have biogas generators attached to their houses. The gas produced is used for cooking and lighting on a relatively small scale. In Britain, refuse dumps produce large amounts of methane, but most of it is wasted. In certain cities, however, methane is collected and piped away from refuse dumps to be used as a fuel for hospitals and other large buildings.

Figure 14.23 *This plant generates electricity from the methane gas released by a waste dump*

Did you know?

In 1988, the Meriden rubbish tip near Coventry was taking over 3500 tonnes of domestic and industrial waste every day. It produced $2\,m^3$ of biogas per minute. When collected and purified, it was compressed with air and fed into a turbine to generate 3.5 megawatts of electricity. Throughout Britain there are well over 650 tips which are large enough to enable gas to be collected and used in this way. Theoretically, 5% of British households could be fuelled by biogas!

In Russia, bacteria from rivers, lakes and the sea bed are grown in salt water. The solution is then pumped into coal seams in coal mines and sprayed on the coal face. Six months later the miners start mining there. As microbes break down methane at the coal face, reducing the level by 50%, there is less danger for the miners and less need for expensive ventilation.

Harmful microbes

Those helpful and essential organisms described previously are probably not the most talked about microbes. The ones that get their names in newspapers and on TV and radio are usually the disease causing types – **pathogens**. They can be killers and, because many can spread from one person to another so easily, many are the cause of important diseases.

How do pathogens cause disease?

Like all living things, pathogens produce waste products. Unfortunately for the infected person, these act like poisons and can kill cells. If the microbes are able to establish themselves and thrive within us, they can overcome our natural defence mechanisms and so produce even more chemicals to poison our organ systems. At this stage we show symptoms of the disease. Our bodies do, however, have some natural defences against invasion by microbes:

- skin acts as a barrier
- tear glands produce an anti-bacterial chemical
- blood clotting provides a temporary barrier before a wound heals
- white blood cells ingest microbes
- the stomach produces hydrochloric acid which sterilises food
- antibodies and antitoxins are produced.

Once established on or in our bodies, many microbes can spread to other people. Some of the transfer methods used are given below:

- through the air
- by direct contact
- in body fluids such as blood and semen
- through food and water
- by carriers such as insects and other animals.

The culprits

Airborne diseases include **influenza** and **tuberculosis**. Influenza is caused by a virus which normally enters the body through the respiratory passages. It attacks the membranes which line these passages and, in doing so, will damage cells in such a way that they can be invaded by bacteria causing secondary infections. Conditions of overcrowding and poor ventilation help to spread the disease because the virus can spread in huge numbers in airborne droplets through sneezing and coughs. There are so many different strains of this virus evolving continuously that vaccination is of limited and temporary value.

Tuberculosis is caused by a bacterium. The bacteria enter the body through the respiratory passages and may reach many parts of the body via the bloodstream. Infection of the lungs is most common and the disease is more likely to develop if a person is living in overcrowded conditions and has a poor diet. Vaccination and mass X-ray programmes to detect the early stages have helped to prevent the spread of the disease. Antibiotics have also been successful in curing infected people. Recently, however, antibiotic-resistant strains of the tuberculosis bacterium have evolved and are proving very difficult to eliminate. An increase in social deprivation, even in developed countries, has also increased the incidence of tuberculosis in recent years, with homelessness and poor diet aggravating the situation.

Athlete's foot is spread by direct contact. It is caused by a fungus which lives off dead superficial skin cells, often between the toes. It is spread as **spores** which are produced by the fungus when it reproduces. The spores can reach the skin of people who share communal bathing facilities or showers. Shared towels can also spread the disease. Careful attention to foot hygiene can help to prevent its spread and it can be cured with creams and powders containing a mixture of fungicides and antibiotics.

Diseases caused by bacteria which are transmitted via food and water include cholera, salmonella and botulism. **Cholera** is spread through drinking water which has become contaminated with infected faeces. The bacteria infect the large intestine and cause severe diarrhoea. Fluid loss can be so great that the person may die of dehydration. Treatment involves antibiotics and the replacement of fluid with saline solution. Spread of the disease can be prevented by not contaminating water supplies with faeces and by having proper chlorination of drinking water. Immunity by vaccination against the disease usually only lasts for six months.

Salmonella bacteria cause certain types of food poisoning. Food may be contaminated with bacteria from an infected person's faeces. The bacteria infect the intestine and their toxins may produce a fever followed by diarrhoea and vomiting. Careful attention to hygiene in the preparation and storage of food helps to prevent the spread of food poisoning. Complete thawing of frozen food before cooking is also essential, with no re-freezing of food after it has thawed.

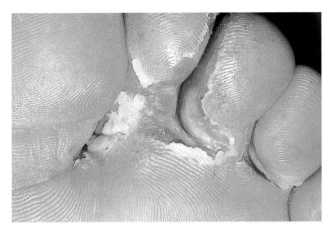

Figure 14.24 *Athlete's foot*

Figure 14.25 *A water supply from a developing country*

Canned food that has not been properly sterilised is an ideal home for a bacterium which causes **botulism** and produces one of the most deadly poisons known. Less than a millionth of a gram of this poison will kill you. Normally the bacterium, called *Clostridium botulinum*, lives in the soil, reproducing only in anaerobic conditions. If canned food is contaminated, it will produce a foul-smelling gas which causes cans to swell (sometimes called 'blown' tins). This is why it can be suicidal to taste suspect food from cans. Symptoms appear about three days after eating poisoned food and include vomiting, constipation and paralysis.

Finally, there are microbes which are transmitted in or on the bodies of carriers. Many of these exist throughout the world but the most important killer is the single-celled animal, *Plasmodium*, which causes malaria and is carried by the *Anopheles* mosquito. This mosquito does not live in Britain. In fact, the only mosquito which does live in this country is the culicine type and it is completely harmless.

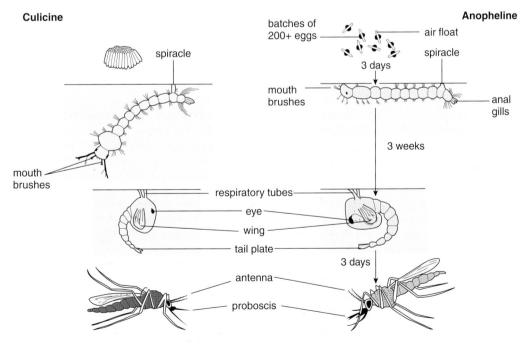

Figure 14.26 *The life history of the Anopheline and Culicine mosquito*

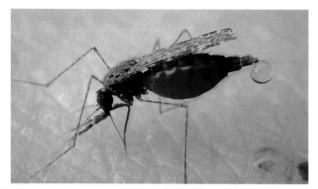

Figure 14.27 *A female* Anopheles *mosquito feeding on human blood*

The female *Anopheles* needs a protein found in blood to make her egg cases and so feeds on humans.

It pushes its needle-like mouthparts into the skin and sucks up the blood. The male feeds on plant cell sap in a similar way. The female injects an anti-clotting chemical into the human so that the blood keeps flowing through its mouthparts. By feeding on more than one person, the mosquito will transmit the malarial parasite from one person to another.

The malarial parasite

If a person suffering from malaria is bitten by a female *Anopheles* mosquito, the parasite passes with the blood into the mosquito's stomach. Here, it reproduces sexually, forming a cyst which bursts and allows the young stages to pass to the salivary glands. If the mosquito bites another person, the parasites are injected

World Health Organisation – malaria
http://www.who.int/health-topics/malaria.htm

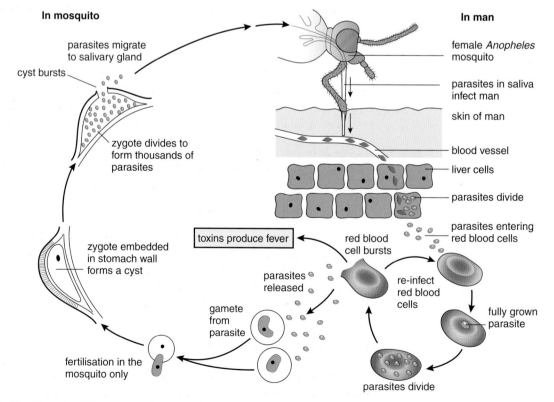

Figure 14.28 *The life cycle of the* Plasmodium *parasite*

into the person's bloodstream. They travel to the liver where they undergo asexual reproduction. They then invade red blood cells from which they obtain food. Poisons are released at this stage causing fever and possibly death.

Control of malaria focuses on eliminating the mosquito and treating the parasite when it is in humans. The mosquito is attacked by:

- use of insecticides
- preventing its reproduction by eliminating its breeding places
- killing the larvae with oil or some form of biological control.

The parasite is attacked with drugs such as paludrine, daraprim, chloroquine and quinine.

Control of disease through prevention

Bacteria are among our chief competitors for food. We cannot even estimate the amount of food spoilage by bacteria, but most food would remain edible for years if bacteria were not present on it. For this reason we have developed efficient methods of preserving food. These methods all depend on either eliminating bacteria themselves or removing one or both of the conditions necessary for their growth – water and a suitable temperature. Killing all the bacteria present, then sealing the food in a container is the basis of canning. Another method involves keeping food in conditions under which bacteria reproduce more slowly or cannot reproduce at all. This includes cooling or freezing, salting and dehydration. Chemical preservatives may also be used, however, their use has declined in recent years.

Radiation may be an important aid in preserving foods. The foods are packaged and sealed, then exposed to gamma radiation (see p. 180) which destroys all bacteria.

A special form of treatment is given to milk. Because it is an ideal food, milk can be a breeding ground for many types of disease-causing bacteria. Tuberculosis, diphtheria, scarlet fever, food poisoning and dysentery can all be spread via contaminated milk unless it is treated by pasteurisation. This is a legal requirement in this country before milk can be sold. There are two methods:

1 The HTST method – high temperature, short time. Milk is heated to 72°C, held at that temperature for 15 seconds, then cooled to about 10°C.

2 The milk is heated to a temperature between 63°C and 66°C, held at that temperature for 30 minutes, then cooled rapidly to about 10°C.

Pasteurisation does not eliminate all bacteria from milk but does destroy pathogenic types. Sterilised milk is also available in which the milk is heated to very high temperatures (Ultra High Temperatures, UHT). Sterilisation kills the majority of bacteria but, as a consequence, the flavour is altered. The shelf-life of such milk is much longer than that of pasteurised milk.

The cellular level of defence

If microbes are able to pass through our first line of defence, such as skin and mucous membranes, they meet a second line of defence in the tissues of the body. Certain white blood cells (see p. 59) can engulf and digest the invaders.

271

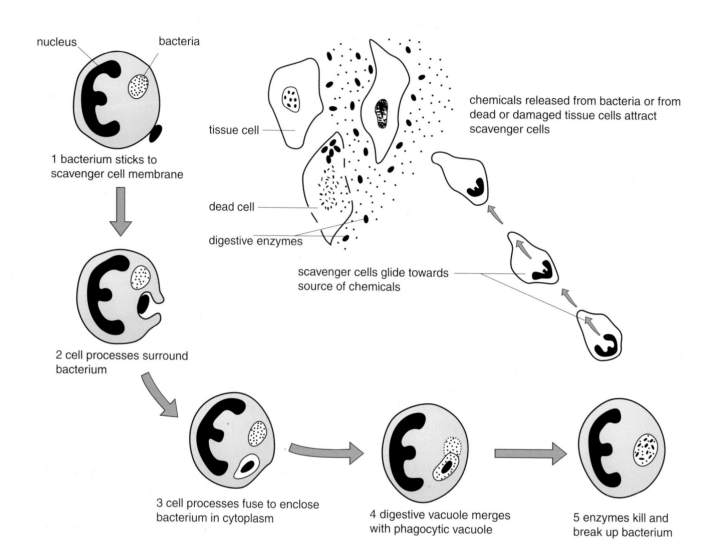

nucleus   bacteria

1 bacterium sticks to
scavenger cell membrane

2 cell processes surround
bacterium

3 cell processes fuse to enclose
bacterium in cytoplasm

4 digestive vacuole merges
with phagocytic vacuole

5 enzymes kill and
break up bacterium

tissue cell

dead cell

digestive enzymes

chemicals released from bacteria or from
dead or damaged tissue cells attract
scavenger cells

scavenger cells glide towards
source of chemicals

Figure 14.29 *Phagocytosis*

As the battle goes on in a wound, a fluid of digested bacteria, broken down cells and blood plasma builds up as **pus**. Often the tissues become inflamed as increased blood flow to the area brings more white cells. Lymph also seeps into the infected region. It carries bacteria and white cells to lymph nodes, where they are filtered out.

A third line of defence involves the production of special proteins called **antibodies** which are specific to a particular disease-causing organism. Invading microbes and their toxins have their own proteins that are alien to the host. These foreign proteins are called **antigens** and can be recognised by body cells. When antigens are detected, the host's lymphocytes (see p. 59) produce specific antibodies. The antibodies combine with the antigens – they fit together precisely due to their molecular shapes.

Production of specific antibodies in the lymph nodes begins within a few hours of an antigen appearing in the body. A few days later, the antibodies enter the blood. They increase in number over three or four weeks, after which time the rate of production slows down. If the host is again exposed to the antigen, production of antibody rises very rapidly and may prevent the development of symptoms.

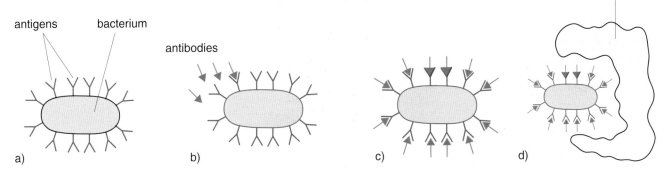

Antibodies produced by the host's body attach to the antigens on the invading bacterium. The bacterium then is easily engulfed by a white blood cell.

Figure 14.30 *Antigen/antibody reaction*

Immunity

'Sarah Portlock, of this place, was infected with the cowpox when a servant at a farmer's in the neighbourhood, twenty-seven years ago. In the year 1792, conceiving herself from this circumstance, secure from the infection of smallpox, she nursed one of her own children who had accidentally caught the disease, but no illness ensued. During the time she remained in the infected room, pus from smallpox blister was inserted into both her arms, but without any further effect and no symptoms of smallpox....'

This was part of an account written by Dr Edward Jenner in 1796. Jenner is known as the 'father' of vaccination.

Edward Jenner (1749–1823), as a country doctor in Gloucestershire, was naturally interested in the diseases that affected the local population. One of these was smallpox, a virus infection transmitted from the udders of cows to those who milked them. In his early years, Jenner had learned of the old wives' tale that an attack of cowpox would give protection against the smallpox. Smallpox was a serious disease of the time, which left those who survived with severe disfigurements. For centuries, inoculation with smallpox had been practiced in China and Siam (now Thailand). Pus from a smallpox blister was injected, **inoculated,** into a healthy person in the hope that the resulting attack of smallpox, induced when the sufferer was in good health, would prove less severe than the naturally occurring disease. The inoculation gave protection against further attacks of smallpox. This practice had long been employed in Wales but it first gained acceptance in England after its introduction from Turkey by Lady Mary Wortly Montagu, in 1717. Its main disadvantage was that no-one could guarantee its success and it sometimes proved to be fatal.

Dr Jenner established the truth of the country tradition that an attack of the mild disease, cowpox, would give immunity against the life-threatening disease, smallpox. In order to test his theory, he took some pus from a blister of someone suffering from cowpox and scratched it into the arm of the young boy, Jimmy Phipps. Jimmy thus became one of the most famous human guinea pigs of all time. He developed cowpox symptoms and, some weeks later, Dr Jenner took a great risk and gave Jimmy a second inoculation which consisted of pus containing the smallpox virus. His calculated risk paid off, fortunately for little Jimmy, because he did not develop smallpox.

www

People and discoveries – smallpox
http://www.pbs.org/wgbh/aso/
databank/entries/dm79sp.html

Figure 14.31 *Dr Jenner inoculating Jimmy Phipps with the smallpox virus*

Did you know?

In 1978, modern vaccines based on Jenner's original ones were responsible for eliminating smallpox from the human population. It was the first example of humans being able to *purposely* eradicate any organism. However, many samples of the virus were kept in a laboratory and they escaped causing two minor epidemics. One person died from a disease which, technically, did not exist!

In 1796, Dr Jenner published his report of 23 cases in which he had successfully used a 'vaccine' (from the Latin *vacca*, meaning cow) to protect his patients. Despite strong opposition from Fundamental Christians, vaccination was adopted in Europe and the United States. Eventually, the British Government was persuaded to use the vaccine on British soldiers in India, where hundreds of them were dying of smallpox.

There were several claims from England, Denmark and Germany, that cowpox vaccination had been used before Jenner's experiments. The validity of these claims does not detract from Jenner's right to the credit of being the first to test, through careful experimentation, what was no more than folk-lore.

Jenner was unable to explain the biology behind his success. The understanding of the principles of natural and artificial immunity had to await the discoveries of the father of bacteriology, Louis Pasteur, and his followers.

The father of bacteriology

Louis Pasteur (1822–1895) had lost two of his daughters to the bacterial disease, typhoid, and he became obsessed with the idea that some bacteria could cause disease. 'In the field of experimentation,' wrote Louis Pasteur, 'chance favours only the prepared mind'. It was this belief that directed him to the discoveries which entitle him to be regarded as the originator of immunology. Just as many previous world-shaking discoveries have been made by accident or coincidence, this particular contribution of Pasteur to Mankind came about by chance.

A culture of bacteria, which causes chicken cholera, was left in his laboratory when he departed in haste for a holiday. When he returned, he was about to discard this old culture, when he suddenly changed his mind. He injected a syringeful of the culture into a hen. Hens were popular as experimental animals in Pasteur's day. He subsequently treated a whole batch of hens in the same way.

Some time later, he treated this batch of hens and another batch of hens, which he had not inoculated, with a fresh culture of chicken cholera bacteria. The original inoculated batch survived, but the others, without exception, died. Pasteur's 'prepared mind' instantly grasped the implications of his experiment. Comparing his work to that of Jenner, he adopted the same term, *vaccination*, for this process of preventative inoculation, or immunisation. He was approaching 60 years of age at this time and devoted the remaining years of his life to this field of medicine.

The principle of his brilliant discovery depended on weakening, or attenuating, a strain of virulent microbes. He wanted to apply this method to as many different diseases as possible. A microbe may be virulent to one species of host but not to others. By 'virulence', he meant the ability of a microbe to multiply in the tissues which it invades.

How vaccines work

Neither Jenner nor Pasteur knew that they were exploiting an animal's natural immune system when they introduced alien microbes into the blood of humans or chickens. Our immune system has the ability to respond to specific microbes as a means of defending against their harmful effects. Such microbes include viruses, bacteria and Protozoa.

- **Viruses** consist of genetic material surrounded by a protein coat. They can reproduce only when inside living cells.
- **Bacteria** are much bigger than viruses and are similar to the cells that make up our bodies. Most obtain their food by digesting living or dead cells of other organisms.
- **Protozoa** are single-celled organisms. Most are harmless aquatic creatures, such as *Amoeba* or *Paramecium* (see p. 125), but some are killers and can cause malaria (see p. 269), sleeping sickness and amoebic dysentery.

All of these microbes which invade our bodies have one thing in common. Their surfaces are covered with molecules of a particular shape and pattern that our immune system can recognise as alien. The molecules are usually proteins and are called **antigens**.

The first step in immunity is taken when protein molecules, called **immunoglobulins**, found on the surface of special white blood cells, bind to antigens. The process of binding causes the white blood cells, called **B lymphocytes**, to divide and form daughter cells. Some of these daughter cells become plasma cells which make large amounts of immunoglobulins. Once they are released from the cell, they are called **antibodies**.

Antibodies of a particular molecular shape will bind to the antigen molecules with which they fit. In doing this they can completely surround the microbe and secure it while phagocytes (see p. 272) gather to ingest it.

Viruses living inside cells stimulate the activity of a different type of white blood cell. These are the **cytotoxic T lymphocytes**, which also bind to antigens, such as the viral proteins that appear on the surface of a viral infected cell. Once the cytotoxic T cell has bound to the antigen, it kills the cell, thus preventing the virus from reproducing and spreading infection.

www

The immune system
http://www.schoolscience.co.uk

Infection does not necessarily result in the host experiencing symptoms of the disease. Infection occurs when microbes enter the host and establish themselves. This invariably results in a race between the immune system and the microbes, which try to multiply faster than the immune system can eliminate them. If the microbes win, the disease symptoms appear but if the immune system wins, there will be no signs of the disease.

After an infection, it may take up to 10 days before the body produces enough antibodies to prevent the symptoms of the disease. However, we have developed a neat trick to speed things up by being able to produce 'memory' cells. These arise from the daughter cells which are produced by B lymphocytes during an initial infection. These memory cells remain ready to react in the event of future infections, when they bring about the production of antibodies within three days of an encounter with the same microbe. Some daughter cells from the cytotoxic T lymphocytes are also memory cells.

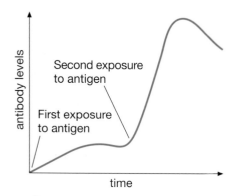

Figure 14.32 *Memory cells ensure that the production of antibodies after the second encounter with the antigen is swift and vigorous*

Because memory cells are produced in response to a particular microbe, they will only respond to that specific microbe. For example, the immune response that protects against chickenpox will not work against any other virus, or indeed that virus if its antigen coat is changed by mutation (see p. 272).

Having antibodies protecting you from a disease makes you immune to that particular disease. It is called **natural active immunity**. In contrast, **passive immunity** may be gained by a child who receives antibodies via its mother's placenta or in her milk, or by someone who has an injection of antibodies, purified from the blood of other people or from animals such as a horse. We are now in the era of 'designer antibodies' when we can genetically engineer antibodies to protect against, or treat, specific diseases.

The aim of vaccination is to induce active immunity without causing the symptoms of the disease. The vaccine prompts the immune system so that it is ready to act when the recipient next meets the disease-causing microbe. Vaccination is **artificial active immunity**.

How vaccines are made

Most vaccines are prepared in one of four ways. The first of these involves killing bacteria or viruses. There are various ways to kill microbes, such as exposing them to high temperatures or by treating them with chemicals such as formaldehyde. The structure of the surface antigen molecules remains unaltered but the microbes are inactivated and cannot cause disease. The Salk poliomyelitis vaccine is an example of a killed virus which is given by injection. It was named after the American, Jonas Salk, who developed the vaccine as a result of his research in 1947 at the University of Michigan.

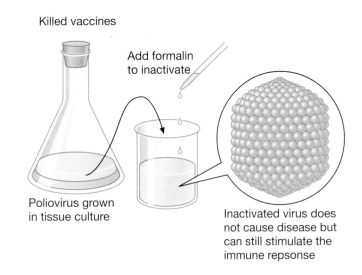

Killed vaccines

Add formalin to inactivate

Poliovirus grown in tissue culture

Inactivated virus does not cause disease but can still stimulate the immune repsonse

Figure 14.33 *Preparation of killed microbes for vaccines*

A second category is one where vaccines are made with live attenuated (weakened) microbes. The microbes still infect the recipient and stimulate an immune response but they do not cause disease. Microbes are attenuated by growing them in experimental animals or in cultures of tissues. Attenuation also takes place if microbes are cultured in conditions which are not ideal for growth. For example, extremes of temperature or absence of oxygen cause weakened mutants to form.

Both Jenner's and Pasteur's methods relied on using attenuated microbes. In Jenner's use of the cowpox virus to protect against smallpox, he was using the attenuated form which existed naturally. The cowpox virus was so similar to the smallpox virus that the antibodies produced in response to it also protected against smallpox. The Sabin poliomyelitis vaccine is an example of a live attenuated virus being used. It was named after Albert Sabin, who was of Russian origin but who became an American citizen in 1930. His development of the attenuated-virus vaccine for polio took place in 1959 at the University of Cincinnati College of Medicine.

A third type of vaccine relies on inactivating bacterial toxins. Some bacteria cause disease by excreting poisons (toxins) into the bloodstream. The toxins can be made harmless without losing their ability to promote the immune response. After inactivation, they are called toxoids. Examples are the vaccines against tetanus and diphtheria.

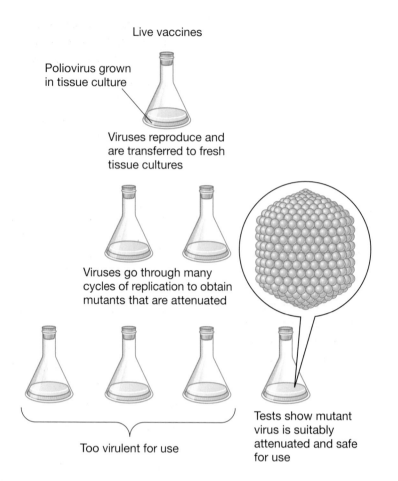

Figure 14.34 *Preparation of attenuated microbes for vaccines*

The fourth category includes subunit vaccines, which are based on only fragments of the microbe. The protein-based antigen coat is separated from the rest of the microbe, and when injected, will promote the antibody–antigen response.

A comparison of vaccines containing live or dead microbes is given below:

- Live microbes multiply within the body, so that a sufficient dose of antigen can be delivered in one injection of low dose. Several injections, delivering high doses of dead microbes, are often needed.
- Live microbes induce long-lasting immunological memory because viral-infected cells stimulate production of cytotoxic T cells and memory cells.
- Live vaccines involve a risk that the microbe may lose its effectiveness through mutation or regain its ability to cause disease. One in about 3 million attenuated poliomyelitis viruses mutates to a virulent form.
- Live vaccines, once prepared, must be kept refrigerated. This form of storage is not always possible in some developing countries.
- Both live and killed vaccines may contain fragments of the cells in which the microbes have been grown. This may lead to the development of the disease in the recipient of the vaccine.

The search for safe vaccines continues. One of the latest techniques harnesses the knowledge gained from genetic engineering. It relies on the fact that one or more genes control the production of the protein-based antigen. Once the genes have been identified, they can be separated from the source DNA and spliced into the DNA of yeast cells. The yeast cells can be made to reproduce in large numbers and produce vast quantities of the required antigen. The antigen can be separated, purified and used in vaccine. Hepatitis B is treated in this way.

There are some diseases against which it will be difficult or impossible to make vaccines. Certain microbes mutate so rapidly that the immune system cannot keep up with them because the antibodies they produce will not fit the constantly changing shape of the antigen coat. The common cold and various strains of influenza are in this category.

Hide and seek

Although progress has been made in applying immunological techniques to combating parasitic Protozoa and worms, there has been very limited success so far. The main problem is that they are much more complex than bacteria and viruses and are able to make a vast arsenal of antigens, as well as being able to cover themselves with a protective coat of molecules that the host does not recognise as alien. In other words, they remain permanently hidden from their host.

Destroying the human immuno deficiency virus (HIV), which causes AIDS presents one of the greatest medical challenges of all time. The antibodies to HIV do not appear to protect people from developing AIDS and, superimposed on this, HIV inserts a copy of its own genetic material into the DNA of human cells. The infective part of the virus hides within the very cells which normally form part of our immune system.

To have or have not

A safe, effective vaccine which prevents disease is still only useful if the public as a whole co-operates and allows it to be used in mass vaccination programs. Much depends on effective health education to ensure that people understand the need for vaccination and 'booster' injections. The whole point about vaccination is that it protects not only the individual, but also whole populations. By reducing the number of hosts available to the microbe, it prevents the spread of disease through a community. As more people are vaccinated, a point arrives when the number of unimmunised people may be too small to sustain the microbe. The risks associated with vaccination may then exceed the perceived risks of the disease.

By definition, a free society has the right to choose, to accept or not to accept medical treatment. But without the full co-operation of communities in vaccination programs, the target of complete elimination will not be attained. The vaccine against whooping cough is an example of this. In the 1970s, there was a 40% drop in the number of people having their children vaccinated against whooping cough. The result was several epidemics of whooping cough and several dozen deaths. Yet the risk of death following natural infection is 10 000 times higher than that following vaccination. A subunit whooping cough vaccine based on bacterial antigen is likely to supercede the whole-cell vaccine on a worldwide scale.

Ironically, multi-national pharmaceutical companies can make more profit from developing a pill to cure headaches than they can from making vaccines for use in developing countries. Developing countries simply do not have the money to pay for them. The hard truth is that the elimination of many diseases through mass vaccination programs in developing nations may be unachievable due to the fact that company profits have a higher priority than the well-being of people.

Did you know?

In the 1890s about one in every 1000 people in Europe and the US caught poliomyelitis each year. In the US about 20 000 cases were reported each year. The Sabin vaccine (see page 277) brought the incidence down to only six cases by the 1980s!

Summary

1 Most microbes are not harmful to Mankind. Some are essential, for example, those involved in natural cycles such as the carbon and nitrogen cycle.

2 Many microbes are used by us to make useful products. These include the types involved in the production of various foods, ethanol, antibiotics and biogas.

3 Microbes are also used in sewage treatment and for the extraction of enzymes which help us in the detergent industry and food technology. Waste disposal and mining are other aspects of technology where microbes are used.

4 Disease-causing microbes are called pathogens and can be transmitted through the air, by direct contact, through food and water, and by vectors (carriers).

5 Control of disease depends on hygiene, including proper handling and storage of food, and vaccination.

6 The body has natural defence mechanisms including natural immunity.

7 Artificial immunity may be acquired through immunisation.

Homework Questions

1 What is the source of the carbon used by plants to make food by photosynthesis?

2 Explain how the constant level of carbon dioxide in the atmosphere is maintained.

3 Outline briefly the cycle of carbon between plants and animals.

4 By what means is atmospheric nitrogen made available to plants?

5 What is the alternative source of plant nitrogen and how is it obtained?

6 Why do plants and animals need nitrogen?

7 What do you understand by the term 'biotechnology'?

8 Describe the various ways in which infectious diseases are spread.

9 How does food poisoning occur? Give one example.

10 List the main structural defences of the body.

In-Depth Questions

1 Summarise the role of bacteria in the circulation of both carbon and nitrogen.

2 Give an account of a food manufacturing process that depends on one or more species of microbe.

3 Justify the statement that 'we could not survive without microbes'.

4 Describe how white blood cells defend us from microbes.

5 How do vaccines protect us from microbes?

Theme 3 Exam Questions

1 The cane toad, a native of Africa, was introduced into the sugar cane plantations of Australia. It was thought to be an effective agent of biological control. It was found to be a predator of Australian organisms and was able to adapt to many different environmental conditions. It has a poison in its skin which is deadly to predators. A single female can produce 30 000 eggs in one year and an individual toad can live for up to 30 years. The food web below shows the feeding relationships in the sugar cane area of Queensland, Australia.

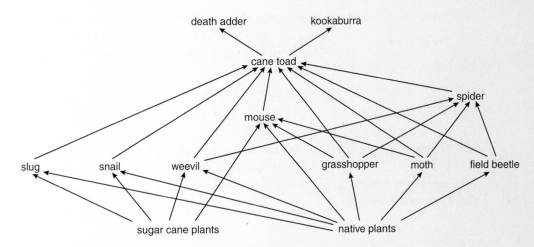

Use the information above and your own knowledge to answer the following questions.

(a) (i) Explain why the cane toad was originally an effective agent of biological control. *(3 marks)*
   (ii) Suggest why the cane toad quickly became a disaster as an agent of biological control. *(3 marks)*

(b) Give one advantage of using an effective agent of biological control compared with conventional methods of pest control.

(1 mark)

EDEXCEL

2 **(a)** The diagram below shows part of the carbon cycle which uses and replaces carbon dioxide in the air.

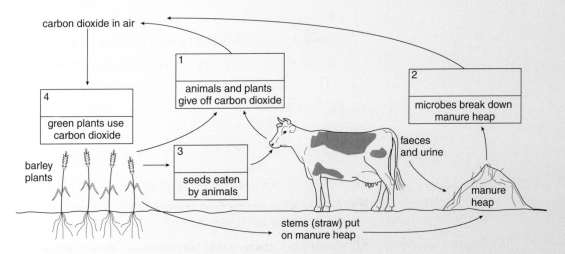

Use the diagram and your knowledge to answer the following questions.

(i)   These processes are part of the carbon cycle.

Decay Excretion Feeding Photosynthesis Respiration

Match each word to the number in each box.   *(4 marks)*

(ii) Until 1993, farmers were allowed to burn straw after the harvest. What effect did this have on the amount of carbon dioxide in the air?   *(1 mark)*

(iii) Some trees and some microbes growing millions of years ago did not decay completely after they had died. Use words from the list to complete the sentences below.

Burned coal fossil gas liquid oil sold solid

These trees became _____ and the microbes became _____.

These are both _____ fuels and can be _____ to release energy.   *(4 marks)*

(b) The list below gives the names of three processes which are part of the nitrogen cycle:

Nitrogen fixation   Nitrification   Denitrification

Match the description of the process, given below, to the name of the process.
(i)   Nitrate is changed into nitrogen gas.
(ii) Nitrogen gas is used by bacteria in root nodules of bean plants which help the plants make protein.
(iii) Faeces are broken down by microbes and used to make nitrates.
(iv) Nitrogen gas and oxygen are changed into nitrates by lightning.   *(4 marks)*

EDEXCEL

3   Enzymes are proteins which catalyse biological reactions.

(a) Diagram A shows one theory as to how the enzyme sucrase is able to catalyse the conversion of sucrose into glucose. Diagram B shows sucrase which has been denatured and is unable to catalyse the reaction.

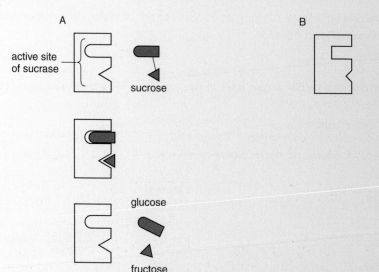

(i)   Suggest why the denatured enzyme is unable to catalyse the reaction.   *(2 marks)*
(ii) State two conditions which could denature an enzyme.   *(1 mark)*

(b) Enzymes are being used increasingly in technological applications. They are usually extracted from bacteria which are grown in bulk cultures in fermenters. The diagram shows a fermenter.
(i)   Suggest how the sensors help to maintain optimum conditions for the multiplication and growth of the bacteria.   *(3 marks)*

(ii) One system of enzymes has been developed to detect heroin which has been mixed with other substances. The enzymes are immobilised and fixed onto a gel strip where they catalyse the following reactions.

$$\text{Heroin} \xrightarrow{\textit{Enzyme 1}} \text{Morphine} \xrightarrow{\textit{Enzyme 2}} \text{Red dye}$$

Suggest how such gel strips could be used in detecting heroin. *(2 marks)*

AQA

4 The diagram shows the flow of energy through 1m of an ecosystem.

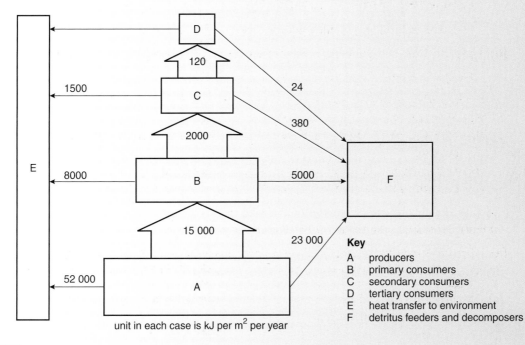

unit in each case is kJ per m^2 per year

KEY

A producers
B primary consumers
C secondary consumers
D tertiary consumers
E heat transfer to environment
F detritus feeders and decomposers

(a) (i) Name the process in which green plants transfer solar energy into chemical compounds. *(1 mark)*
(ii) Name the process in living organisms which results in the transfer of heat to the environment. *(1 mark)*

(b) (i) Tertiary consumers receive energy from secondary consumers. Calculate the amount of heat energy which tertiary consumers transfer to the environment as a percentage of the energy received from secondary consumers. Show your working. *(2 marks)*
(ii) Tertiary consumers transfer a high percentage of their energy intake to the environment as heat. Primary consumers transfer a much lower percentage. The tertiary consumers are mainly mammals and birds. The primary consumers are mainly insects and molluscs. Explain why mammals and birds transfer a higher percentage of their energy intake to the environment as heat than insects and molluscs do. *(2 marks)*

AQA

5 The graph shows how vaccination has helped to control whooping cough.

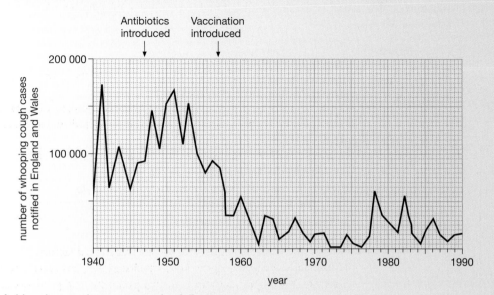

(a) Use the graph to answer the following:

    (i) In what year was the highest number of cases of whooping cough? *(1 mark)*

    (ii) In what year did vaccination first appear to eliminate whooping cough in England and Wales?

    (1 mark)

    (iii) How many years from 1940 did it take for whooping cough cases to stay below 100 000? *(1 mark)*

    (iv) Fears about the safety of the vaccine led to a drop in the number of children being vaccinated. Suggest when this occurred. *(1 mark)*

(b) State how the vaccine for whooping cough is produced. *(1 mark)*

(c) The diagram shows stages in a type of genetic engineering which produces a vaccine based on the mass production of an antigen.

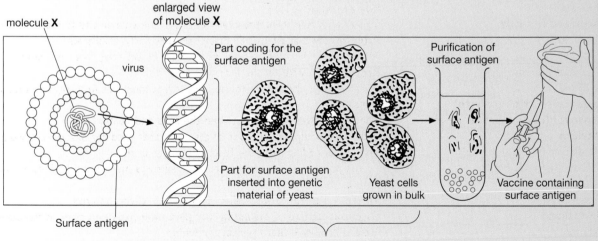

    (i) What type of chemical is an antigen? *(1 mark)*

    (ii) Name the molecule labelled X. *(1 mark)*

    (iii) What name is given to the part of this molecule that codes for the antigen? *(1 mark)*

(d) During stage Y millions of genetically identical copies of the yeast cell are produced by mitosis. Name this process. *(1 mark)*

(e) Name the disease which is vaccinated against using antigens which are separated from a virus. *(1 mark)*

WJEC

Glossary

A

Abdomen	The area between the thorax and the pelvis.
Actin	Slender filaments of protein arranged in bundles in the composition of muscle fibrils.
Active transport	The passage of a substance through a cell membrane requiring the use of energy.
Adaptation	The process by which a species becomes better suited to survive in an environment.
Addiction	The body's need for a drug that results from the use of the drug.
Adrenal glands	Two ductless glands located above each kidney.
Aerobic	Requiring free atmospheric oxygen for normal activity.
Aerosols	Tiny droplets suspended in air.
Air sacs	Thin-walled divisions of the lungs.
Alimentary canal	Those organs that comprise the food tube.
Allele	One of a pair of genes responsible for contrasting characters.
Alveoli	Microscopic sacs in the lungs in which exchange of gases takes place.
Amino acids	Substances from which organisms build protein; the end products of protein digestion.
Amnion	The innermost fetal membrane, forming a sac surrounding the fetus.
Amniotic fluid	Secreted by the amnion and filling the cavity in which the embryo lies.
Anaerobic	Deriving energy from chemical changes other than these involving oxygen.
Anther	The part of the stamen which bears pollen grains.
Antibiotic	A bacteria-killing substance produced by a microbe.
Antibody	A substance in the blood that helps lead to immunity.
Antigen	A substance, usually a protein, which, when introduced into the body, stimulates the production of antibodies.
Antitoxin	A substance in the blood that counteracts a specific toxin.
Anus	The opening at the posterior end of the alimentary canal.
Aorta	The largest artery in the body which leads from the heart.
Aquatic	Living in water.
Aqueous humour	The watery fluid filling the cavity between the cornea and the lens of the eye.
Arteriole	A tiny artery that eventually branches to become capillaries.
Artery	A large muscular blood vessel that carries blood away from the heart.
Asexual reproduction	Reproduction without the fusion of sex cells.
ATP (adenosine triphosphate)	A high-energy compound found in cells that functions in energy storage and transfer.
Atrioventricular valves	The heart valves located between the atria and ventricles.
Atrium	A thin-walled upper chamber of the heart that receives blood from veins.
Auditory nerve	The nerve leading from the inner ear to the brain.
Autonomic nervous system	A division of the nervous system that regulates involuntary actions in internal organs.
Autosome	Any paired chromosome other than the sex chromosomes.
Autotroph	Organism capable of organising inorganic molecules into organic molecules.
Auxin	A plant hormone that regulates growth.
Axillary buds	Buds formed in the angle between a leaf stalk and a stem.
Axon	A nerve process that carries an impulse away from the nerve body.

B

Bacteria	A group of microscopic organisms without nuclear membranes.
Bile	A brownish-green emulsifying fluid secreted by the liver and stored in the gall bladder.
Binary fission	The division of a single-celled organism into two similar cells.
Biodegradable	Material decomposed by natural processes.

Biomass	The mass of living material per unit area or volume.
Biome	A large geographical region identified mainly by its major vegetation.
Biosphere	The area in which life is possible on Earth.
Blastula	An early stage in the development of an embryo, in which cells have divided to produce a hollow sphere.
Bowman's capsule	The cup-shaped structure forming one end of the tubule and surrounding a knot of blood capillaries in the tubule of a kidney.
Brain stem	An enlargement at the base of the brain where it connects to the spinal cord.
Breathing	The mechanism of getting air in and out of the lungs.
Bronchiole	One of numerous subdivisions of the bronchi within a lung.
Bronchus	A division of the lower end of the wind pipe leading to a lung.
Bud	An undeveloped shoot of a plant, often covered by scales; developing young forming on some simple animals such as *Hydra*.
Bulb	A form of underground stem composed of thick scale leaves e.g. onion.

C

Calorie	A unit used to measure the energy in food. It is now outdated and should by substituted by the joule as a unit. A kilocalorie is the amount of heat needed to raise the temperature of 1 kg of water (1 litre) by 1°C.
Canine	Tooth for tearing.
Cambium	A ring of dividing cells in roots and stems that forms new xylem and phloem.
Capillary	The smallest blood vessel in the body through which exchanges occur between blood and tissue fluid.
Cardiac muscle	Muscle composing the heart wall.
Carnivore	A meat eater.
Cartilage	A strong, pliable, smooth tissue which supports structures and lines bones at joints.
Catalyst	A substance that accelerates a chemical reaction without being altered chemically.
Cell	A unit of structure and function of an organism.
Cell theory	The cell is the unit of structure and function of all living things and arises from a pre-existing cell by division.
Cementum	The covering of the root of the tooth.
Central nervous system	The brain and spinal cord and nerves arising from them.
Cerebellum	The brain region between the cerebrum and medulla, concerned with balance and muscular coordination.
Cerebrum	The largest region of the brain, considered to be the seat of emotions, intelligence and voluntary activities.
Cervix	The neck of the uterus.
Chlorophyll	Green pigment essential to food manufacture in plants.
Chloroplast	A structure in a plant cell that contains chlorophyll.
Choroid layer	The layer of the eye beneath the sclera which prevents internal reflection and contains the most blood vessels.
Chromatid	During cell division, each part of a double-stranded chromosome.
Chromosome	A rod-shaped gene-bearing body in the cell, composed of DNA joined to protein molecules.
Cilia	Tiny hair-like projections of cytoplasm.
Ciliary muscles	Those that control the shape of the lens in the eye.
Cleavage	The rapid series of divisions that a fertilised egg undergoes.
Cochlea	The hearing apparatus of the inner ear.
Co-enzyme	A molecule that works with an enzyme in catalysing a reaction.
Cohesion	The clinging together of molecules as in a column of liquid in transpiration.
Coleoptile	A protective sheath encasing the primary leaf of the oat plant and other grasses.
Cone	Cells in the retina responsible for colour vision.
Colloid	A gelatinous substance, such as protoplasm or egg albumen, in which solids are dispersed throughout a liquid.
Colon	Part of the large intestine.

Connective tissue	A type of tissue that lies between groups of nerve, gland and muscle cells.
Consumer	An organism that feeds on another organism.
Contractile vacuole	A cavity in some single-celled organisms associated with the elimination of excess water.
Cornea	A transparent bulge of the sclera of the eye in front of the iris, through which light passes.
Corpus luteum	Refers to the follicle in an ovary after an ovum is discharged.
Cortex	In roots and stems, a storage tissue; in organs such as the kidney and brain, the outer region.
Cotyledon	A seed leaf present in the embryo plant that serves as a food store.
Cowper's gland	Located near the upper end of the male urethra. It secretes a fluid which is added to the sperms.
Cytoplasm	The protoplasmic materials in a cell lying outside the nucleus and inside the cell membrane.

D

Daughter cells	Newly-formed cells resulting from the division of a previously existing cell, called a mother cell. The two daughter cells receive identical nuclear materials.
Decomposers	Organisms that break down the tissues and excretory material of other organisms into simpler substances throughout the process of decay.
Deficiency disease	A condition resulting from the lack of one or more vitamins.
Dentine	A substance that is relatively softer than enamel, forming the bulk of a tooth.
Denitrification	The process carried out by denitrifying bacteria in breaking down ammonia, nitrites and nitrates and liberating nitrogen gas.
Depressant	A drug having an anaesthetic effect on the nervous system.
Diaphragm	A muscular partition separating the thorax from the abdomen. Also, a contraceptive device used as a barrier at the cervix.
Diastole	Part of the cycle of the heart during which the ventricles relax and receive blood from the atria.
Diffusion	The spreading out of molecules in a given space from a region of greater concentration to one of lesser concentration.
Digestion	The process during which foods are chemically simplified and made soluble for absorption.
Diploid	Term used to indicate a cell or an organism that contains a full set of homologous pairs of chromosomes.
DNA (deoxyribonucleic acid)	A giant molecule in the shape of a double helix, consisting of alternating units of nucleotides, composed of deoxyribose sugar, phosphates and nitrogen bases.
Dominance	The principle first observed by Mendel, that one gene may prevent the expression of an allele.
Duodenum	The region of the small intestine immediately following the stomach.

E

Ecology	The study of the relationships of living things to their surroundings.
Ecosystem	A unit of the biosphere in which living and non-living things interact, and in which materials are recycled.
Egestion	Elimination of insoluble, undigested waste.
Egg	A female reproductive cell.
Embryo	An early stage in a developing organism.
Enamel	The hard covering of the crown of a tooth.
Endocrine gland	A ductless gland that secretes hormones directly into the bloodstream.
Endoskeleton	Internal framework of vertebrates made of bone and/or cartilage.
Environment	The surroundings of an organism; all external forces that influence the expression of an organism's genes.
Enzyme	A protein that acts as a catalyst.

Reflex action	A nervous reaction in which a stimulus causes the passage of a sensory nerve impulse to the spinal cord or brain, from which a motor impulse is transmitted to a muscle or a gland.
Renal	Relating to the kidney.
Replication	Self-duplication, or the process whereby a DNA molecule makes an exact duplicate of itself.
Reproduction	The process through which organisms produce offspring.
Respiration	The release of energy from glucose in every living cell.
Response	The reaction to a stimulus.
Retina	The inner layer of the eyeball, formed from the expanded end of the optic nerve.
RNA (ribonucleic acid)	A nucleic acid in which the sugar is ribose. A product of DNA, it controls protein synthesis.
Rod	A type of cell in the retina of the eye that responds to shades of light and dark but not to colours.
Root cap	A tissue at the tip of a root protecting the growing region.
Root hair	A projection of the outermost layer of a root which increases the surface area for absorption of water and minerals.
Root pressure	The pressure that is built up in roots due to water intake.

S

Saliva	A fluid secreted into the mouth by the salivary glands containing the enzyme, amylase.
Salivary gland	A group of secretory cells producing saliva.
Saprophyte	A fungus or bacterium that lives on dead organic matter.
Sclerotic layer (sclera)	The outer layer of the wall of the eyeball.
Scrotum	The pouch outside the abdomen that contains the testes.
Sedative	An agent that depresses body activities.
Seed	A complete embryo plant surrounded by a food store and a protective coat.
Selectively-permeable membrane	One that lets some substances pass through more readily than others depending on their molecular size.
Semen	Fertilising fluid consisting of sperms and fluids from the seminal vesicle, prostate gland and Cowper's gland.
Semi-circular canals	The three curved passages in the inner ear that are associated with balance.
Semi-lunar valves	Cup-shaped valves at the base of the aorta and the pulmonary artery that prevent back flow of blood into the ventricles.
Seminal vesicles	Structures that store sperm.
Seminiferous tubules	A mass of coiled tubes in which sperms are formed in the testes.
Sensory neurons	Those that carry impulses from a receptor to the central nervous system.
Sepal	The outermost part of a flower, usually green, which protects the bud.
Serum	Plasma without clotting factors.
Sex chromosomes	The two kinds of chromosomes (X and Y) that determine the gender of a person.
Sex-linked character	A recessive character carried on the X chromosome.
Small intestine	The digestive tube, about seven metres long, that begins with the duodenum and ends at the colon.
Smog	Combination of smoke and fog.
Smooth muscle	That which is involuntary and is found in the walls of the intestine, stomach and arteries.
Sperm	Short for spermatozoon – a male reproductive cell.
Sphincter muscle	A ring of smooth muscle that closes a tube.
Spinal cord	The main dorsal nerve of the central nervous system.
Spinal nerves	Large nerves connecting the spinal cord with the organs of the body.
Spongy mesophyll	Loosely connected leaf tissue with many air spaces.
Stamen	The male reproductive organ of a flowering plant.
Stigma	The part of the female reproductive organ of a flowering plant that receives pollen during pollination.

Stimulant	An agent that increases body activity.
Stoma	A pore regulating the passage of air and water vapour to and from leaves and stems.
Style	The stalk of the female reproductive organ of a flowering plant.
Stomach	An organ that receives ingested food, prepares it for digestion and begins protein digestion.
Symbiosis	The relationship between two organisms of different species for mutual benefit.
Synapse	The space between nerve endings.
Synovial fluid	A secretion that lubricates joints.
Systole	Part of the cycle of the heart during which ventricles contract and force blood into arteries.

T

Taste buds	Flask-shaped structures in the tongue containing nerve endings that are stimulated by chemicals.
Tendon	A strong band of connective tissue which connects a muscle to a bone.
Testa	The outer seed coat.
Testes	The male reproductive organs which produce sperms.
Thorax	The middle region of the body between the neck and the abdomen.
Thrombin	A substance formed in blood clotting as a result of the reaction of prothrombin, thrombokinase and calcium ions.
Thrombokinase	A substance essential to blood clotting formed by the breakdown of platelets.
Thyroid	The ductless gland, located in the neck, that regulates metabolism.
Tissue fluid	That which bathes cells of the body. It is called lymph when in vessels.
Trachea	The windpipe taking air to the bronchi.
Transfer RNA	A form of RNA which delivers amino acids to the template formed by messenger RNA on the ribosomes.
Translocation	The movement of manufactured dissolved food substances in the phloem.
Transpiration	The loss of water from plants.
Transpiration pull	The pressure which forces water to rise in a stem as cells lose water to the atmosphere by transpiration.
Tropism	A growth response in a plant due to a uni-directional stimulus.
Turgor	The stiffness of plant cells due to the pressure exerted by contained water.
Tympanic membrane	The ear drum.

U

Umbilical cord	The link between the embryo and the placenta.
Urea	A nitrogenous waste substance made in the liver from excess amino acids.
Ureter	A tube leading from the kidney to the bladder.
Urethra	A tube leading from the bladder to an external opening of the body.
Urine	The liquid waste made in the kidney and stored in the bladder, consisting mainly of water and urea.
Uterus	The organ in which developing embryos are nourished and protected until birth.

V

Vaccination	Method of producing immunity by inoculating with a vaccine.
Vaccine	A substance used to produce immunity.
Vacuole	One of the spaces scattered through the cytoplasm of a cell, containing liquid.
Vagina	Cavity in the female immediately outside and surrounding the cervix of the uterus.
Vas deferens	Tubes that transport sperms from the testes.
Vascular bundles	Strands of phloem and xylem found in roots, stems and leaves for transporting materials in solution around the plant.
Vector	A carrier of disease.
Ventricle	A muscular chamber of the heart for pumping blood.
Vertebra	A back bone.
Vertebrate	An animal with a back bone.

Villi
Microscopic projections of the wall of the small intestine or the placenta for increasing the surface area.

Viruses
Particles that are non-cellular and have no nucleus and no cytoplasm. They cannot reproduce unless they are inside living cells.

Vitamin
An organic substance that helps enzymes work in the body.

Vitreous humour
A transparent jelly-like substance that fills the interior of the eye ball and maintains its shape.

Vocal cords
Those structures within the larynx that vibrate to produce sound.

Voluntary muscle
Striated muscle that can be controlled at will.

W

White blood cells
Colourless nucleated blood cells for defence.

X

X chromosome
A sex chromosome present singly in males and as a pair in females.

Xylem
The woody tissue of plants that conducts water and dissolved minerals.

Y

Y chromosome
A sex chromosome found only in males.

Z

Zygote
The product of fertilisation.

Exam answers

Note that the following answers are the responsibility of the author and not of the examination boards from whose papers they originate.

Theme 1

1 a) A = Epidermis, B = Spongy mesophyll, C = Guard cell

   (b) i) In June, the amount of carbohydrate is highest in the leaves because photosynthesis is at its highest and potatoes have not yet formed as storage organs. In September, the amount of carbohydrate is highest in the potatoes because it is being stored as starch. The rate of photosynthesis would be less in September because of the shorter days resulting in less light. Carbohydrate is taken from the leaves and is stored in the potatoes.

      ii) Starch

    iii) Energy for growth and reproduction

    iv) Phloem

  c) i) See graph

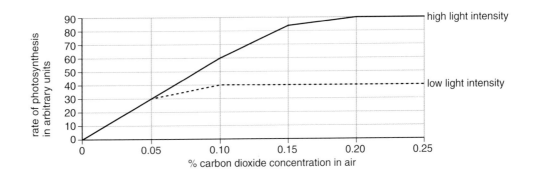

    ii) Low light intensity = 30 units. High light intensity 584 units.

   iii) Temperature or pH

2 a) See graph

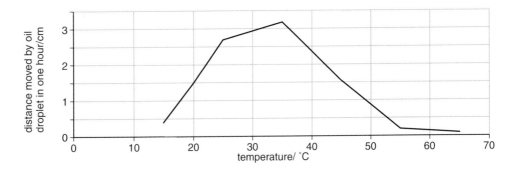

b) There are no data from 36°C to 44°C.

c) Sodium hydrogencarbonate breaks down to form carbon dioxide. This must be kept constant for photosynthesis because it is a limiting factor. All other factors must be kept constant if only one is being investigated.

3 a) (i) Yellow-brown

   (ii) Brick-red

b) (i) Black

   (ii) Clear blue

c) Boiling denatures enzymes.

d) A protein which speeds up the rate of a reaction.

e) The optimum means the quantity at which a reaction takes place at the fastest rate.

4 a) 5. There was no digestion of starch. This can be deduced because the hole is still surrounded by blue/black agar. The enzyme is denatured.

b) 2. This contains 2% enzyme which is the optimum concentration of enzyme to digest starch at 37°C. 3 contains 1% enzyme at 37°C. Maximum digestion of starch does not take place at this concentration.

c) You would boil a piece of the agar with an equal volume of Benedict's reagent. The Benedict's reagent would change from clear blue to brick-red if sugar was present.

d) Set up four test tubes, each with 2% salivary amylase at 37°C and add sodium hydroxide or dilute hydrochloric acid to have a range of pH e.g. 2, 4, 7 and 9. Repeat the experiment as before by adding the mixture to the holes in the starch agar. After flooding with iodine, note the area that was cleared.

5 a)

Process	Apparatus letter	Gas produced by process
Photosynthesis	C	Oxygen
Respiration	A	Carbon dioxide
Transpiration	B	Water vapour

b) The rate of water loss could exceed the rate of water absorption thus causing wilting.

6 a) To carry blood from the heart towards organs.

b) i) Coronary

   (ii) Cholesterol

c) i) The narrowing of the artery causes an increase in pressure. The blood is forced through the artery by the heart.

   (ii) Cholesterol narrows the artery, eventually blocking it. The heart muscle becomes starved of oxygen and glucose. The tissue dies and the heart stops beating.

d) Reduce fats in the diet and increase the amount of exercise to use the energy in stored fat.

7 a) At rest the heart rate after training is lowered. This is because the volume of blood pumped out at each beat is greater than it was before training. During exercise the heart can increase faster in the trained person and can become higher without straining the heart muscle. This allows more blood with oxygen and glucose to reach muscles more efficiently. After exercise the recovery rate of the heart beat is faster in the trained person. The overall effect is to improve fitness.

b) i) $6000\,cm^3$

ii) Ventricles

iii) By muscular contraction which decreases the volume and increases the pressure.

c) Improves the efficiency of breathing and improves muscle tone. It also prevents obesity.

8 a) Stomata

b) (i) Transpiration

ii) Transports water and minerals from the roots through the stem to the leaves.

c) (i)

	A	B
Numbers of stomata	8	18

ii) A, because it has fewer stomata and therefore a reduced rate of transpiration.

9 a) i) A

ii) It has a thicker wall to withstand higher pressure of the blood.

b) i) A

ii) The rhythmic muscular contraction of the ventricles of the heart causes the arteries to recoil after dilation.

iii) Place your middle finger on an artery which is near the surface of the skin e.g. the radial artery in the wrist or the carotid artery in the neck, and count the pulsations in 15 seconds, then multiply by four to find the number per minute.

10 a) One would expect a greater loss of water in the plant with roots because roots provide a greater surface area for absorption of water.

b) (i)

Plant with roots	Plant without roots
6	0.06

     ii)   Yes, because water loss is 100 times more in plants with roots once the leaf surface area is taken into account.

c) To prevent evaporation from the surface of the water to prove that all the water lost was via the plant.

d) Maintain equal temperature, light, air flow and ensure that the plants are of the same species.

11 a) i)   A

     ii)   Contraction of the diaphragm muscles increases the volume of the thorax and decreases the pressure. The atmospheric pressure is greater than that of the thorax so air is forced into the lungs during inspiration.

b) From the graph, inspiration + expiration = 3.25 s $= \dfrac{60}{3.25} = 18.5$ per min

c) The diaphragm muscles relax. The pressure inside the thorax increases as the volume decreases. The elasticity of the lungs also forces air out during expiration.

12 a) Sugar + oxygen $\rightarrow$ water + carbon dioxide + energy

  b) i)   Total intake = 2500 cm³

         Water in urine = 2500 − 1000 = 1500 cm³

     ii)   A lower water intake causes an increase in production of anti-diuretic hormone (ADH) from the hypothalamus in the brain. This causes the kidney tubules to re-absorb as much water as possible into the blood. High water intake causes less ADH and therefore less reabsorption of water.

c) The dialysis machine allows urea to diffuse through the selectively permeable membrane, but, because the dialysate contains a mixture of glucose and salts similar in concentration to the blood, these substances do not diffuse out of the blood. So as the blood passes through the machine it loses urea but not essential glucose and salts.

  d) i)   Cost and convenience to the patient because of the mobility that a transplant allows.

     ii)   Problems of rejection. Problems of finding donors with a perfect tissue match.

13 a) The blood sugar of a healthy person is kept constant. When the blood sugar level tends to rise above 0.1 g per 100 cm³ blood, insulin lowers the level by changing excess glucose into glycogen which is stored in the liver.

b) Person B was not producing enough insulin and was possibly suffering from diabetes.

c) The rate of a reaction being controlled by the accumulation of a product of that reaction. For example, when a substance builds up in the blood, production of that substance is decreased by the activity of a hormone.

14 a) Phototropism

　　b) i)　The tip

　　　　(ii)　The plant does not respond when the tip is covered or when it is removed.

　　c) (i)　Auxin

　　　　ii)　It causes elongation of cells at the growing region.

　　　　iii)　Light causes the auxin to migrate to the opposite side of the stem.

　　d) These are controls to show that only one factor is causing the response.

15 a) i)　Pupil's diameter is larger than A.

　　　　ii)　Reflex

　　　　iii)　I light. II retina. III brain. IV iris.

　　　　iv)　Co-ordinator.

　　b) i)　0.05

　　　　ii)　0.16

　　　　iii)　The person has 'got used' to the flashes or the eyelid muscles are tired.

16 a) Day 17

　　b) Menstruation

　　c) i)　Oestrogen causes egg release

　　　　ii)　Progesterone prepares the uterus for implantation and further development of the embryo.

　　d) The level of progesterone increases and remains high.

　　e) It would rise, then fall back to 6 units.

　　f) It becomes thicker by being richly supplied with blood vessels for implantation and the development of the placenta.

Theme 2

1　a) One that can be inherited or passed on via genes through generations.

　　b) Air cannot reach the air sacs because the bronchioles of the lungs are blocked with mucus. This prevents the exchange of gases at the air sacs.

　　c) Antibiotics will kill bacteria which may be trapped in the mucus.

　　d) I) Nn　**iii)** Nn　**iii)** nn　**iv)** NN or Nn.

　　e) Examples are: Huntington's disease, Sickle cell anaemia, haemophilia.

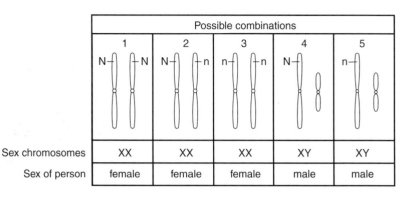

	Possible combinations				
	1	2	3	4	5
Sex chromosomes	XX	XX	XX	XY	XY
Sex of person	female	female	female	male	male

2 a) See diagram

   b) 22

   c) $X^N X^n$, because one of the offspring is a female haemophiliac. In order to produce this genotype, the mother must have been a carrier.

   d) A haemophiliac female is rare because she would not survive after puberty because of the severity of blood loss during menstruation. The only way that she could survive would be if she did not begin to menstruate due to abnormalities in sex hormone production.

3 a) There are three X chromosomes and three of chromosome number 21.

   b) Female, because there is no Y chromosome.

   c) $24 + 23 = 47$

   d) Mutation

   e) Nuclear radiation increased the rate of mutation.

   f) Leukaemia.

4 a) They would be seen by birds and eaten, therefore reducing their numbers.

   b) The number of pale moths would decrease and the number of black moths would increase because the pale ones would be eaten in greater numbers than the black ones. The black moths would therefore survive to breed.

5 a) Fewer predators would be able to attack it as it became larger. This would increase its chances of survival.

   b) i) The digits have been reduced from four, to three, to one.

      ii) For locomotion on soft marshy ground because there would be a greater surface area of the feet preventing sinking.

   c) Natural selection is the result of survival in the struggle for existence among organisms that have those characteristics that give them an advantage to breed and pass on the characteristics to their offspring.

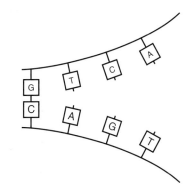

6 a) i) See diagram

   ii) Mitosis

b) i) methionine – glycine – proline – tyrosine

   ii) valine – glycine – proline – histidine

   iii) The correct sequence of amino acids for a particular protein cannot be present because of the reversal of their codons.

7 a) The gene for insulin production is removed from a human chromosome with the use of enzymes. The bacterial DNA is split to allow for the insertion of the human gene. Enzymes are used to seal the human gene into the bacterial DNA.

   b) Bacteria are given the ideal conditions for growth i.e. suitable temperature, water and food and allowed to reproduce in large numbers. They will then produce the amount of insulin that is required.

   c) Many people object to the killing of animals for human needs.

   d) To regulate the concentration of blood sugar.

   e) Carbohydrate is digested to glucose and this would increase in concentration in the blood to a dangerous level.

Theme 3

1 a) i) It can eat all the pests of sugar cane.
It has a high reproductive rate.
It can adapt to different environmental conditions.

   ii) It eats animals which are not pests.
It produces a poison which kills predators which are not pests.
It has a very long life span so it is difficult to eliminate after it has eaten the sugar cane pests.

b) Conventional pest control may result in the build up of concentration of pesticides in food chains so that animals at the top of food chains are poisoned.

2 a) i) 1 = respiration, 2 = decay, 3 = feeding, 4 = photosynthesis

ii) It increased

iii) The trees became *coal* and the microbes became *oil*. These are both *fossil* fuels and can be *burned* to release energy.

b) i) Denitrification, **ii)** nitrogen fixing, **iii)** nitrification, iv) nitrification.

3 a) i) The structure of the active site of the enzyme is altered so that the substrate cannot fit into it.

ii) Boiling and extremes of pH.

b) i) They can monitor the temperature, pH and oxygen.

ii) The strip is dipped into the mixture and if heroin is present, the enzymes would change it to morphine and then to the red indicator.

4 a) i) Photosynthesis, **ii)** respiration.

b) i) $120 - 24 = \dfrac{96}{120} \times 100 = 80\%$

ii) They are more active and lose more heat during respiration which releases energy in all cells of the body.

5 a) i) 1941 **ii)** 1972 **iii)** 14 **iv)** 1976

b) Use of killed microbes

c) i) Protein **ii)** DNA **iii)** Gene

d) Cloning

e) Influenza or hepatitis

Index